ROBERT BLY IN THIS WORLD

Robert Bly In This World

Proceedings of a Conference

held at Elmer L. Andersen Library

University of Minnesota

April 16–19, 2009

Thomas R. Smith, Editor
with James P. Lenfestey

UNIVERSITY OF MINNESOTA LIBRARIES
Archives and Special Collections
Minneapolis, Minnesota, 2011
Distributed by the University of Minnesota Press

Copyright © 2011 by the Regents of the University of Minnesota

ISBN 978-0-8166-7770-2

Excerpt from *Unpacking the Boxes: A Memoir of a Life in Poetry* by Donald Hall. Copyright ©2008 by Donald Hall. Reprinted by permission of Houghton-Mifflin Harcourt Publishing Company. All rights reserved.

Laurie Hertzel story, *The Poet Comes Home*, used by permission of the author and the StarTribune.

Prose excerpt from Paul Gruchow, *Journal of a Prairie Year* (Minneapolis: Milkweed Editions, 2009). Copyright 1985 by Paul Gruchow. Reprinted with permission from Milkweed Editions. www.Milkweed.org.

"Sioux Metamorphoses" by James Koller is reprinted from *Shaking the Pumpkin: Traditional Poetry of the Indian North Americas*, ed. Jerome Rothenberg (New York: Doubleday, 1972). Reprinted with permission.

"In Fear of Harvests" by James Wright is from *Above the River: The Complete Poems* (New York: Farrar, Straus and Giroux and University Press of New England, 1990). Reprinted with permission.

All quotations from poetry, prose, and interviews by Robert Bly are reprinted with the permission of Robert Bly. Thanks, as ever, to Robert for his generous cooperation.

Special gratitude to:

Robert H. Bruininks, President, University of Minnesota
Wendy Pradt Lougee, University Librarian and McKnight Presidential Professor
Kris Kiesling, Director, Archives and Special Collections
Ann Mulfort, Bly Archivist
Katherine McGill, Director of Development
Marlo Welshons, Director of Communications
Linda Greve, Community Outreach
Lanaya Stangret, Friends of the Libraries

A Man Writes to a Part of Himself: Robert Bly,
film by Mike Hazzard and Greg Pratt (57 minutes).
Copyright 1978. www.thecie.org.

Designed and typeset by Scott King using Quadraat OT,
a digital typeface designed by Fred Smeijers

Published by University of Minnesota Libraries
Archives and Special Collections
Minneapolis, Minnesota
Distributed by the University of Minnesota Press

CONTENTS

PREFACE: THE PROPHET SPEAKS FIRE FROM THE PROVINCES

By James P. Lenfestey

> *A great poet and a great critic are like the mule who can smell fresh water ten miles away. There is a sense that tells us where the water of poetry is, abroad or at home, West or East, even under the earth.*
>
> —Robert Bly, *American Poetry*

As renowned poet, critic, social transformer, teacher, editor and translator, Robert Bly has been invited to perform, read, recite, and speak all over the world—from the Russia of Andrei Vosznesensky to the England of Ted Hughes, the North Africa of the Berber poets to the Innisfree isle of Yeats.

He has drawn vast crowds sprawling over hillsides in California, requiring the police, and a small, attentive congregation in the Little Stone Church on Mackinac Island in Lake Huron. The listeners hear something in his poems, translations, activism, and inquiries into ancient and contemporary ideas that echoes their own deep wonderings and longings, like finding fresh drinking water in a desert.

As coordinator of the conference, *Robert Bly in This World*, I welcomed to the Elmer L. Andersen Library at the University of Minnesota scholars, colleagues and students of Bly from as far away as England, Maine and Washington state, as close as Illinois, Wisconsin and the Twin Cities. They were charged with illuminating the many facets of the presence of Robert Bly in this world, no easy task. The results, published here, succeed handsomely.

The world of poetry is in many ways like the world of religion. It has its saints and sinners, its suffering Jobs and prophetic Jeremiahs, its many lovely singers, its psalmists, its wandering ascetics and devoted apostles. But poetry has very few who stride forth like Moses from the wilderness challenging nearly everything. Ezra Pound played that role in the first half of the 20th century, Robert Bly in the second. In his essay, "A Wrong Turning in American Poetry," Bly baldly stated about Eliot's influential formulation, the "objective correlative," "The tone is authoritative, but the statement is not true." Bly led the charge instead toward poetry of "spiritual as well as psychological intensity" represented by the image, which is "the natural speech of the imagination." Where did such fresh authority come from?

Born and raised on a farm in the productive wind-swept plains of western Minnesota, the son and brother of farmers, Robert Bly did not spring full blown from the whirlwind. He grew from an early love and study of poetry coupled with an encyclopedic intellect and fearless curiosity. At Harvard University he edited the literary magazine *The Harvard Advocate*, publishing soon-to-be famous friends and unknowns and, impishly without permission, T. S. Eliot's student poems. He fell in love with Yeats and still recites swaths of Yeats's poems by heart with the fire of delight. On a Fulbright fellowship to Norway in 1956, he discovered in an Oslo library a book of translated poetic voices of an intensity he had not heard before, which became the model for his transformative magazine of "poetry, translation and general opinion," *The Fifties, The Sixties, The Seventies*. And he sprang from reading, with his friend James Wright, the wise and funny old Chinese poets of long ago. Out of this brew, and the silent spaces of the landscape around him, grew a poet conversant in the psychological power and deep resonance of language, and also its meditative stillness.

One of the tasks of the prophet is to send out thundering pronouncements that roil the oceans. This offends some who practice other religions or who adhere to previous commandments. Robert made enemies from the beginning of his career with the first words out of his mouth in the first issue of *The Fifties*: "The editors of this magazine believe most of the poetry published in America today is too old fashioned." That statement angered poets, such as Allen Tate, immersed in practices of the previous half-century, but went to the heart of the problem for many. Bly's *Fifties* howl was heard all over the country by bodies suddenly able to breathe freely again, most famously James Wright in Minneapolis, but countless others. Poet William Matthews, writing in the winter, 1969 issue of *The Ten-*

nessee Poetry Journal, said, "It is nearly impossible to over-emphasize the importance of Bly's criticism [begun in *The Fifties*]. John Haines was the first to say in public that there has been nothing so interesting or influential since Ezra Pound began sending reviews to *Poetry*." MacArthur-winning poet and memoirist Patricia Hampl remembers, "I read Bly's magazine, and his good-spirited but deadly attacks on the literary establishment, and I knew I was reading the future.... There are many of us who will never forget that generosity and the bracing experience of editorial honesty."

Like other prophets, Bly disseminated his own sacred texts. Many are collected today in *Eating the Honey of Words*, his second volume of new and selected poems, *American Poetry: Wildness and Domesticity*, his influential essays, *Iron John*, the mythopoetic international bestseller, *The Winged Energy of Delight*, selections from his translations of twenty-two poets from ten different languages, and the three great anthologies he edited: *News of the Universe*, *The Rag and Bone Shop of the Heart*, and *The Soul Is Here For Its Own Joy*.

If Robert Bly's work has one unifying theme, it is entering "the inward world" of human grief. Perhaps due to his remote, alcoholic father, or his bookish mother who accepted in silence her hard life, or the harsh horizontal landscape of his youth—whatever the cause, Bly proved well-equipped to take on that neglected dimension of the modern psyche. Men particularly do not easily visit that vast and wild terrain inside them, even if it can be transformed into sweet honey. Yet Bly insisted on grief as a step into a fully lived life, and utterly necessary to create substantial poetry. As always, he preached in images.

WARNING TO THE READER

Sometimes farm granaries become especially beautiful when all the oats or wheat are gone, and wind has swept the rough floor clean. Standing inside, we see around us, coming in through the cracks between shrunken wall boards, bands or strips of sunlight. So in a poem about imprisonment, one sees a little light.

> But how many birds have died trapped in these granaries. The bird, seeing freedom in the light, flutters up the walls and falls back again and again. The way out is where the rats enter and leave; but the rat's hole is low to the floor. Writers, be careful then by showing the sunlight on the walls not to promise the anxious and panicky blackbirds a way out!
>
> I say to the reader, beware. Readers who love poems of light may sit hunched in the corner with nothing in their gizzards for four days, light failing, the eyes glazed ... They may end as a mound of feathers and a skull on the open boardwood floor ...

In the end, the thunder of Robert Bly's voice resolves itself, like Whitman's, into tinkling bells of sweet music under our ears. A new form of poetry he invented later in his prodigious career consists of eight lines driven entirely by "friendly little sound particles," a form he has named the "ramage." Sense must be there, of course, and rhythm, and images, and fun, but the music of language itself drives the poem's joy.

With the annunciation of the first issue of *The Fifties* in 1958, the world has been unable to ignore the presence of Robert Bly. He opened wounds of grief many did not want opened, and some have never forgiven him. He put his body as well as his poems on the line against "the insanity of empire" whenever he saw it, and some never forgave him. He named the names of tyrants who "counted small-boned bodies" and the vassals to those tyrants never forgave him. He called for modern men to study the ancient story of an iron-colored man, and some men and women never forgave him. He called many poets "old-fashioned"—some mistakenly—and told some aspiring poets harshly their poems felt like "two-day-old lettuce." No surprise that many of the poets he has publicly admired—Lorca, Machado, Neruda, Hafez, Mirabai—were also pariahs to political or religious establishments. No surprise either that he built his own education/creative arts institutions—the Great Mother Conference and the Minnesota Men's Conference—well outside the halls of established academic, arts and spiritual institutions.

But wherever he went, he gathered devoted disciples and students who crowded halls in Minnesota, New York, San Francisco, London, or who read his poems, ancient stories and translations in lonely farmyards in Kansas, single apartments in Boston, along the Rio Grande border and under the coastal redwoods of California. And he has influenced countless people outside the poetry world. The renowned Shakespearean actor Mark Rylance, master of London's Globe Theatre, agreed to play the title role in Henrik Ibsen's *Peer Gynt* if Bly would translate it, which he did, masterfully, for the Guthrie Theater. After the triumph of the opening night performance in Minneapolis in 2008, Rylance halted the thunderous applause to speak directly to the audience, reminding them—reminding us all—what an extraordinary international resource is Robert Bly.

The one shocking fact of Robert Bly's career is that he has won so few major prizes—a National Book Award, two Guggenheims, the early Fulbright to Norway—although he is well honored in his state as the first literary winner of the McKnight Award for Distinguished Achievement in the Arts, and as Minnesota's first Poet Laureate. Bly's restless intellect never stood still long enough. By the time the critics caught up with him he had moved on, from the stillness of *Silence on the Snowy Fields*, to the "deep image," to William Stafford's practice of *Morning Poems*, to adaptations of the Persian ghazal, to homegrown ramages. Yet his poetic taste proved unfailing—three of the poets he early translated into American English went on to win Nobel Prizes. The 14th century Sufi mystic Rumi, whom Bly first brought into modern American consciousness through his "versions," has become, through the translations of Bly's friend Coleman Barks, the most widely read poet in English today.

Bly's wide-ranging, game-changing influence is well represented at this conference, beginning with the remarks of keynote speaker Lewis Hyde. As a University of Minnesota student, Hyde first met Bly in 1965 on a bus from Minneapolis to a Vietnam War protest in Washington, and they later worked together on translations of the Spanish poet Vicente Aleixandre. When Aleixandre won the Nobel Prize in 1977, their book, *Twenty Poems of Vicente Aleixandre*, was one of the few editions of his work available in English. Hyde soon won a MacArthur "genius" grant after publication of his first major prose book, *The Gift*.

Current US Poet Laureate W. S. Merwin said of *The Winged Energy of Delight* that Bly's translations "helped broaden the horizon for generations of readers of poetry." It is rare indeed to find such a sweeping prophetic voice walking the earth, as the following essays make abundantly clear. The Elmer L. Andersen Library and the University of Minnesota deserve great credit for their visionary purchase and careful archiving of Robert Bly's papers for future generations, and for sponsoring and hosting the conference *Robert Bly in This World*. My special gratitude to the tireless, careful and detailed editing of these manuscripts by Thomas R. Smith into the accurate historical assessment of the career of Robert Bly they surely will become.

INTRODUCTION: ROBERT BLY IN THIS WORLD (AND THE OTHER)

By Thomas R. Smith

This book is the harvest yield of a weekend in April, 2009, when scholars, writers, and readers assembled at the University of Minnesota to retrace the rich path that brought Robert Bly to international prominence. Bly has mattered to his audience as few poets have, not only as poet but as one of those rare and valuable artists and thinkers whose work has helped to shape the sensibility of his time.

This volume strives in its outline and particulars to approximate in print that symposium, *Robert Bly in This World*, held on April 16-19, 2009. The descriptive copy for that gathering reads: *A creative/academic conference to celebrate Robert Bly's career and influence in poetry, translation, political protest, the Men's Movement, and cultural transformation.* When organizer James P. Lenfestey put together the appropriately varied program, he sought out poets, translators, teachers, and cultural historians to expertly survey the dauntingly vast field of Robert Bly's distinction over the past six decades.

The title *Robert Bly in This World* indicates an intention to follow some major threads through the broad tapestry of Bly's multifarious activity and industry, particularly his far-ranging influence. That influence is real, though incalculable, so thoroughly has Bly redrawn the contours of American poetry in his time. It would be difficult to find a contemporary poet not indebted to him in some way.

Still, the phrase "Robert Bly in this world" tells only half the story. The title of Bly's 1985 poetry collection, *Loving a Woman in Two Worlds*, is more suggestive of the whole. In truth, Bly's extroverted public persona, which is outsized, has been consistently nurtured by an underground spring of reflection, inwardness, receptivity, and silence. It's no accident that Bly's debut collection in the turbulent, clamorous Sixties was titled *Silence in the Snowy Fields*. The fact that Bly has so steadfastly insisted that *both* worlds—the inward world of introspection and the outward world of action—be present in his work has made him an arresting and profoundly necessary figure for our time. The critic Charles Molesworth said that Bly writes "religious meditations for a public that is no longer ostensibly religious." It is surely the highest tribute to Bly's integrity and perseverence as an artist that he has succeeded in speaking of spirit and that "other world" to a milieu that would often rather deny both.

Just as no single collection of papers, no matter how diverse, can pretend to be the last word on Bly, so this book itself inevitably falls short of the moment-to-moment live electricity of that April weekend in Minneapolis. Nonetheless, considerable pains have been taken by the contributors and myself to give the reader the next best experience to actually attending this scintillating forum. I've edited with a light hand to preserve the wide variety of voices and vocabularies, which all partake to varying degrees in the announced "creative" and "academic" foci of the conference. It's my hope that the very individuality of the pieces will suggest the scope of Bly's appeal and the gift he has given to so many in our literary, artistic, and cultural communities.

While some live ambiance is lost in the print incarnation of these proceedings, there are also bonuses, in the form of solicited contributions by the two renowned storytellers, Gioia Timpanelli and Daniel Deardorff, who performed the evening of Friday, April 17th to a capacity crowd of conference-goers and general public but did not present papers. Also invited to contribute was poet and translator Coleman Barks, who shared the stage with Robert Bly himself the following evening. These additions have further enriched this volume, as has an appreciation by the poet Jane Hirshfield, who was unable to come to Minneapolis due to scheduling conflicts. Other notable non-attendees are represented here by a series of brief tributes. Finally, as a coda to the sessions at the University of Minnesota, on Sunday afternoon William Booth, William Duffy, and Patricia Kirkpatrick gave flavorful presentations at the Lac Qui Parle County Museum, not far from Robert's old writing studio, a remodeled country schoolhouse, now permanently installed on the county fairgrounds.

All, originally present or not, are happily united in these pages in tribute to our mentor and friend, Robert Bly.

My gratitude to James P. Lenfestey for his editorial contributions to this book and for envisioning and then actually pulling together this mammoth undertaking, and to the supportive staff of the University of Minnesota libraries for making this celebration and publication possible.

I'll conclude on a more personal note.

In the early afternoon of Sunday, April 19, 2009, after those days of glorious talk at the Elmer L. Andersen Library on the U of M campus, I found myself with dozens of fellow travelers gazing from a tour bus at the flat western Minnesota fields under a mild spring sun. This bus trip served as dessert to the conference's main courses, a tour of Bly's Madison places, and first encounter with Bly's hometown for many who had previously visited those locales only in poems. Presenters and attendees passed the three-hour ride in animated conversation. Texas filmmaker Farid Mohammadi darted up and down the aisle documenting the occasion with his video camera. Laurie Hertzel, who wrote about it marvelously for the Minneapolis *StarTribune*, was on board. And Robert Bly, along for the ride with his wife Ruth, supplied occasional commentary via intercom, by turns acerbic and wistful. He was obviously enjoying himself. And why not? It was like a combination birthday party and literary soiree on wheels.

And yet, given the retrospective nature of the weekend, how could this outing be without some melancholy? On the Madison trip, an especially strong presence in his absence was Bly's great friend and co-conspirator in the poetry of the "new imagination," James Wright. (Anne Wright remembers the farm in her essay in this book as a "heavenly place" for the visiting newlyweds in the late 1960s.) At the Lac Qui Parle County Museum, another of Bly's co-conspirators from Madison days, William Duffy, was in fact very much with us, delivering his high-spirited recollections of helping Bly edit the seminal *Fifties* and *Sixties* magazines. Patricia Kirkpatrick, in her museum talk, invoked the late Carol Bly, another crucial missed presence.

For me, the mood of the trip crystallized in a single unforgettable image just down the road from the old Bly farmstead. A sudden hush descended as the bus paused a moment before the modest house set back among the budding trees. All quiet, as if the lingering calm after the long storm of creative energy and intellect that marked Bly's passionately intense Madison years.

As we glided slowly past the farm, I happened to look the other direction down the road, to glimpse as if in a dream two white-tailed deer kicking up dirt as they fled our intruding juggernaut. I had hardly a moment to mention the occurrence to others before two more deer broke together from fields dry with lack of rain, their hooves striking up puffs of ditch dust. I don't think Robert was able to see them from his front seat on the bus, and later I could hardly believe I'd seen them myself. So strange, the apparition of those two deer couples, synchronized as horse teams, keeping to the dirt road. Later, when I mentioned it to the English storyteller and vision quest leader Martin Shaw (another great student of Bly), he replied, "I really believe something otherwordly happened with the Deer, or I'm no kind of wilderness guide." This is how it came out in a poem I jotted in my notebook that day:

NEAR THE BLY FARM OUTSIDE MADISON, MINNESOTA

The thickening buds need one good rain
to leaf forth in the late April sun.
Already the willow groves are misting
yellow-green across the dusty fields.

The old farmhouse back among the trees
and sheds recedes into stillness. Where are
the ideas, the talk, and high spirits now?
They're not here anymore, they've gone on.

I watch two deer running beside the mile-
section dirt road, then a second pair
closely following. They move away from us,
the friendship of James Wright and Robert Bly.

> The horizon here is so limitless
> you can hear the wind of the End blowing.
> Don't worry about those old ones, they're
> all right, what they've accomplished is safe.
>
> Find that other, silent legacy,
> all the things they have not said. It waits
> for us along the roads, glinting like
> the Minnesota River at Montevideo.

Indeed, the Madison farm long ago ceased to be the epicenter of the revolution Robert Bly fomented in American poetry. That epicenter has moved with the seasons of Bly's restlessly Protean life to Kabekona Lake, to Moose Lake and then to Minneapolis, where he has made his home for the past two decades. In his poem, "When Threshing Time Ends" (*Morning Poems*), he writes with Ecclesiastes-like directness and honesty:

> The Bible was right.
> Presences come and go.
> Wash in cold water.
> The fire has moved.

By the time this book sees print, Robert will have celebrated his 84th birthday. His new volume of poems, *Talking into the Ear of a Donkey*, will have seen print. That forthcoming collection is as astonishingly rich in spirit and accomplished humanity as anything Robert has written. Meanwhile, the changes he has wrought in poetry and culture are significant and secure. Because of him, we will never be the same. The contributors to this volume all demonstrate in their varied ways that his work is far larger and wider than the singular human being who is Robert Bly. That work belongs to a tradition—or perhaps several of them—of perennial wisdom, rediscovered by Robert for a generation that had virtually forgotten it, and in a place where few besides the indigenous people of the land had thought to look. To paraphrase Keats, the poetry of earth is never finished. Robert helped put the western Minnesota prairie earth on the world literary map. In the process, he has enabled many to discover for themselves that "poetry of earth" under their feet, and running alongside their lives like a river, in Minnesota and elsewhere.

LESSONS FROM ROBERT BLY'S BARN

By Lewis Hyde

Although I was born in Boston and grew up on the east coast, my parents were both from Minneapolis and so, when it came time to go to college, I applied to the University of Minnesota and—having been denied admission to several fancy East Coast schools—arrived on campus in the fall of 1962. One evening when I was still a senior in high school I took out the University catalog so as to daydream about my future as a college boy. The map of the campus was a bit of a surprise. In the middle sat a large building labeled Cow Barn. Nearby were others: Sheep Barn, Pig Barn, Cereal Rust Lab, Weed Research .... Down at the bottom right was a tiny building: Liberal Arts. I hadn't realized how far west I was about to travel!

It was a great relief, of course, when my grandfather picked me up at the train depot and took me to the Minneapolis campus, not to what we used to call the Cow Campus over in St. Paul. Then as now the Minneapolis campus itself was huge—I think there were 30,000 students at the time, a large number to be sure but useful to me because out of all those thousands it turned out that there were half a dozen who became real soul mates: Jim Moore, Patricia Hampl, Garrison Keillor, Sam Heins, Francis Galt, and more.

The first time I met Robert Bly we were both on a bus going to an antiwar march held in Washington, D.C. on November 27, 1965. I had no idea he was a writer until, a few months later, Garrison invited him to give a reading on campus. Robert would have been in his mid-thirties then; he was full of energy, full of opinions, highly knowledgeable about modern poetry, and editing a wild little magazine called *The Sixties*. It soon developed that some of us would drive out to Madison, Minnesota to try to figure out what this fellow was all about. The first time Jim Moore and I made that trip we stopped on the way and bought a pork roast, my mother having taught me that guests should always arrive with a house gift of some sort. This was a raw roast of course, not a prepared meal, but I think it was gratefully received nonetheless. In those days lots of young poets showed up in Madison bearing no meat at all.

At the time of that first visit, Robert had just moved an old one-room schoolhouse onto his farm to use as his study. Initially, however, it was going to serve as a honeymoon cottage for James and Annie Wright. Jim and I were put to work helping to fix it up for them. Our first job was to dig the outhouse pit. Such were the entry requirements for those wishing to enter the world of poetry in the mid-1960s.

On a later trip to Madison I interviewed Robert for *The Lamp in the Spine*, a little magazine edited by Jim Moore and Patricia Hampl. Looking back at the interview now I see that I had big questions on my mind: "Do you believe in God?" I asked, and "Are you afraid of death?" In his answers Robert kept refusing to engage with my abstractions, his habit always being to think in images. In response to one question about spiritual life he had this to say:

> There's a skin or hide between ourselves and our inner being. And in the West that skin is very thick. Inside us there's a sea and that sea is your inner life, your spiritual life, and your sexual impulses—everything you've gotten from the memory stores of evolution. Then there's the outside world made of buildings and automobiles. And these two worlds can't rub against each other. It's too painful. Therefore you develop a hide exactly like a cow develops a hide. You don't want her guts to rub against the barn. [Hyde 50-51]

Thus did my studies begin on the Cow Campus after all, with Farmer Bly as one of my tutors.

He had many lessons to teach. A primary one had to do with solitude, something that has since played an important role in my own life. Robert has often told the story of his own initiation:

> I went to New York and I lived in a room by myself.... I had about two and a half years of solitude which troubled me and which drove me out of my mind; but nevertheless, in the course of that I understood something.

There are many things to be understood through solitude. All cultures seem to have the idea that human beings can be renewed by quitting the familiar, either in fact or in imagination, and going into the desert. In some traditions the young must go into silence for a period before they can emerge as real human beings. It isn't enough to take instruction from the community; you must also become aware of our collective ignorance, as Henry Thoreau used to say, with how vast it is and how fertile it can be. Thoreau is the great example in this country of a man experimenting with solitude. He went to Walden Pond to step outside the village proper, on the chance he might learn something not talked about in the town. The silence of solitude is itself a teacher. "Silence is audible to all men...," Thoreau once wrote. "She is when we hear inwardly, sound when we hear outwardly." [Thoreau 391]

There is a narrative, a plot as it were, to the experience of solitude. Certain things happen as the time unfolds. At one point in an interview collected in a Michigan Press book, *Talking All Morning*, Robert remarks on what happens if we quit the chatter of social life:

> Psychic energy can be drained by talking. My experience is that when, by means of solitude, the psychic energy is prevented from dispersing, then, after five or six days the psychic energy takes rhythmic forms.... [*Talking* 121]

That's actually quite deep into solitude: if you've made it to day five or six, you are doing very well. The first few days are very hard, or at least they have usually been for me. This is partly because going off by yourself is an implied insult to the community or to your loved ones and they may threaten to withdraw their affection if you leave, or at least you imagine that they might. We desire the love and respect of our community; if you step away from it, "a terrible fear comes," as Robert has said. And yet: "What the collective offers is not even love..., but a kind of absence of loneliness." [*Talking* 308]

Clearly, there are gates or barriers standing in the way of solitude. Fear is one of them; depression is another. To speak only of my own experience, for years now I have arranged periods of retreat for myself, time simply to read and to write. Years ago when I began such retreats I would often find myself depressed for the first day or two. I'd lie on the floor wondering why I had been so stupid as to be a writer. Why hadn't I become a carpenter or car mechanic? Why hadn't I found something useful to do with my hands? In this state my own work always looks stupid and obvious, my sentences stumbling and labored. I mention this period of gloom and doubt partly because if that's what's waiting for you then you'd better have some sort of container to hold you while you go through it. Time and enclosure: these are what a writer must have. Talent helps, but the yield may be small without time and enclosure.

My retreat depressions are usually followed by simple acceptance rather than elation. Gary Snyder has a poem called "Why Log Truck Drivers Rise Earlier than Students of Zen" that describes waking early to drive the rig up into the mountains for a day's labor. It ends with flat declarations: "Thirty miles of dust. / There is no other life." There is no other life. You may as well get to work.

And once you get to work you can sometimes, in solitude, forget your own self-judgment. I recently had a chance to spend three weeks alone in a house in a very small town in West Texas; during the second week I ran into a friend on the street who asked "How are things going?" I couldn't say! I had no idea how things were going. In solitude, if you are lucky, there comes a point when you are just doing the work, not thinking about whether it will please someone else, or even whether it pleases you. As Flannery O'Connor once wrote, "in art the self becomes self-forgetful in order to meet the demands of the thing seen and the thing being made." There is judgment internal to the art, to be sure ("Does this work on its own terms?") but blessedly the other sorts of judgment can fall away. The work can absorb you the way good soil can absorb the rain.

The final piece of the narrative of solitude appears when you reenter the world. If you've really made contact with inner life, or really become self-forgetful, then you return with a different quality of attention. When I was done with my weeks in Texas I found myself in the El Paso airport where the loudspeakers were saying, over and over again, "The Department of Homeland Security Authority has set the terror alert level at orange." Every so often they would also announce that there were hand-held defibrillators located near the restrooms. I'd heard none of these things before my retreat; they were surely there, but as accepted background noise. Now they seemed ominous and weird; I'd somehow walked into a land whose citizens heard disembodied voices constantly warning of bombs and heart attacks.

To spend time away from the culture's repeating noise allows you to notice the incongruity between what might be and what actually is. In solitude lies a promise of fresh speech and fresh action. Again I think of Thoreau: having spent two years at the pond he was able to say clearly why he was a tax resister. He had something new to say, a translation for his neighbors of what the inner ear hears in silence.

Which brings me to a final point about solitude, one that I don't think people always understand, and that is that being alone is connected to being with other people. "It was first in solitude that I really felt an affection for the human community," Robert has said. [*Talking* 10] After all, if you can't be at ease with yourself, how can you be at ease with others? If you feel no affection for yourself, good luck feeling affection for your homeland.

This brings me to a second lesson that many of us studied in Robert Bly's barn, one having to do with the soul work of connecting the inner and the outer worlds. I'm going to build my description of this work around two of Robert's sentences, the first of which comes from his great antiwar poem published in 1970, "The Teeth-Mother Naked at Last": "[The Vietnamese] are dying because gold deposits have been found among the Shoshoni Indians." [*Teeth-Mother* 18] The second sentence is not printed anywhere I know of; it's inscribed in my memory. At one of the many public events around the Vietnam war protests I remember Robert saying something like this: "We are killing men with black hair because the Minnesota Historical Society owns the scalp of Little Crow."

Nobody in my family ever spoke sentences like these; very few people do, actually, and I'm going to spend a minute reflecting on how they operate.

The first thing to say is that they contain history and some history about Little Crow is therefore in order. Little Crow was a Dakota Sioux, one of the leaders of the Sioux Rebellion of 1862. A decade before that date the Sioux had entered into a treaty with the U.S. government in which they agreed to settle along the Minnesota River in exchange for land, annuities, and certain other goods. The U.S. Senate then reneged on this deal whereupon the Sioux tried to drive European settlers out of Minnesota. This act of rebellion failed and a year later Little Crow was shot by a farmer while foraging for berries near Hutchinson, Minnesota. The farmer took the body into town where the townspeople mutilated it, dragging it through the streets with firecrackers stuck in the ears and dogs picking at the head. The farmer scalped him, there being a bounty on the Sioux in that time and a double bounty for Little Crow. When I was in college, both the scalp and the skull were owned by the Minnesota Historical Society.

The sentence about "the scalp of Little Crow" contains history, then, but it is swift history. It isn't a meditation on the past; it isn't an ode to the Confederate dead. The sentence jumps between two moments in time and in doing so reveals a connection to the Surrealists. The Surrealists famously juxtaposed things that no one would normally think of putting together as in the famous line from Lautréamont: "The chance meeting on a dissecting table of a sewing machine and an umbrella." Such juxtapositions are the stuff of dreams of course, the Surrealists in the 1920s being very much interested in the dream work of Freud and other early psychoanalysts.

Knowledge in each of these cases—in dreams, in Surrealism, and in Robert's practice—comes to us in images. Regarding Little Crow and history you could of course say something like "There is a statistical correlation between nineteenth-century racial attitudes among immigrant populations from Northern Europe and the difficulty of winning the hearts and minds of our allies in Southeast Asia." But that would be a scalped sentence. It has no living animal body in it and therefore no feeling life and therefore little chance of giving birth to ethical or spiritual consciousness, let alone to action. Images in Robert's works are not simply a technique or a matter of craft; they arise from a sense of how the human mind functions in its fullness, how it engages with the world. In an early essay of his about working with images he reminds us that we had a period of "imagism" in this country, one associated with Pound and Williams. Robert differentiates that movement from what he and others were trying to do in the sixties by saying that the earlier "imagism" was largely "picturism":

> An image and a picture differ in that the image, being the natural speech of the imagination, cannot be drawn from or inserted back into the real world. It is an animal native to the imagination. Like Bonnefoy's "interior sea lighted by turning eagles," it cannot be seen in real life. A picture, on the other hand, is drawn from the objective "real" world. "Petals on a wet black bough" can actually be seen. [*American* 20]

In one sense the lines I've quoted contain the kind of pictures that can be found in real life; you could actually go see Little Crow's scalp if you wanted to. But you cannot see the whole of what that line contains because the full image leaps between two centuries. This is a dissecting table where the Indian Wars have bumped into napalmed Vietnamese farmers. That juxtaposition departs from what a few of the Surrealists did, for some were not so interested in politics. Marcel Duchamp, for one, spent the second war in Argentina playing chess.

The surrealism of the "Teeth-Mother," on the other hand, is closer to that found in poems written by Pablo Neruda during the Spanish Civil War. Its imagistic density manages to combine spiritual questions (can you feel compassion for distant strangers?), psychological claims (unexamined inner life produces violence in the outer world), and political demands (the war must be stopped). It is political poetry in the simple sense of speech that cannot be aligned with the speech coming from the government or the television.

There was, after all, an official narrative about the Vietnam War that included things like the Domino Theory (if Vietnam fell, so would Laos, then Thailand...); to speak of Little Crow's scalp in that context was to offer a counter narrative (of the kind most likely to arise in solitude and retreat).

"Political concerns and inward concerns have always been regarded in our tradition as opposites, even incompatibles," Robert has said; the promise of what might be called "active solitude" is that it can dissolve that supposed opposition: "the political poem comes out of the deepest privacy." [*Talking* 98-99] Where that isn't the case, where inner and outer remain unrelated, then the task of the poet is to thin out the husk, the skin or the hide that we grow to separate the two—to thin it out *not*, however, to be that poor cow dragging her guts against the barn, but to replace the protective skin of indifference and inattention with a better, livelier membrane. The name of that membrane is poetry.

In this case it is a poetry of both belief and action. Notice that the quotations I've offered are both declarative sentences. Each declares its given perception to be true. They are assertions of faith, therefore, of the faith that the world can be read coherently, that there is a way to do the Hermes-task of drawing meaning from apparent nonsense, or from beneath the false-meanings that the collective offers.

> We know the road; as the moonlight
> Lifts everything, so in a night like this
> The road goes on ahead, it is all clear. [*Selected* 37]

First comes faith, then comes action. For if these perceptions are clear and true, what shall we do? There are many stories about action from that period, of course. To speak of only one of these, in the spring of 1968 Robert received the National Book Award for *The Light Around the Body*. The date matters because a few months earlier our government had begun to arrest a number of public figures who were counseling draft resistance. The Reverend William Sloane Coffin, Dr. Benjamin Spock, and three other men had been indicted for conspiracy and put on trial. Robert gave his Book Award acceptance speech on March 6, 1968 and at the end of it he gave his award check to Mike Kempton of The Resistance, saying: "I hereby counsel you... and other young men...to defy the draft authorities—and not to destroy [your] spiritual lives by participating in this war." [*Talking* 108] That sentence is what language theorists call "a speech act": it didn't just say something, it did something (it broke the law).

We often speak of Henry Thoreau as having been a solitary or asocial person but in doing so we forget that *to publish* means *to make public*. We forget, that is, that writing and publishing are forms of social engagement, of combat even. There is a wonderful essay by the British psychoanalyst Adam Phillips that touches on this matter of public combat. In an essay called "Superiorities" (in his book *Equals*) Phillips set out to imagine what equality might really mean, and why we often resist it. In the course of his argument he makes a nice distinction between two kinds of fighting: *antagonism* and *agonism*.

With antagonism we try to crush our opponents and silence them; agonism, on the other hand, welcomes conflict, entertains it, enjoys it even. An *agon* in ancient Greek drama was a verbal contest between two characters on the stage, each of whom appeals to the audience, neither having any necessary claim to the truth. Greek democracy borrowed from drama in this case, for democracy flourishes whenever antagonism can be converted into agonism, the contending of equals. Robert's literary criticism and his political interventions have always been democratic in the sense of welcoming agonistic exchanges. He once said that most American criticism is out to either destroy enemies or praise friends. He suggested and practiced a third form: "Those who are interested in the same sort of poetry [should] attack each other sharply, and still have respect and affection for each other." [*Talking* 160]

Whether they were directed toward friends or not, there were always fighting words in Robert's little magazine. As if to announce what was to come, the first issue of *The Fifties* contained these lines from William Blake:

> O young men of the New Age! Set your face against the ignorant hirelings! For we have hirelings in the Camp, the Court, and the

> University who would, if they could, forever depress mental and prolong corporeal war. [*Fifties* 1 44]

Depress mental and prolong corporeal war: Robert's antiwar poetry does the opposite. It engages in mental combat so as to depress the corporeal. I deeply believe that there are men and women my age who are alive today because we had people like Robert doing that work in the sixties. We cannot know who they are but they are among us. The sixties are often now maligned, imagined only in terms of sex, drugs, and licentiousness; but to describe them as such covers up the more significant story line. The antiwar movement actually did something; so did the civil rights movement; so did the wave of feminism that began at the end of the sixties. Each of these changed our world immeasurably. "You can't fight City Hall" is a rumor spread by City Hall. There were and there are hierarchies in this nation that depend on gender inequality, racial inequality, wealth inequality, and military force; in the late sixties they briefly lost control. They would like us to forget that and so they mock that period, but don't believe them. Ruth Bader Ginsburg now wears a black robe because Richard Nixon arrested Dr. Spock for burning draft cards.

I began with a story about visiting Robert in Madison; I'll end with a related story told to me by John Stratton Hawley, professor of Hinduism and Indian religions at Columbia University. Hawley once told me about a famous Sanskrit scholar who lived in Berkeley, California; this man was working at home one day when there came a knock on the door. When he answered a man was standing there who said he wanted to see him. The scholar said that he was very busy; perhaps they could make an appointment. The visitor explained that he had come all the way from India, that he was an admirer of the man's work, and that he just wanted to see him for fifteen minutes or so. The scholar relented and admitted his visitor asking him what specifically he wanted. "Oh nothing," the man said, "I really just wanted to see you." He sat there for fifteen minutes watching as the scholar went back to work. Then he left.

There is a tradition in Hindu culture called *darshan*. It means *to lay eyes on* or *to behold*. When we were undergraduates at the University of Minnesota it was important to us that we see some poets. There were several in the state, and we used to go look at them. All young people do this, I think. Robert did it when he was young—he went to see William Carlos Williams; he went to see Pablo Neruda. Surely there is a *darshan* of the book as well, a laying of eyes on authors and traditions long past, in Robert's case a witnessing of Rilke, Juan Ramón Jiménez, Jakob Böhme and so many others. I mention these long-dead spirits partly to move away from the necessary grandiosity that attends a celebration like this. We're here to celebrate Robert Bly, but to say only that is like saying we honor the door of a barn when the point is to open it and see the animals inside.

I brought one of those animals with me, something I found in Robert's barn forty years ago: a pamphlet of ten poems by Issa. Here are three of them:

> Now listen, you watermelons—
> if any thieves come—
> turn into frogs!
>
> This line of black ants—
> Maybe it goes all the way back
> to that white cloud?
>
> The old dog bends his head listening...
> I guess the singing
> of the earthworms gets to him.

On the first page of this little pamphlet we read: "This booklet is a gift, and is not to be sold." I've had this pamphlet for forty years; I brought it along to give away—to Jim Lenfestey who helped to organize this conference.

As you must know, I've written a book about gift-exchange and poetry, and I sometimes wonder if this sentence from this pamphlet wasn't a seed for that work. I recently read a remark by Bob Dylan about the first time he listened to Woody Guthrie: hearing Guthrie's songs, Dylan says, left him "feeling more like myself than ever before." That's a very strange remark if you think about it. A young man of 18 or 19 listens to an older man's art and it makes him feel like himself.

As for me, I've spent many days with Robert Bly during which I have felt quite like myself. It's quite mysterious, really. Mysterious to be born into a human body. Mysterious to have the gift of consciousness. Mysterious to mingle one mind with another. Wonderful to find friends and companions whose spirits enter into our own, enlarging us and letting us know we are not alone. How fine for many of us to have found, when we were young, such a roomy cow barn out in western Minnesota.

SOURCES

The Fifties. Number 1 (1958). [Published at Pine Island, Minnesota; edited by William Duffy and Robert Bly].

Bly, Robert. *American Poetry: Wildness and Domesticity*. New York: Harper & Row, 1990.

———. *Selected Poems*. New York: Harper & Row, 1986.

———. *Talking All Morning*. Ann Arbor: The University of Michigan Press, 1980.

———. *The Teeth-Mother Naked at Last*. San Francisco: City Lights Books, 1970.

Hyde, Lewis. "An Interview with Robert Bly." *The Lamp in the Spine*. Number 3 (Winter 1972): 50-65. (The interview was conducted in March 1969 by Lewis Hyde and Franz Allbert Richter at Madison, Minnesota).

Thoreau, Henry D. *A Week on the Concord and Merrimack Rivers*. Princeton, NJ: Princeton University Press, 2004.

SHADOWS ON THE PRAIRIE: WHERE THE GIFT GATHERS

By Patricia Kirkpatrick

I

Robert Bly was born in Madison, Minnesota, the son of Norwegian immigrant farmers Jacob and Alice Bly. He graduated from Madison High School where during his senior year, he and a young woman classmate were named "King and Queen of the Snow." After serving two years in the Navy, he attended St. Olaf College for a year, then transferred to Harvard, where he joined the writing class of Archibald MacLeish along with Adrienne Rich, Donald Hall, and John Ashbery. He lived several years in New York after college. In 1955 he married Carol MacLean—the late writer Carol Bly—and returned to Minnesota, settling on a farm near Madison where they raised four children. There Bly wrote the poems published in his first book, *Silence in the Snowy Fields*. Although he has lived in other places and traveled widely, he has always kept a home in Minnesota.

"I worked in the *Snowy Fields* poems," he has noted, "to gain a resonance among the sounds, and hidden below that there is a second resonance between the soul and a loved countryside, in this case the countryside of my childhood." The resonance between the soul and the countryside is what I want to talk about here. The soul—or "soul-making," the subjective experience of the inner life—traditionally has been a subject of lyric poetry, going back to John Keats and before. The countryside of Bly's childhood is western Minnesota: the river valleys, fields, farms, small towns, birds and animals of the prairie, the dark earth left by retreating glaciers which rises ultimately to become the great American plains of the Dakotas. Once inhabited by the Dakota people, forcibly removed from it onto reservations, the land was settled by Scandinavian and German immigrants. Bly grew up, in his own words, as a "Lutheran boy-god"—a special son somehow floating above the "stream of life"—and as a farm boy, with grass at his feet, a horizon in the distance, and the height of sky, clouds, and sun overhead. Before he went to Harvard, he knew where split-tail swallows build nests in spring and how box-elder leaves smell in fall. He also knew the labor of the seasons, how to shock grain, how to bring in hay, first with horses, later with machines. "If the senses are sharpened by labor," he writes in *A Little Book on the Human Shadow*, "you begin to merge with the creatures and objects around you." Here is a poem of such merging.

WAKING ON THE FARM

I can remember the early mornings—how the stubble,
A little proud with frost, snapped as we walked.

How the John Deere tractor hood pulled heat
Away from our hands when we filled it with gas.

And the way the sun brought light right out of the ground.
It turned on a whole hill of stubble as easily as a single stone.

Breathing seemed frail and daring in the morning.
To pull in air was like reading a whole novel.

The angleworms, turned up by the plow, looked
Uneasy like shy people trying to avoid praise.

For awhile we had goats. They were like turkeys
Only more reckless. One butted a red Chevrolet.

When we washed up at noon, we were more ordinary.
But the water kept something in it of the early morning.

Vowels make the resonance among the sounds in "Waking on the Farm." Just as the poem's speaker recalls that the grass stubble "snapped as we walked," so the poem's vowels snap as we read: the short *a*'s of "snapped," "hands" and "gas"; the long o's of "stones" and "goats"; the long e's of "heat" and "breathing." I always have thought the lines of this and other Bly poems look something like the fields described, long straight lines of free verse that resemble row-crops of corn and soybeans and give a tremendous sense of space. The lines carry clear images of animals and objects, what Bly's fellow poet Galway Kinnell has called "the creatures of the world" necessary to poetry: angleworms, shy people, turkeys. Finally the poem suggests power below and beyond the surface of what can be seen: light being brought out of the ground, water keeping something of the "unordinary" morning.

When morning gives way to afternoon, Bly describes the snowy fields themselves.

SNOWFALL IN THE AFTERNOON

I

The grass is half-covered with snow.
It was the sort of snowfall that starts in late afternoon,
And now the little houses of the grass are growing dark.

II

If I could reach down, near the earth,
I could take handfuls of darkness!
A darkness that was always there, which we never noticed.

III

As the snow grows heavier, the cornstalks fade farther away,
And the barn moves nearer to the house.
The barn moves all alone in the growing storm.

IV

The barn is full of corn, and moving toward us now,
Like a hulk blown toward us in a storm at sea;
All the sailors on deck have been blind for many years.

I like the plain, colloquial language of this poem, the sentence of the second line especially, and the subtle but steady interplay between literal physical description and metaphorical suggestion. Sometimes it's hard to tell the difference between those last two: for me that's what gives the poem its tension between senses of calm and alarm. Yes, there's darkness near grass but are there houses? (I thought there were when I was a child and watched snow fall in the afternoon.) Yes, the snow grows heavier, cornstalks fade, the barn is filled with corn. But the barn can't really move. Suddenly there are blind sailors: where do they come from and what should we make of them? These kinds of leaps and associations of imagery characterize many Bly poems.

Lewis Hyde has said that the declarative sentences of Bly's poems are "statements of faith: they declare 'I can read the world.'" With such sentence statements, Bly reads the world of a prairie childhood informed by years of education, his curiosity about what he has called the shadow or "dark" side of personality, American history, and perhaps also a visionary dread toward the the "weather ahead" in America.

Grass growing dark, and *handfuls of darkness*. It's a physical description, of course, but for Bly, darkness has always been a psychological matter as well. Over the years he has urged himself and readers to explore the dark, hidden or "shadow" parts of the personality; to allow, in poetry and in life, those moments when unconscious material "shoots up into the conscious mind."

On the prairie, to speak of grass means to speak of the earth. Bly's psychological portrait of an individual personality, what can shoot up from below, parallels a scientific description of the dark earth where prairie grasses root. The late Paul Gruchow, who grew up in the Chippewa River Valley outside Montevideo fifty miles or so from Madison, describes the prairie ecosystem in his book *Journal of a Prairie Year*.

> Grasses are wonderfully well suited to the capricious prairie winds. For one thing, they grow from the roots up. A grass seedling shows only modest top growth for the first three or four years of its life. It spends much of its energy in building a dense underground support system. Its roots grow deep enough to take advantage of subsoil stores of water in times of drought, and they grow wide enough to catch the nutriment and moisture in the upper levels of the soil in times of normal rainfall. The grasses make

> a forest that grows undergound instead of aboveground, and an incredible thicket it is. A square meter of prairie sod might contain twenty-five miles of roots.

The energy of those subsoil stores is the stuff Bly is after. "In a poem, as in a human body, what is invisible makes all the difference," he writes in his essay "A Wrong Turning in American Poetry." In poetry and on the prairie the invisible subsoil drives a life force that offers nourishment from darkness.

Bly always has insisted that the shadow side of the self must not only be brought up but *lived*, being careful to clarify that the human shadow isn't necessarily evil, but often simply unknown, undervalued. In this way he has related the individual human personality to the larger directions of culture. He believes that, untended, the human shadow can be acted out in dangerous ways, including ways that are "cruel, selfish, can kill people," and that is how he interprets much of the violence in American history, including on the prairie. Regarding the indigenous people driven from the land, he reads the world of western Minnesota like this in the poem "A Pint of Whiskey and Five Cigars": "We all knew what was at stake; both/ The Europeans and the Sioux wanted holy ground."

Holy ground. Of his own holy ground, he spoke of his book, *Silence in the Snow Fields*, in a 2000 *Paris Review* interview with Francis Quinn, saying, "I never could have written a book that interesting without being in the landscape of my childhood." In an unpublished interview in 2002, I asked him why that landscape was so important. "Well, you know you learn a lot of things when you go to school and you read Nietzche and Kierkegaard and you learn a lot of new words. How well do you know what the words mean? Are they words that your family ever spoke? Probably not. Certainly you don't know what the word *justice* means. Even the word *heaven*. But coming back to a place of my childhood I knew what the word *dusk* meant. The word *snow*. So with the help of the old Chinese poets, Du Fu and others who always wrote about a quiet landscape, I was able to talk about the things I knew, experiences I had in childhood, only with a better sense that I was being true to them."

Here we detoured a bit from the subject of landscape to Minnesota culture in general. Bly told the story of a Lutheran minister serving as a missionary in China who questioned the dishonest way Lutherans counted their Chinese converts, because many converts "recycled" from Lutheran to Baptist to Methodist and so on. For his question the minister was removed and sent to Madison, not allowed to transfer to "better churches," nor to teach at St. Olaf in Northfield. But the minister knew a lot about China, had Chinese objects all over his house and was a wonderful man, Bly recalled. "One time, maybe when I was in college, I had said something like 'I am the master of my soul' from that old poem by Thomas Henley, the English imperialist. I remember Tetley, the minister, heard about it and he drove all the way out to the farm, asked to see me and said, 'Listen, I can understand how you feel but that 's not right. We aren't the master of our souls.' Isn't that touching? So there, right inside that Minnesota culture, was a strange little opening for China, and an urge to be a bit suspicious of Lutheran purity and the anger and hatred of the truth. That opening was a lot of help to me."

At the time Robert and I spoke he was writing the introduction to James Wright's *Selected Poems*. "For Jim, a part of his whole life was anger and disgust at the mood of Ohio, because that's a part of the life of the United States, that horrible destruction of landscape by the mining companies. In Minnesota there's more of a sense of blessing. I think Jim was healed by coming out here and feeling the land that hadn't been destroyed. You don't want to compliment Minnesota too much, but you could say one can feel blessed by those fields and our own moral history. A lot of good things have come politically out of this state." He named the *Star Tribune* newspaper and the late senator Eugene McCarthy as examples.

Coming back to the fields and moral history of his childhood countryside enabled Bly to do these two things. First he moved himself to a landscape *empty of cultural expectation*—notice I do not say empty of culture because I don't believe that's true—a place, in his own words, removed from the "seats of power," even the cultural power of museums, symphony orchestras, ivy-league universities.

Second he used the imagery of that landscape to show that the place itself is not only a source of literal nourishment and spiritual sustenance but also a playing field for historic events and their political consequences.

The Minnesota prairie grounded some of Bly's most political poems. In "A Poem for the Drunkard President," Bly describes the fate of Little Crow, the chief of the Mdewakanton Dakota Sioux who participated in the 1851 negotiations for the Treaties of the Traverse des Sioux and Mendota which sent his people to the west side of the Minnesota River. "Little Crow died with skunk-fur bands on his wrists," Bly writes in that poem from the 1950s, belatedly published in his second selected poems, *Eating the Honey of Words*, in 1999. Little Crow, born in 1810, had tried to adapt to the ways of the white settlers, even became a farmer, then fought in the 1862 Dakota War, ultimately fleeing to Canada when his people lost their territory. When he came back to Minnesota in 1863 for horses, Little Crow was shot and killed by a European farmer for a $500 bounty, his mutilated body dragged through the streets of Hutchinson. In a poem from *The Light Around the Body* (1967), "Hatred of Men with Black Hair," Bly links the story of Little Crow to the 1960's struggles of African people for independence from colonial powers—Belgium and Portugal—in the countries now known as the Democratic Republic of Congo and Angola, finally implicating himself and others who have spent time in the hardware stores and tack rooms of Minnesota:

> I hear voices praising Tshombe, and the Portuguese
> In Angola, these are the men who skinned Little Crow!
> We are all their sons, skulking
> In back rooms, selling nails with trembling hands!
>
> We distrust every person on earth with black hair....

"So what do you look for now in a political poem?" I asked in 2002.

"Now I'd have to look for the word 'we.' I think that's what my generation of poets learned. And if we don't raise our voices—if you don't cry out in a fragrant language, because fragrance comes out of the shadow—it means you're still being trapped by rationality."

In the book *The Light Around the Body*, and others after it, Bly would move increasingly to the word 'we.' But in *Silence in the Snowy Fields*, the solitary poet still speaks often of the counryside in a first person singular voice.

> I am driving; it is dusk; Minnesota.
> The stubble field catches the last growth of sun.
> The soybeans are breathing on all sides.
> Old men are sitting before their houses on car seats
> In the small towns. I am happy,
> The moon rising above the turkey sheds.
>
> ("Driving Toward the Lac Qui Parle River")

2

The lyric poem, its little song: its flicker, cry, and hum. Fireflies light the prairie night then suddenly disappear. *Lit and gone.* The critic Helen Vendler writes that "lyric requires not a character but a voice," its purpose is "to represent an inner life in such a manner that it is assumable by others." The voice of a lyric poem holds the listener—with image and sound—to a single moment in time, fleeting yet eternal.

When my children were babies I realized the lyric, its little song, propels the first voice of the child. Repetition helps. What does the sheep say? *Baa, baa.* What does the duck say? *Quack, quack.* The baby alone in her crib sang the sounds to herself. *La la la la la.* I listened. Such sounds are called, such songs sung, by people all over the world. Here are workings by James Koller from Frances Densmore's translations of "Sioux Metamorphoses."

> At daybreak
> I go
> I gallop
> I go

.....

I thought I saw buffalo
& called out
I thought I saw buffalo
& called out
let them be buffalo

They were blackbirds
I walked toward them
& they were blackbirds

I thought I saw buffalo
& called out
I thought I saw buffalo
& called out
let them be buffalo

They were swallows
I walked toward them
& they were swallows

How assumable is the inner life of one person by others? It's a challenging question, and much of the challenge I think is related to the qualities of a poem's speaker, that voice a poet creates. I have never hunted buffalo, but when I read it aloud, I can assume the straightforward hope and expectation, even the restrained disappointment carried in the voice of "Sioux Metamorphoses." These are not so different from what Bly expresses in the poem "Waking on the Farm": "I can remember the early mornings—how the stubble, /A little proud with frost, snapped as we walked." There is little sense of character in either poem: we don't know how old the speakers are, what they look like, nor even if the speakers are male or female. But both poems offer an urgent, direct voice, punctuated by short words, bound by the repetition of sounds. Would a New Yorker be able to assume—or feel—the inner life these poems present? Would a citizen of Elizabethan England, accustomed to the metrical line of a Shakespearean sonnet? I don't know.

Contemporary poets, influenced by everything from philosophy, literary theory, and neuroscience have been debating whether there can be a single voice and speaker for a poem, whether one inner life experience can center a poem. Some poets want to go beyond Rimbaud's "'I' is an *other*" to "'I' is many," or perhaps 'I' is nobody at all. Emily Dickinson was there in the 19th century: "I'm nobody. Who are you?" In the early 20th century, Virginia Woolf, among others, was asking such questions in prose. In her essay "Evening Over Sussex: Reflections in a Motor Car," she juggles four selves at once, writing "it is well known how in circumstances like these"—the circumstances being a ride in a car—"the self splits up and one self is eager and dissatisfied and the other stern and philosophical...." Yet as the ride in the car continues, Woolf concludes, "Now we have got to collect ourselves; we have got to be one self. Nothing is to be seen any more, except one wedge of road and bank which our lights repeat incessantly."

Woolf's "wedge of road and bank" reminds me of Bly's poem "Driving Toward the Lac Qui Parle River," and also of the process of making a poem. "To make a poem we must make sound," Mary Oliver writes in her fine book *A Poetry Handbook*, "not random sound but chosen sounds." The expectations for what sounds a poet will choose change from one time and place to another. But again and again a lyric poem offers an invitation to establish a relationship between writer and reader, between speaker and listener. In the poem "Come With Me," Bly extends this invitation:

> Come with me into those things that have felt this despair for so long—
> Those removed Chevrolet wheels that howl with a terrible loneliness,
> Lying on their back in the cindery dirt...

The poem's invitation to visit the broken lives of the prairie is underscored by an even more essential call to make the sounds of language: the "o," "s" and "t" sounds in words the poet has chosen. The sounds of our language: Bly chooses them in his poems; the speaker chants them in "Sioux Metamorphoses"; the baby practices them alone in her crib as she sings.

3

Robert Bly was the beginning of poetry for me. I loved—and wrote—poetry as a child but cared more about history and politics when I got to college. It was the end of the 1960's, the beginning of the 1970's: on Wednesdays I stood with others on the Pentacrest of the University of Iowa campus to protest the Vietnam War. For three spring semesters in a row, my university of 20,000 students was shut down by protests. I thought we were going to change the world.

A friend gave me copies of *Silence in the Snowy Fields* and James Wright's *The Branch Will Not Break*. For me these poems were the revelation of an inner life that took place in a landscape I knew from my childhood in Iowa. They showed me what poetry could be in contemporary life. But I was coming at the poems backwards. I had barely taken a college English course beyond the requirements. Others spoke of the freshness of Bly's poetry, its bolt from the strictures and poses of metered verse. Patricia Hampl has written that she found in the poetry and translations of *The Fifties*, the magazine Bly edited with William Duffy, "an immediacy and pulse" she hadn't found in her classes as an English major. "I read Bly's magazine, and his good-spirited but deadly attacks on the literary establishment, and I knew I was reading the future."

I only knew I was reading poetry—and I loved it. There was plenty of poetry in Iowa City: I took courses in the Writer's Workshop, devoured the Paul Carroll anthology *The Young American Poets*, heard readings by Marvin Bell, Jack Marshall, Albert Goldbarth, Louise Gluck. The night I heard poet Galway Kinnell, introduced by Richard Hugo, read his poems, including "The Bear," I walked home looking at the stars and decided I wanted to be a poet. The naivete of it all still astounds me, but at the time, it was so.

There also was a burgeoning women's movement in Iowa City as well as across the country: more demonstrations, newspapers like *Ain't I a Woman*, anthologies like *Sisterhood Is Powerful*, Adrienne Rich's poetry in *The Will to Change*. Extraordinary public events seemed to prompt continual changes in daily life. It was a heady if slightly capricious time to graduate from college and want to be a poet. Yet my degree was in sociology and I knew little about the history of poetry in my language. When I went to graduate school in San Francisco, to study with a woman poet I'd met in Iowa City who became a mentor, I realized how truly behind I was. Not only were there centuries of literary history to address but many poetry factions in the Bay Area itself: language poets, feminists, remnants of the Beats, the Berkeley Poets Coop, Tassahara Buddhists, and many poets new to me whose work I wanted to read—George Oppen, Robert Hass, Kathleen Fraser. One day in class my mentor said that Robert Bly had been a terrible influence on women writers, and to be fair I don't think Bly had much regard for her or her work. It wasn't a good time for women to name male writers as models, and I had come to my own misgivings about aspects of Bly's work. I was distressed as Bly championed "the Great Mother" while seeming to ignore writing by women and the influence of the women's movement itself. Suffice it to say that the subject of gender in literature was—and is—difficult and deserves more discussion. Additionally, West—and East—Coast writers were not inclined to appreciate work by Midwestern writers. Meanwhile I had oral exams to study for, the poetry of Emily Dickinson, the modernism of Virginia Woolf.

Fast forward ten years. I had married a writer and we moved to Minnesota where he had a playwrighting fellowship. We bought a house, I got a teaching job, he published novels, I wrote poetry, and together we raised a daughter and son in a wonderful Saint Paul neighborhood. Then the bridge came falling down. In 2005 my mother died after the sudden and grueling onset of a rare disease. Her death was followed by others, then family crises, finally my own major health blow. In the same period, I received a generous poetry grant. But I had lost my way as a poet. In my own darkness I remembered how my way to poetry began. I wanted to see where and perhaps how *Silence in the Snowy Fields* came into being. I began driving regularly to western Minnesota, to the towns of Sacred Heart, Montevideo, Milan, Bellingham, and of course Madison. I was glad to see the fields, the dull stares of Black Angus cattle, the unspooled shimmer of the Lac Qui Parle River, yellow meadowlarks punching out of ditches, stalls of red sumac along the roads. Yet if homage initiated my drives, the spirit of the prairie soon took over. I began to write my own prairie poems.

4

In his magnificent book, *The Gift*, Lewis Hyde writes, "The spirit of the artist's gifts can wake our own." Robert Bly's gifts have awakened many readers and writers. The Minnesota landscape of his childhood awakened him. And that gift—the spirit of a particular land—has been given to many, whether the land was, to use the terms of James Baldwin, a *birthright* the writer was born to or a *heritage* the writer sought. I am thinking not only of Robert Bly, but of James Wright, Carol Bly, Paul Gruchow, Thomas McGrath, Jim Moore, Phebe Hanson, Bill Holm, Joyce Sutphen, many others. Go north from Madison and find the land of Black Elk, Louise Erdrich and Heid Erdrich, David Treuer; go south and find the land of Meridel LeSueur, Frederick Manfred, and Freya Manfred.

"The gift must always move," Lewis Hyde tells us. The gift must be given, accepted, and reciprocated. Perhaps I write here to keep the gift of land and literature moving. I know I received Bly's poetry of an essential if undervalued American landscape as a gift, and I write of it now when the landscape, as well as ways of life that have been rooted there, are increasingly at risk. You can still find beauty on the prairie. But a multinational company owns the patent for the seeds of corn. Family farms are threatened by corporate farming; top soil is eroded; chain stores ring the edges of towns.

I admire other aspects of Bly's work I haven't discussed, his fierce moral vision for example, and the raging Whitmanesque protest of his long poem "The Teeth Mother Naked at Last." Yet even there, in the most surrealistic charges of that political poem, I find evidence of the prairie. Of Vietnam he writes: "Engines burning a thousand gallons of gasoline a minute sweep over the huts with dirt floors." Of the use of napalm he writes:

> But if one of those children came near that we have set on fire,
> Came toward you like a gray barn, walking,

> You would howl like a wind tunnel in a hurricane,
> You would tear at your shirt with blue hands,
> You would drive over your own child's wagon trying to back up,
> The pupils of your eyes would go wild—

5

When I interviewed Bly in 2002, his book *The Night Abraham Called to the Stars* had just been published. We sat upstairs in his Minneapolis writing studio on an August afternoon, Bly in front of a window overlooking a branch outside where a cardinal perched. The position of his chair to the window, branch, and cardinal made it look like the bird sat on him. It's an image I'll never forget: Robert Bly with a ruddy red bird on his head.

We talked about the changes in form and line of his new poems compared with those in past books. One of the biggest changes was the "escape from free verse" which he explained like this. "My whole generation, you know, led the attack against meter and I was just as mouthy as anyone about it. Our free verse had to do with rebellion against rationality and English models, how to speak deeply from the 'I' and so forth. I remained in that place, with free verse, until I could understand a form that was not English."

The understanding came when he discovered the Mideastern form of the ghazal. In the ghazal form the stanzas don't rhyme but they repeat words as they continually change subjects. Bly said such repetition creates a pleasure the audience feels. " The audience knows that the writer has gone through a lot of trouble in order that the audience can have this strange pleasure. From that point of view, free verse has a lot to do with your self will. Writing in form has to do with service. In the *Snowy Fields* poems I used free verse and I would have cheered you up in some way. In 'The Teeth-Mother' it's sort of the Whitman line. Whitman blesses you with the long line. But I throw out the long line like a whip: I sting you! That long line is not a form of blessing and it's not a form of service."

"I came to the ghazal form of service at the same time I'm trying to learn service in my own life," he concluded. But his ghazal poems don't leave behind the farm. "In the *Abraham* poems when I'm talking about Rembrandt and Newton, I know those poems are grounded by my life as a farm boy." He started reading aloud some lines which became stanzas of the poem "Eating Blackberry Jam" in a later book.

> When I hear that we all belong to nonexistence,
> I drop my eyes, but then I raise them out
> Of love for the little creatures of nonexistence.
> ...
>
> The cries of the infant barn-swallows rising from
> The mud-nests fastened ingeniously to the rafters
> Taught me to love the skinny birds of nonexistence.

"You see I could float off on this existence and nonexistence. It's a Buddhist concept. What anchors it is that I remember those swallows and the nests they made."

Because Bly talked so much about being anchored to the landscape of his childhood, I asked why the new poems reference so many philosophers, artists, religions, and rulers.

"Because! I want to remind people, if you don't know this, look it up! I'm not making my poems simple just because you didn't read your god-damn books in high school and college!"

"So your service to the reader comes with lessons?" I pressed.

"Yes!"

Blessings, service, lessons: it seemed that the Lutheran boy-god was back, and that he had been joined by a Jewish mystic and a private school headmaster. Indeed the *Abraham* poems reference a multitude of cultural figures from many centuries and countries. But the poems are intimate too, and the Minnesota countryside still hovers in the lines. I asked what would happen to a culture that doesn't live closely with animals, to generations of children who grow up without feeding goats or gathering eggs, knowing how a barn smells, or watching swallows build their mud nests. Bly paused a long time.

"I think that's something my generation grieves about."

In 2005 Bly published his second book of ghazals, *My Sentence Was a Thousand Years of Joy*. At times these poems shriek and wail harsh cries. Yet even when he stings us—and himself—most intensely with our failures, with the war and waste of cities and countryside, he offers a scene of hope from the prairie. I'll end with lines from "The Buff-Chested Grouse":

> It was only when I was out in the fields, hiding
> From the winds, that I understood that what fell
> To pieces last night could be whole this morning.

BIRTH OF A REVOLUTION: THE FIFTIES

By William Duffy

It has been over a half-century since Robert Bly and I first met. He was on his way back to his Madison, Minnesota farm and I was a graduate student at the University of Minnesota, where we were introduced to each other by a mutual friend. He was 28 years old and I was 25. There weren't more than a few casual remarks about poetry and my reference to teach at Clara City in the fall. Since we'd be only a short distance from each other, we agreed that we'd be getting together in a few months. Our meetings in the fall of 1955 turned out to be extended conversations about our own poetry, but even more intensively about the state of modern American poetry, its pitfalls, its shortcomings, and basically what poetry really needed then. We concurred that the life blood of American poetry had become so infused with English traditions that it didn't have distinctive characteristics of its own. Surely, there had been attempted revivals of American poetry in New York, North Carolina, and, of course, in the blaring iconoclastic Beat movement, mainly issuing its fuming poetry from San Francisco, but all falling short to us.

And it was wasn't long before I realized that Robert was a benevolent genius with a photographic memory. He had an interesting anecdote about every literary person he had ever met, listened to, or read about. As many know, he has this fascinating manner in the way he describes people, incidents, and places where he had lived. With his seemingly encyclopedic mind, one could surmise that he has on tap the last hundred years of European, South American, and North American poetry.

But poetry didn't always occupy our time in those early days. We'd go pheasant hunting in the long corn fields and soybean fields of Lac Qui Parle County. Or we'd visit interesting places, attend auctions, and talk to old neighbors. Occasionally, we would drive over to Jacob and Alice's place on an errand. One time there was the all-night New Year's Eve party that dozens of local friends attended. But

I remember that the next day was a little too bright and sunny for most of us who went over to Jim Bly's farm for dinner.

Curiously, we never spent any of our time in cities or larger towns, except once to attend a play in Minneapolis, which, I believe, featured Marilyn Monroe. But always there were the long dinners and longer discussions about poetry following the dinners. Since we both had farm experiences, there was an unsaid mutual understanding in our references to rural life.

But then there was that inevitable moment when we both sensed that perhaps we could realistically do something ourselves about the predicaments of American poetry. Outside of what we thought was a handful of good American poets at that time, the poetry of America in the Fifties was mainly represented by the Beats sect and the college and university mills who wrote mostly in intellectual and regressive English styles. It was obvious to us that this kind of poetry didn't represent the true and authentic American culture.

Our discussions paused for a moment. While Robert preferred the rows of flat corn fields and a landscape of towering grain elevators every six miles, I really needed the hills and trees I had always known in southern Minnesota, so I accepted a new teaching job in Pine Island, Minnesota. Here I bought a house high on a hill overlooking the town. Then Robert and I would split our time between Pine Island and his Madison farm.

By 1957 we both understood what we thought were the key deficiencies of the current poetry and what we presumed American poetry desperately needed to flourish and represent our present culture. Just as an artist "paints" the history of his era, we knew that the poet also must be the poetic recorder of his own culture in his own time.

Oddly enough, the majority of American poets then were still using rhymes, meters, and constricting forms modeled after the great days of English poetry. This was especially true of many university poets who were constantly attempting to write their inspirations in the styles of Shakespeare (sonnets), Donne, Byron, Keats, and Shelley. So without any trepidation, Robert and I took a bold stance and declared all that kind of poetry to be "old-fashioned." This became a mantra for us. We were not denigrating the English poets of the past. We were just boldly stating that modern American poets should no longer continue to resurrect the old syntax, forms, styles, and meters from the ancient trunks of English antiquity. We hoped that American poets would find new methods in our own country and write poems in an American way. We favored a poetry with passion, new imagination, and dense texture. We would rather see that the poem expresses the emotion rather than explains the emotion. We felt there was no need for iambs, caesuras, rhymes, patterns, or constricting forms as in the sonnet. In fact, we felt there was no need for form itself. Modern poets who had captured their own culture's new imagination and methods were writing fine poems, especially in South America and in Europe. We found excellent examples from Neruda, Vallejo, Lorca, Trakl, and Machado.

In fact, we mostly agreed with Machado when he said, "...the substance of poetry does not lie in the sound of the word, nor in its color, nor in the poetic line, nor in the complex sensations, but in the depth of the spirits and this deep pulse is what the soul contributes, if it contributes anything, with a voice appropriate to itself, in a courageous answer to the touch of the world." (*The Fifties*, #4)

We wanted our own modern American poetry to have a deep understanding of our life today along with a keen display of new imagination. So the founding of *The Fifties* came to Robert and me rather simultaneously. We felt we could only show American poets what we believed was acceptable in the United States by starting our own literary magazine. We were well aware that the Beats would not approve of our own poetry, nor would the university presses that really only published "their own." But that simple decision of publishing a literary magazine was elementary compared to all the practical details. We decided that a four-prong approach might suit us best. In each issue we would have a few American poets, some European or South American poets in translation, an essay or two explaining our positions and thoughts on what modern American poetry should be, and lastly, a few pages of sarcasm, humor, and irony. Fortunately, while Robert was in Norway, he had discovered some present-day

Scandinavian poets, so we decided that some of their poems would be the translations for our first issue, since we believed some of these poems might elucidate our poetic beliefs. Since there were no poetry submissions for the first publication, we solicited poems from contemporary American poets who reflected the kind of poetry that should be written in the Fifties. We knew that most small poetry magazines fail because they simply publish poems. So for us, there also had to be teaching in the early issues by not only showing, but explaining to our poetry audience what we conceived was truly American poetry. This procedure obviously set a tone of "We're taking a definite stand here and now, whether anyone else does or not." Because of this editorial attitude in our essays, we would surely gain support and enemies.

Before the first issue could be printed, there were dozens of practical decisions to make—choosing type, advertising, distribution, payments, and publisher. The first production of 1,000 copies cost us more than we could recover from subscriptions, so we certainly knew it was a money-loser. But the promotion of new American poetry was our primary goal. Surprisingly, the majority of new subscription requests came from colleges and universities. This is what we had hoped for because that meant multiple readers per copy.

When the presses had finally rolled, Robert sent me the first copy and brought all the rest back with him from New York. With further distribution, letters and poetry submissions started appearing. Sometimes my Pine Island mail box would contain ten to twenty letters a day—some of indignation and horror and many shouts of approval. Complimentary copies were sent to a number of contemporary published poets and other famous world writers which resulted in dozens of commentaries from them. But by far the longest and most detailed letter was from James Wright. And I mean long—his letter was six single-spaced typewritten pages. Obviously the new *Fifties* magazine had been a catharsis for him. Jim had recently published a book of poetry in the style that we had labeled "old-fashioned" in our first issue. Interestingly, he had received compliments from his peers (professors at the University of Minnesota) comparing him to John Keats! Jim's poetry immediately went through a complete transformation. And two of his "new modern American style" poems were quickly published in our second issue. One of these poems was "In Fear of Harvests." This poem, one by Robert, and one by me were published by *The Fifties* and *The Sixties* press.

IN FEAR OF HARVESTS

It has happened
Before; nearby,
The nostrils of slow horses
Breathe evenly,
And the brown bees drag their high garlands
Heavily,
Toward hives of snow.
—James Wright

POEM IN THREE PARTS

I
Oh, on an early morning I think I shall live forever!
I am wrapped in my joyful flesh,
As the grass is wrapped in its clouds of green.

II
Rising from a bed, where I dreamt
Of long rides past castles and hot coals,
The sun lies happily on my knees;
I have suffered and survived the night,
Bathed in dark water, like any blade of grass.

III
The strong leaves of the box-elder tree,
Plunging in the wind, call us to disappear

Into the wilds of the universe,
Where we shall sit at the foot of a plant,
And live forever, like the dust.
—Robert Bly

POEM ON FORGETTING THE BODY

Riding on the inner side of the blackbird's
Wings, I feel the long
Warm flight to the sea;
Dark, black in the trees at night.
Along the railroad tracks
In men's minds wild roses grow.
Lingering as ripe black olives
I go down the stairs of the little leaves,
To the floating continent
Where men forget their bodies,
Searching for the tiny
Grain of sand behind their eyes.
—William Duffy

These three poems represented what we believed were examples of modern American poetry of that period.

With Jim's letter came his long association with *The Fifties* and with Robert particularly. One weekend during the summer of 1958, I believe, Robert and Jim came down to Pine Island to spend a few days. While Robert and I were occupied with "magazine" work, Jim was upstairs writing poems. Later that afternoon I remember Jim standing in front of the kitchen window and reading to us his first draft of "In Fear of Harvests" and asking us whether the last few words should be "hives of snow" or "hooves of snow." I think we suggested the latter, but he said, "I believe I'll go with 'hives of snow.'"

I'm sure that *The Fifties* would have always been a popular literary magazine, but it became a trend-setter and notoriously influential because of many other reasons. Even James Wright's so-called conversion made readers more aware of it and what it stood for. Robert had involved himself in various literary activities. *The Fifties* became widely discussed in New York where Robert was head of the poetry readings at New York University. It was at NYU where Robert invited Louis Simpson, Donald Justice and me to read our poetry one December evening. And we all had a grand time before, during, and after the readings. Robert's associations with poetry readers at NYU and the "Y" certainly promoted our magazine and its affirmations. Besides that, he taught university classes at various places and gave his poetry readings throughout the United States for many years. I'm saying that *The Fifties* magazine was the instrument of our ideas, examples, and goals, but it was Robert on the road, so to speak, who helped bring *The Fifties* to fulfill its purposes.

Being in New York with Robert led to exciting times. We had tea with Stanley Kunitz, visited the Hechts, lunched with Denise Levertov, met with elegant Spanish poets, went to E. E. Cummings's home, etc., etc. Besides all that, we attended many literary parties and even played some practical jokes on Columbia University faculty members.

Then one morning in New York, Robert and I got a call to pick up the second issue of *The Fifties*, which had just arrived from Ireland, so we had to go down to the docks. On the way we were thinking about the big duty tax we'd have to pay. But inside we immediately noticed that the agent in charge was named O'Grady. Robert quickly noted to me to do the talking. Agent O'Grady quickly located the box and lovingly exclaimed that it was from old Ireland. He studied the papers, asked my name and identification, and finally with a big smile on his face told us since we were Irish and the box was from Ireland, it just wasn't right for him to take our money.

As usual, with Robert there were many pleasures whether seriously appraising poetry submissions, making editorial choices, or writing rejection slips. Friends of Robert all agree about his generosity. He always has a gift for you along with that inimitable broad smile. But his material gifts dwindle compared to the attention and support he has given to beginning writers and poets. He'll spend hours with novitiates suggesting how and what they should concentrate on. Hundreds of young writers will assure you of his kind, encouraging, and helpful suggestions he has given to them. Bill Holm, just recently deceased, exclaimed about the wonderful insights that Robert had given him, and considered him one of his mentors.

When I left to teach in North Africa in the fall of 1960, it was Jim Wright who slipped in to aid Robert with parts of the magazine, especially with the translations. When I was leaving for Tangier, I had asked Robert if he could get the basement door repaired on my Pine Island home. So in late September in 1960, Robert and Jim came down to stay at my empty Pine Island home. Robert went about getting a carpenter to repair the door while Jim was lying in the hammock under the trees. And this is when he wrote the famous poem, "Lying in a Hammock at William Duffy's Farm in Pine Island, Minnesota." *The New York Times Book Review* said this was probably the best poem written in the twentieth century. Robert and Jim took short trips also down toward Orinoco and Rochester. Somewhere along the way, Jim wrote about the pastured horses. So the basement door was fixed, a few poems were written, and I brought the hammock with me when I moved to Grand Marais, Minnesota.

Now, more than a half-century later, we see that most of American poetry has changed and has been rejuvenated. Most literary historians say that *The Fifties* magazine did play a crucial role in modernizing American poetry. And Robert and I are grateful to accept that conclusion.

Even though Robert and I took different paths in the Sixties, our old seasoned friendship remains strong and steadfast. For me, it has been one memorable and glorious expedition with some of the world's most gifted poets. A half-century later, my great admiration and love for Robert has only grown stronger.

UNDER THE SIGN OF ODIN: ROBERT BLY'S WILD LITTLE MAGAZINE[1]

By Mark Gustafson

How did a publication from rural southern Minnesota, with just eleven individual issues over a period of fourteen years, manage to be one of the most talked-about and argued-over literary magazines of its time? That is the question. By writing a book-length narrative in answer, I have reconstructed how each issue of *The Fifties/Sixties/Seventies* came together and how it was received. It is an epic story, closely intertwined with many of Bly's other activities, and with his community of fellow poets.[2]

In this essay, instead of merely summarizing that larger report, trying to hit all the high points, I have limited myself to two tasks: first, to account, in chronological fashion, for the magazine's gestation period; and second, to use a conceit—which I will develop in the first part—as a means to explore some (but not all) of the more obvious traits of the magazine and its effect on its readers. The latter part is more impressionistic and uneven, exemplary rather than exhaustive, a stew consisting largely of quotations. Thereby I hope to clarify why adjectives such as the following have been used to describe the magazine: lively, intelligent, fresh, pugnacious, uncompromising, serious, hard-hitting, courageous, maddening, controversial, erratic, and funny.

---

1 Thanks to Robert Bly for, among many other things, permission to quote from his correspondence and other writings. Most of the research on which this essay is based was done at Bly's log cabin in Moose Lake. His papers are now located at the University of Minnesota Libraries.

2 The book-length narrative, tentatively entitled *The New Imagination: Robert Bly, Editor & Firebrand*, is forthcoming. A fully detailed examination of the magazine and press, *The Odin House Harvest: An Analytical Bibliography of Robert Bly's Fifties, Sixties, Seventies, Eighties, Nineties, and Thousands Press* (with a foreword by Robert Bly), will be published by Red Dragonfly Press in late 2011.

I. The Beginning

What are the origins of Bly's decision to edit a little magazine? His automatic response is that it happened when he was in Norway (1956-57). But a fuller explanation takes us back to the previous decade. Among Bly's papers is a book he made in high school (in the early 1940s), with "POETRY" on the cover in red, white, and blue letters. It is an anthology of poems by, among others, Longfellow, Poe, Stevenson, Bryant, Whittier, Kipling, and Whitman, all carefully typed and illustrated. The youthful enthusiasm and the wartime fervor are plain, and the dedication to his English teacher is touching.[3] It is a start at editing, even if not a particularly auspicious one, for young Bly gathered these poems into three sections which he entitled: "Liberty and Patriotism," "The Door of Death," and "The Better Life." After the Navy (1944-46), he went to St. Olaf College, and was an assistant editor of the college annual literary magazine. But this editing experience did not amount to much, either.

In 1947 he transferred to Harvard College, and joined the staff of the venerable *Harvard Advocate*. At the end of his sophomore year, Bly was chosen to be the *Advocate*'s literary editor, a position that came with the moniker "Pegasus." This, the winged horse of Greek mythology, and a traditional symbol of poetry, was the magazine's official emblem.[4] In his first issue as Pegasus, his first significant experience as editor, there were poems by his classmates John Ashbery, Donald Hall, Kenneth Koch, and Frank O'Hara, all of whom went on to extraordinary poetic careers.[5]

This surely is the cornerstone of Bly's career as an editor and critic. He started to evaluate the poetry of both peers and established poets, began to formulate his own notions about poetry and poetics,

---

3 "Dedicated to: Miss Puerner /Whose untiring efforts to/get me to like poetry/were finally rewarded."

4 Pegasus, who had sprung full-grown from the neck of the dying Gorgon Medusa, was tamed by Athena and then presented to the Muses. With a stomp of his hoof, he created the Hippocrene, the sacred spring of the Muses on Mt. Helicon. Pegasus also carried the thunderbolt of Zeus. He was captured by Bellerophon, who rode him through many adventures, including killing the Chimaera.

5 *Harvard Advocate* 131.6 (May 1948).

got an idea about what it took to crank out a magazine, and learned about maintaining standards (usually erring on the side of rejecting rather than accepting poems). The sixth and last issue of the *Advocate* that Bly's Pegasus oversaw bears a characteristic mark of his later magazine—his hand seems to be everywhere. He contributes a poem, a short story, and a review (not to mention a couple of unattributed pieces).[6] With this impressive breadth and versatility, his Pegasus was flying out in a blaze of glory.

From 1954 to 1956, Bly was enrolled in the Iowa Writers' Workshop. After he and Carol McLean were married, in June 1955, they moved back to Madison, Minnesota. Carol had made the acquaintance of Christina Duffy (in classes at the University of Minnesota), who, together with her husband Bill, was living in Clara City, fifty miles east of Madison. Bill proved to be another excitable farm boy who loved poetry and ideas and talking about them. In late January 1956, having seen the Duffys three times that month, Bly wrote in his journal: "In bed I thought of gathering a first issue of the magazine, The Poet's Magazine, a Poet's Review, and inquiring about [the] cost of publishing." A few months later, he submitted his M.A. thesis in Iowa City, and then talked to Paul Engle, the workshop's director: "I told him I'd like to start a magazine and publish some decent stuff," Bly told me. "But he wasn't very sympathetic. He thought I was simply confused."[7]

Now came a Fulbright grant to translate Norwegian poetry in Norway. Discovering not only Scandinavian poets, but also Trakl, Neruda, Jiménez, and others, Bly had found—at last—a remedy for his festering dissatisfaction with English language poetry. He also

6 *Harvard Advocate* 132.5 (March 1949). "Letter from a Wedding Trip," consisting of 19 lines of conventional rhythm (iambic pentameter) and rhyme scheme (beginning A-B-A-B-C-C), stands as his first published poem. The short story is entitled "Fish, Flesh, and Fowl" (an apparent allusion to Yeats's "Sailing to Byzantium"). The review of a book by Peter Viereck (who had been published in the *Advocate* a decade earlier), *Terror and Decorum: Poems, 1940-1948*, is almost uniformly negative. "Notes from 40 Bow" is the usual Pegasus editorial, and the unattributed "The Club System, Pro, Con," was Bly's as well.

7 MG interview with RB, 30 July 1999.

met a young poet there, Paal Brekke, who had recently put together an anthology of modernist poetry from eight countries. Bly determined to do something along those lines, and more. He began brainstorming. Here's one example from his journal: "For the magazine, this principle: that a poem or any art should not be the emotion of the moment..., [but] the expression of emotions felt over many years...as many as possible."[8]

Near the end of that year, Bly wrote to Hall (his best friend from college):

> I am more and more convinced that our generation has a real destiny in the course of American poetry. But I think the destiny lies in an opposite direction to where it has been living so far, namely it lies in revolution [underscored three times]. If the writers of the 30's think we are too tame, let them watch: I will take them apart, brick by brick! How could the time of advance and radicalism be over, when the imagination has hardly touched the density of modern life?[9]

When Bly returned to Minnesota, he and Duffy (now living in another small town, Pine Island) decided to start a magazine and to split the costs, scraping together what they could. There was an early wrinkle, as Bly told Hall:

> Bill Duffy, and myself, and another man named [Roland] Tweet are starting a magazine called *The Nineteen Fifties: A Magazine of Poetry and General Opinion*.... This magazine is going to publish nothing but poems, and then articles of opinion on either poetry or politics.... Then there will be my own magazine, ...called THE DARK REPUBLIC, over which I reign in solitary glory. It turns out that the greatest expense in publishing a magazine is paying the contributors; consequently we will have no contributors. That settles that problem—no envelopes to return, no time reading MS, etc., no overhead. We will have only two or three poems in every issue; the rest will be quotations, myths, translations, articles.[10]

8 RB journal, n.d. (late 1956 or early 1957)

9 RB to DH, 15 June 1957.

10 RB to DH, 23 November 1957.

Obviously, there would be several modifications to this plan.

At the same time, an anthology edited by Hall, Louis Simpson, and Robert Pack, *The New Poets of England and America*, was published. Bly was tickled, as he told Hall:

> "Of course it is always a thrill, even of a sort of degenerate variety, to see your name blazing or bubbling out in a book for the first time, as, thanks to you, it is here; and one has a sad feeling too, as if part of one were already dead, and we were reading the epitaph. (God knows, my poems looked dead enough to me!)" He continues: "... the sameness of form in the book is horrifying to me. The number of rhymes in the book would make even Milton turn over in his grave. Everybody writes a poem with lines all the same length... and this old iamb clopping along clippiecloppieclippiecloppie. I think I'll go crazy listening to it...."[11]

In February 1958, an advertisement in *Poetry* magazine announced the impending publication of a new literary quarterly, *The Fifties*, edited by Duffy and Bly, not from New York, Paris, San Francisco, or even Chicago, but from Pine Island, Minnesota.[12] They chose *Poetry* because of its established position and its broad circulation (it being entirely coincidental that, ever since Harriet Monroe started the magazine in 1912, Pegasus—that traditional horse again—had consistently appeared on the cover). The first issue came out in July 1958. The horse was loose, so to speak. (It may be interesting to note that *The Sixties* #4 [1960] has a poem by Duffy, "The Horse Is Loose," which Bly was also thinking would be a good title for a book of his and Duffy's poems.) The horse (though not Pegasus) was loose indeed, and, as another saying goes, the rest is history.

II. Odin

The cover of each and every issue of *The Fifties*, *Sixties*, and *Seventies* has a bold image of a horse with a rider, armed with spear, shield, and helmet, two birds in the air, and a serpent rearing up

11 RB to DH, 29 October 1957.

12 *Poetry* 91.5 (February 1958), 341.

at the horse's feet.[13] The armed man doesn't look particularly menacing, only peculiar. The horse may be an intentional echo of Pegasus, but, if so, a distant one, as it is wingless. (Another apparent coincidence—or not—is that the first issue of *The Paris Review*, originating from Paris in 1953, with which Bly's Harvard pals Hall and George Plimpton were involved, and in which Bly had two poems, had that by-now-familiar winged horse on its cover, but with a rider [apparently Bellerophon].) Inside the front cover is a single declarative sentence: "The editors of this magazine think that most of the poetry published in America today is too old-fashioned." Suddenly the horseman does seem combative; we hear saber rattling from the middle of nowhere.

Though never explicitly identified as such, this is Odin, the Scandinavian god, and his speedy horse Sleipnir. Odin has many faces. He is the God of War, or the Terrible One, in his primary aspect. He is called Allfather, the first and foremost of the gods. Furthermore, like a shaman he can journey between worlds. He is also the god of poetry and inspiration.

Thus Bly's and Duffy's feisty and adventurous little magazine was launched not under the sign of Pegasus, but under the sign of Odin. (We notice Bly's progression from Greek to Norse mythology.) Setting out on what was to be a long, strange trip, this god proved to be almost alarmingly suitable. I mean to suggest that it is remarkable how these four aspects of Odin, the patron god of the magazine, are reflected in the magazine itself. I also submit that it is impossible not to see the magazine, and therefore Odin, as a reflection of Bly. Odin, then, is my conceit, a sort of *deus ex machina* (though brought in early rather than late in the game), the means to manipulate the rest of my otherwise scattershot discussion of this wild little magazine.

One last thing to add here. After the third issue, when Duffy's editorial involvement ceased, the business operations moved from Pine Island to Madison (where they were ably handled by Carol). Bly wrote to Hall about this change: "How do you like Odin House? (That is the chickenhouse.) I...had to find some sort of address, since sim-

13 Carol Bly was the artist.

ply 'Madison, Minn.' looks too unreliable. Do you think Odin House is all right?"[14] "Odin House is great," Hall replied.[15] Well, it wasn't quite Valhalla, at least not yet.

—As God of War

Let us start with Odin as God of War. In our context, this means polemic and criticism of the harshest kind. Any writer intent on maintaining the *status quo* (that is, old-fashioned, academic, and formalist poetry, the outlook of New Criticism, abstract language, etc.) was at risk. We might see Odin's magic spear (Gungnir) as Bly's pen, attacking, skewering, and deflating. Paul Carroll, editor of *Big Table*, wrote to Bly in 1960: "What I most admire about *Fifties/Sixties*... is the type of muscular, good criticism you produce. Most criticism is, I think, lenten stuff. One reads it as penance. But yr criticism, clear and virile, seems to me not only valuable, provocative, often irritating (in the good sense), but also seminal."[16] John Haines said in 1964: "[Bly] has...written some of the best criticism American poetry has received. In fact, it is the only new criticism we have had since Pound began sending out his blasts from London around 1912."[17] William Matthews wrote at the end of the decade: "... Bly has come to dominate American poetry.... [His] incendiary criticism and crusade for the poetry he admires have annoyed many and threatened not a few." He continues: "It is nearly impossible to over-emphasize the importance of Bly's criticism."[18]

Some of his extraordinary audacity was fostered at Harvard. One teacher there was Archibald MacLeish, who, as Bly says, "brought a poem of Ezra Pound and read it to us, making sure we understood that Pound was his friend. One of us asked, 'Do you have any friends

---

14 RB to DH, n.d. (September 1960).

15 DH to RB, n.d. This was also a destination or stopping point for poets from far and wide. See: "Odin House: A Literary Crossroads in the Middle of Nowhere," *Rain Taxi Review of Books* 15.1 (Spring 2010), 38-41.

16 PC to RB, 19 December 1960.

17 *Kayak* 1 (Autumn 1964), 57.

18 *Tennessee Poetry Journal* 2.2 (Winter 1969), 49, 52.

that write better poetry?'"[19] As Bly has put it elsewhere, "Our behavior was outrageous...."[20] The class was full of veterans. "There was... this feeling that, if we survived World War II, and we won that war, we could do anything we wanted to do."[21] That grandiosity was a driving force.

Bly writes to Hall with a prediction: "... if we can continue this revolution, we will be a generation as famous as the 10s! And we will have laid down some important ideas for poetry, and perhaps even some important poetry!"[22] And that would be worth all the fighting.

First, the literary establishment was one target of Bly's aggression. In *The Fifties* #2 (1959), in "Madame Tussaud's Wax Museum" (a regular satirical feature), Bly went after the routine use of classical references in poems. There are three suggested resolutions for young poets: "I promise I will neither write nor read another poem on the death of Orpheus as long as I live. I promise I will never describe the sad fate of Oedipus in a poem again, on pain of losing my eyes. I promise I will never capture poor Perseus and drag him into my poems, nor Aeneas, nor good Achilles, nor Telamon, nor Penelope...."

In response to Bly's anti-formalist stance, Thom Gunn wrote a letter, practically daring Bly to say that he would reject Shakespeare's sonnet #129 ("The expense of spirit in a waste of shame...."). Bly responded in *The Fifties* #3 (1959), with a short essay entitled "The Necessity of Rejecting a Shakespeare Sonnet," saying that Shakespeare's language was "striking and new" when he wrote it, but for now such language is "exhausted, dead." So, yes: If Shakespeare submitted a sonnet to *The Fifties*, Bly would reject it (probably, I like to imagine, with a pointed comment along the lines of: "This horse died 350 years ago. We think it's time you found a new horse."). "But, of course," he continues, "he wouldn't; he would write today

19 MG interview with RB, 31 July 2001

20 Robert Bly, "When Literary Life Was Still Piled Up in a Few Places," in *A Community of Writers: Paul Engle and the Iowa Writer's Workshop*, ed. Robert Dana (Iowa City: University of Iowa Press, 1999), 39.

21 MG interview with RB, 30 July 1999.

22 RB to DH, 8 August 1958.

in a language as fresh as his was in 1600. What that might be is hard to estimate, but I would guess it might resemble the language of Lorca or perhaps Neruda."

Somewhat more recent poets, like Longfellow and Tennyson, whose influence was, unfortunately, still apparent, were disparaged. Bly printed up a small card for those who submitted such old-fashioned poems. It said: "This entitles you to buy the next book of Alfred Lord Tennyson as soon as it appears. A Public Service of the Sixties Press."

Living writers of an earlier generation, especially exponents of New Criticism, including Allen Tate, John Crowe Ransom, Yvor Winters, Randall Jarrell, Jacques Barzun, and Lionel Trilling, were relentlessly criticized. Here Bly also found satire an especially effective weapon. In *The Sixties* #5 (1961), "The Order of the Blue Toad" is awarded to Robert Penn Warren and Cleanth Brooks for their *Understanding Poetry*. "This book was really written by Joe Friday. When discussing poems, if a poet shows any sign of generous feeling or whimsy, the authors say in a flat voice: 'We just want the facts, ma'am.' ... It is sad to think that this absurd book is used in almost every American university."

Bly's review of Robert Lowell's *For the Union Dead* (in *The Sixties* #8 [1966]) was especially severe. Bly had loved Lowell from the time he was in college, and he respected his enormous talent. But, he says, most of the poems in his new book are "bad poems," "stale and cold." It is "a counterfeit book of poetry."

Second, Bly fought a never-ending battle with other publications that consistently offered weak criticism and/or insipid poetry. In the first issue is his interview with Francis Brown, editor of the *New York Times Book Review*. (This was expanded and published separately by the Sixties Press in 1961 as *A Broadsheet Against the New York Times Book Review*.) It begins: "How long is [this] farce...to continue?" Reactions tended to be vehemently supportive. Rob Cuscaden wrote: "... it's about time somebody said (in writing) what most of us have felt for a long time."[23]

23 RC to RB, 26 October 1961.

Similarly, in *The Sixties* #4 (1960) was "A Note on Miss Irita Van Doren," editor of the *New York Herald Tribune Book Section*, who refused to run a review of Babette Deutsch's new book by an unnamed young poet (Hall), since it was highly critical, and gave it to Marianne Moore instead. Bly writes: "Behind such chicanery lies the typical American fear of harsh criticism, as well as a certain lack of intellectual honor.... This is a sure way to kill the country's intellectual life."

In 1960, Wright said to Bly: "...you must surely realize how very many editors and reviewers are noticing the magazine, and noticing it with the deepest interest.... If they don't understand quite what you are doing yet, that isn't the point. If they understood already, there would be no place for the magazine.... You have started this fire of response...."[24] From Bly's perspective, that fire was still far too limited. His continued disillusionment with the preponderant poetic ethos is clear in his critique of *Paris Review* #21. He tells Hall, then the poetry editor: "Of the poems as a whole, which are very likely the best you received, I think they show that American poetry now hardly needs *The Fifties* or anyone else to whisk it away; it is already dead on its feet."[25] Soon Bly continued this discussion:

> Did you see Richard Foster's article in the new *Perspective?* ... At the end, he blasts *The Fifties*..., and calls me a jackass, but I like the article as a whole. He tends to be a nay-sayer, but that is the first step toward sanity, after all.
>
> More and more I am struck by the incredibly poor criticism in this country.... The reviews show timid and provincial ignorance of the most squalid sort....
>
> The "new criticism" should be called the "no criticism".... And don't tell me England is any better—they remember what criticism is like—the same way one remembers a bad-mannered cousin, now fortunately dead.[26]

Printed in the first "Letters to the Editor" feature, in *The Sixties* #6 (1962), is a long one from Norman Moser, which begins: "Dear

24 JW to RB, 28 November 1960.

25 RB to DH, 28 October 1959.

26 RB to DH, 7 October 1960.

God, So nice to hear from you. Poetry is serious, you are right, and the poem must be good in itself. But must it be only what you say it is, you silly pedantic slob?" Bly wrote to him before publication:

> I decided to publish a group of insulting letters in order to try to break the air of impeccable dignity—over-dignity—that hovers about the literary magazine. Editors usually preserve an utterly smooth surface on the magazine, like unruffled water. This is reassuring, but not very interesting. One would think there were no reactions, or that the reactions were all favorable.... The purpose is to enjoy the criticism we receive as much as the praise (if any)—and if the criticism is more interesting, publish it, whether we look "undignified" or not. What's the difference? No one knows how a magazine "ought" to be run anyway.[27]

When LeRoi Jones reviewed *The Sixties* #5 (1961), and Gilbert Sorrentino *The Lion's Tail and Eyes* by Duffy, Wright, and Bly (The Sixties Press, 1962), using mockery and sharp rebukes, Bly seems to have relished it. He wrote to Hall: "...be sure to buy the new *Kulchur*.... –[It h]as wonderful attacks on everything *The Sixties* stands for—[the] only thing they didn't attack is the paper!"[28] A noticeable increase in the number and the ferocity of skirmishes was a good sign. There was a renewed vigor in American literary life, and *The Sixties* was in the thick of it. Bly plainly enjoyed a good battle; the shield and helmet were sufficient protection.

A third major way in which Bly and the magazine manifest the violence of Odin is in attacks against contemporary poets now clearly beyond help. "The Collapse of James Dickey" (in *The Sixties* #9 [1967]) was a review of his new book, *Buckdancer's Choice*. Bly and Dickey had become fast friends in the late 1950s, and Bly's Sixties Press published a book of Dickey's criticism, *The Suspect in Poetry*, in 1964. But while he was shepherding that book through to publication and writing the Crunk article on Dickey, his opinion of his friend was plummeting. The war in Vietnam only made matters

---

27 RB to NM, 13 February 1962.

28 RB to DH, 15 July 1963. The reviews were in *Kulchur* 10.3 (Summer 1963), 83-6.

worse, much worse. Found among Bly's papers is a contemporary (but never printed) Blue Toad award to Dickey. But Bly apparently decided that, for the abomination he saw in Dickey's new book (and behavior), mere satire was inadequate. It required the punch of full-blown invective.

This became the most notorious piece of criticism ever published in his magazine. Bly gets straight to the point: "I thought the content of the book repulsive. The subject of the poems is power, and the tone of the book is gloating—a gloating about power over others." The book had been positively reviewed elsewhere (winning the National Book Award in 1966), and when this review appeared, Dickey was Poetry Consultant at the Library of Congress (the equivalent of the current position of U.S. Poet Laureate). Bly ends the review:

> ...his decline...is catastrophic, enough to make you weep. One cannot help but feel that his depressing collapse represents some obscure defeat for the United States also. He began writing about 1950, writing honest criticism and sensitive poetry, and suddenly at the age of forty-three, we have a huge blubbery poet, pulling out Southern language in long strings, like taffy, a toady to the government, supporting all movements toward Empire, a sort of Georgia cracker Kipling.

Bly told Hall: "The letters on Dickey have only two forks—half of them say, Great, Socko, It's true. The other half, a little more forward looking, wonder aloud when the other shoe will fall."[29] Peter Schjeldahl (now art critic for *The New Yorker*) wrote: "I just read your essay about [Dickey]....it is...brave, passionate, and clear-headed.... it reminds me a little (its tone) of Pope on Addison, though Dickey's no Addison, of course. The trick is in saying hateful things with love. You turned it, I think."[30] Instead of Pope, Hall had another worthy in mind:

> Wow, that Dickey piece. Seriously I think you ought to have a gun in the house in case he comes out to break you. He'll want to

29 RB to DH, 3 September 1967.

30 PS to RB, 1 June 1969.

> hurt you a lot....
> ...That ending is the best vituperation since Mencken. You may not like that comparison, but by God, "Georgia cracker Kipling" is something like that--& also like Shakespeare. Wow.

Finally, another friend wrote:

> Your essay on [Dickey's] "collapse" is still the best thing that has been done on his negative aspects. And no doubt he deserved it.... No one else in this country had either the courage or the insight to do it but you.... But harsh criticism is like acid too; a little goes a very long way, and now many people fear and hate you who should not.[31]

To this sort of attack we might add some of the rejection slips, which, while undeniably nasty, were required now and then to deflect repeated submissions from poets who had not been paying attention.[32] Bly rejected one poem this way: "We hate Troy, and academic poetry; and academic poetry <u>about</u> Troy—that's the end!"[33] Another rejection said, simply: "Terrible! These corny rhymes are straight out of 1825."[34]

Some rejectees were hardy enough to take it. One said: "Thanks again for the ferocity of your rejections. I've come to see you as a kind of sumo wrestler whose tactic is to toughen other wrestlers by driving them, skull first if need be, into the mat. It's probably the best technique around...."[35] Another, if not unequivocally grateful, wrote: "By God, it's refreshing to get an honest rejection slip even if it is a kick in the ass."[36]

Others responded angrily. Bly received this letter (from a man with a Greek name, I should add):

---

31 Barent Gjelsness to RB, 22 September 1969.

32 For more on this, see "Rude Awakenings: Rejections from *The Fifties, Sixties, and Seventies*," *Great River Review* 52 (Spring/Summer 2010), 35-52.

33 RB to Mr. Cuddihy, 4 May 1960.

34 RB to M. Turner, n.d.

35 John Eshors to RB, n.d. (1970?).

36 Sandy Taylor to RB, 14 January 1960.

> When you read my poems you must have been either on some kind of trip, drunk, or insane.... If you don't see that meaning in my poetry, then you are just plain stupid. Odin House indeed! I hope your dour Nordic gods betray you when you most need them; and I hope that moment is when my rational Greek god Zeus anoints you with a jet of holy piss.[37]

Bly liked this letter so much that he flagged it for a third "letters to the editor" section (which never appeared). Odin was not afraid to take on Zeus.

The magazine's satiric penchant was a highlight for many readers, especially in the Wax Museum and the Blue Toad features. There were parodies of poems by Howard Nemerov, Lowell, Dickey, Charles Olson, A.R. Ammons, and Charles Bukowski (none of which were by Bly). And there was one of Bly himself, "And Robert Bly Says Something, Too," by Henry Taylor (in *The Sixties* #9 [1967]):

> I raise my head and turn on my side
> And see a horse's tail swishing at flies.
> It is attached to the end of a horse.

It seems he could take as well as he gave.

Bly's fighting sense found a fourth outlet in moral and political engagement. In *The Fifties* #3 (1959) appeared "A Note on Hydrogen Bomb Testing," saying: "We believe that artists above all are not exempt from fighting in national issues." He mentions the Middle Ages, and then: "Just as the Church was indifferent to freedom of thought, scientists like those of the Atomic Energy Commission are indifferent to human suffering. Unless these men are fought, in their inquisition millions will die."

Political poems regularly appeared. And of course, in early 1966, Bly and David Ray formed the American Writers Against the Vietnam War and started barnstorming college campuses across the country. In March 1968, he received the National Book Award for *The Light Around the Body*, and electrified the audience, first with his acceptance speech which decried the widespread institutional collusion

37 Alex Karanikas to Mark Wilson (Bly's assistant), 6 June 1969

in the war effort, and second by giving away his award check to a young member of the Resistance, in order that it be used to help others evade the draft. It was an act of civil disobedience. *The Nation* had this to say:

> For many years Bly has been an important influence in American poetry, as much through the work of his magazine, *The Sixties*, as through his own poetry. His critical articles, his translations of the German and Spanish poets, his extensive and impressive work in opposing the war..., culminating in his splendid action at Lincoln Center, are exemplary for our time.[38]

Along these same lines, Philip Levine responded to *The Sixties* #9 (1967): "I enjoyed it very much and don't quite understand why the magazine manages to seem fresh & important. Most poetry publications crap out in a year. Thanks too for fighting against the war & the wars ahead."[39]

In 1965, Bly received a grant and citation from the National Institute of Arts and Letters.[40] Signed by George Kennan, it says: "To Robert Bly.... A poet of verve and toughness, an editor who stands his ground against the encroachments of establishmentarianism, a translator who has vigorously continued his ancestral traditions of Viking exploration." Ancestral traditions, indeed! Odin could be proud.

—As Allfather

Odin, foremost of the gods, is often called Allfather. Snorri Sturluson, in the *Prose Edda*, says: "Odin is the highest and oldest of the gods. He rules all things and, no matter how mighty the other gods may be, they all serve him as children do their father...."[41] This too is indicative of many aspects of the magazine and Bly's role in it.

---

38 "The National Book Awards," *The Nation* (March 25, 1968), 413.

39 PL to RB, 29 September 1967.

40 John Hersey to RB, 2 March 1965.

41 Quoted in Kevin Crossley-Holland, *The Norse Myths* (New York: Pantheon Books, 1980), xxv.

First, Bly fiercely maintained the conviction that criticism, to be of any value, must always be honest and direct (including, as appropriate, both praise and blame). One feature of every issue (except the last) is a critical essay by "Crunk," on the work of one young poet whom Bly admired and respected. (Bly was Crunk, eight times out of ten.) All these poets had faults and stood in need of some fatherly correction, some tough love. With those he didn't yet know face-to-face, Bly was especially concerned that the criticism be taken in the right way.

Crunk (in *The Fifties* #2 [1959]) has some misgivings about the poems of Robert Creeley, that their lack of images indicates dangerous isolation from Europe. "The American Tradition is not rich enough; it is short, Puritanical, and has only one or two first-rate poets in it, and the faults of the lesser poets are always the same—a kind of barrenness and abstraction." Creeley responds: "Your kind and good note on my work (I take it as having been written by you) was a great pleasure to have. I.e., whatever differences of attitude or opinion might exist between us would god knows be vitiated by the term of your dignity, and care to read rightly what I'd written."[42] As a few letters went back and forth, Creeley asked Bly for help in getting a job. Bly had several suggestions, including taking over for him as director of the Poetry Reading Series at NYU. Creeley wrote: "No matter what comes, so to speak, it will have been a pleasure to have known someone so completely willing to be of use."[43]

On "The Work of W.S. Merwin" (*The Sixties* #4 [1960]) Crunk says: "Mr. Merwin's best poems...show a strange kind of genius; still....I am trying to show that Merwin's work...lacks poetry." Bly was concerned that Merwin would be upset, but he responded: "... all the criticisms you made of my work I'd levelled at myself, not at the time perhaps, but since, and fairly thoroughly. Please don't feel that I was or am offended by your piece. And the respect and interest which prompted it were apparent to me."[44] Their mutual friend Gal-

42 RC to RB, 18 November 1958.

43 RC to RB, 4 December 1959.

44 WSM to RB, n.d. (1961 or '62)

way Kinnell told Bly that the essay "was just, & of all criticism of him is the only piece likely to force him to think over his art. My guess is he will do something tremendously good next time, & very new."[45] That was the tonic effect this father-critic was aiming for.

Crunk said on John Logan (*The Sixties* #5 [1961]): "There is a tendency to use four-letter words, or to be temporarily the tough guy, which is nothing but an embarassment at being a poet." That has the ring of paternal chastisement. After Crunk wrote on Snyder (*The Sixties* #6 [1962]), Snyder replied: "Mr. Crunk is much too nice." He was right. James Wright, who apparently lacked some of that fierce Papa Odin energy, had written it.

A second characteristic of Odin as Allfather can be seen in Bly's relationship with the poets who became his close friends, almost like family. As letters and poems were pouring in after the first issue, Bly wrote to Wright: "...after being for years absolutely worthless to everyone, I suddenly find myself with advice which is of help to other people, and this tends to throw me off balance."[46]

Now Bly was regularly seeing and sharing ideas with Wright, Dickey, Simpson and Kinnell (as well as Duffy and Hall). Dickey said: "you talk about poetry as though you were the other half of my own mind...."[47] Wright, despite some disagreements with Bly, told Hall:

> ...I really do think he is a great man....he is an innovator—you get one in a generation, if you're fabulously lucky. I really believe it's the duty of anyone who recognizes the original man to believe in him; and this belief consists, I have finally realized, not in discipleship, but in searching and serious questions, in *criticism*.[48]

Bly was always reluctant to allow the existence of a clique or school of "Sixties" poets. He wrote to Hall:

45 GK to RB, 12 March 1961.

46 RB to JW, 15 October 1958.

47 JD to RB, 8 June 1959.

48 JW to DH, 19 November 1958 (also in *Wild Perfection: The Selected Letters of James Wright*, eds. Anne Wright and Saundra Rose Maley [New York: Farrar, Straus and Giroux, 2005], 187-8).

> I want to avoid the sense that the magazine is partial to anyone.... Jim's dignity has been somewhat affected, at least temporarily, by statements... implying that he is my disciple or something.... Talk of this kind merely confuses the issues of the magazine. The value of the magazine lies in its independence from the older generation, and its belief in the significance of what the younger ones are doing, not in any single association or in the printing of a single sort of poem.[49]

Despite his intention to assist, Bly was the man with the megaphone, and his growing predominance is undeniable. While these men were exchanging poems and criticism, he was becoming the chief theorist. We may remember: Odin was a member of a group of warrior gods (the Aesir), but he was also its leader.

Dickey, submitting poems in 1959, freely admitted he was under Bly's sway: "I just wanted you to see what influence *The Fifties* is... having on at least one American!"[50] In the early 1960s, Wright's book *The Branch Will Not Break*, Hall's *A Roof of Tiger Lilies*, and Simpson's *At the End of the Open Road*, all manifestly exhibit the effect and strength of Bly's ideas. John Haines, anticipating his first book, *Winter News*, wrote: "...I'm going to have a little note on the title page—co-authored by Robert Bly!"[51]

And then Simpson wrote to Bly a year later:

> Did you see the article in the *N. Y. Review of Books*...in which Wright, Dickey, Simpson, Hall and Bly were described as "the group"? And he said that Bly was the most talented of the lot.... My own opinion is, it's a plot, to make us all start being envious of each other. Of course, you may be the most talented, but it's terrible when people come right out and say so.[52]

By the early 1970s, father-remarks were even more common. Russell Edson wrote, praising *The Seventies*: "I suppose every one of

---

49 RB to DH, n.d. (November 1961).

50 JD to RB, 19 August 1959.

51 JH to RB, 5 September 1964.

52 LS to RB, 1 April 1965. See Robert Mazzocco, "Mixed Company," NYRB 4.5 (April 8, 1965).

your writing friends will have a Bly essay from the issue that doesn't hit right with him. It's like belonging to a big terrible family."[53] William Matthews wrote: "Remember how I wrote...that friends should be people you love no matter what? We talked when you were here about people's need to kill off their literary fathers. Well, you are probably mine, but to hell with killing off people you love."[54] Another friend wrote: "It seems to me that your critical positions have been the most sobering and salutary, and effective, on the very youngest of the poets in this country. The youngest and most gifted. They identify with you as they do with Ho Chi Minh, say; a strong Father-image. This generation needs that image, and I think you have helped to give it a conscience too."[55]

Bly was learning that his high visibility brought the burden of increased expectations, and, occasionally, psychological projection. A couple of years after "The Teeth Mother Naked at Last" was published, a diatribe, cleverly entitled "The FameGreed Father Bare-Assed at Last," excoriated Bly for what its writers perceived as his selling-out. They used to look up to him, said one, for his magazine, his poetry, his criticism, as the "Big Bill Haywood of Poetry," "a model for struggle" with "a good understanding of corporate-monopoly capitalism and the commodity spectacle."[56] Now, I would add, they felt hurt; Daddy had disappointed them.[57]

A third place we see Bly's fatherly generosity and caring (in a gruff, Odinesque kind of way) is in other rejection slips and responses to them. There was teaching going on here, and of course the classic relationship between teacher and student is akin to that between parent and child. When Bly detected even a faint glimmer of hope, he went out of his way to encourage and instruct. For example: "There's liveliness in these poems, which is rare, but you're not even

53 RE to RB, 14 April 1972.

54 WM to RB, 8 July 1970.

55 Barent Gjelsness to RB, 22 September 1969.

56 Jerry Gorshine (signed: "BareAss") to RB, 30 March 1971.

57 A fuller discussion of this dispute, and more, is in "Robert Bly and the Buddha on the Road," forthcoming.

trying to be serious."[58] This one is more directive: "The trouble is that your feelings are too cloudy to you. You don't see into them, they loom like a mist. When you hear bluejays, you're not sure what it is you feel. So you need to spend more time by yourself."[59] There were many responses like the following: "Thank you for the rude awakening. I needed it...."; and: "Your letter was the first honest, direct and clear commentary I have received and the only one to be of any help."[60]

Adrienne Rich said in 1961: "Perhaps you will really succeed in giving this generation of poets an important part of its education."[61] And he did. In 1969, Lisel Mueller wrote: "I become more and more aware of the influence you are having on young poets and poetry-reading students. I see it every time I meet with college students; every time I see an anthology by young poets."[62]

Bly's former teacher, MacLeish, reacted to *The Seventies #1* (1972) as follows: "I like the feel and sense of your metaphor of the leap. [He quotes some of Bly's statements.] ...you are now the teacher and I the learner."[63] Many others also discerned its educational value. One writer said: "It is the best document I have seen on modern poetry. It should serve as a text book for young poets, as both theory & practice."[64] Another wrote: "Should be read by every aspiring or practicing American poet, should be distributed to every elementary and high school, should replace all textbooks in all university seminars. I mean it."[65] And a third said: "I think I need you for a guru. I'm not kidding.... Your mind, your whole self is large, huge—I want you to lead a movement or something. Start a commune and be the guru. Start a school and be the president. Make a movie and put all of us in it."[66]

58 RB to Ruth Bodner, 6 July 1972.
59 RB to Mr. Linder, 26 December 1969.
60 Again, see "Rude Awakenings."
61 AR to RB, 28 April 1961.
62 LM to RB, 20 January 1969.
63 AM to RB, 11 December 1972.
64 Roger Sauls to RB, 17 December 1972.
65 Barbara Riddle to RB, 26 September 1972.
66 Barbara Gibson to RB, 17 June 1969.

Not a few editors of little magazines were also looking to Bly. Harry Weber, editor of *The Minnesota Review*, said: “It’s hard to believe that the most influential magazine in the country, at least as far as poetry is concerned, comes from Madison, Minnesota, which somehow makes me believe in God.”[67] George Hitchcock told Bly of his plans for a magazine, *Kayak* (probably the most important offspring of *The Sixties*): “Since *Kayak* is going to owe a great deal to the critical leadership you have given so many poets, myself included, I am extremely anxious that you be represented in the first issues, either by an article...or by poems or both.”[68] So Bly gave him an essay in 1967 on “The First Ten Issues of Kayak.” He declares that they have been “on the whole clogged and bad. As an editor, George Hitchcock is too permissive.” The result was “an unprecedented amount of comment,” so *Kayak*’s next issue included excerpts from ten of the many letters received.[69] In response to those comments, Robert Peters wrote to Hitchcock:

> I know of no contemporary poet-editor more generous with his encouragements, criticisms than Bly—I have a file here to prove it. So: may he continue tramping through the landscape publishing his magazine whenever he feels like it, delivering his bunyanesque judgments at every opportunity, and continuing to write some of the best poetry going. Creatures nibbling at his ankles and toes will drop off into the muck as soon as he is well into the next swamp, their suffocations sounding like so much fart music.[70]

It is fitting that Bly’s aggressive stance, his fatherly teaching method, is taken to be essentially benign.

—As Shaman

Odin, we are told, “could...act as a seer. Like a shaman, he could send out his spirit, sometimes riding on his eight-legged steed Sleipnir, sometimes in another shape, on journeys between worlds;

67 HW to RB, 25 June 1963.
68 GH to RB, 23 June 1964.
69 “Letters,” *Kayak* 13 (January 1968), 12-21.
70 RP to GH, 22 January 1968. (Peters sent Bly a copy of the letter.)

like a shaman, he could win wisdom from the dead."[71] The shaman also evoked animals as spirit guides or message bearers. One of Gary Snyder's poems in *The Fifties #1*, felicitously, is "First Shaman Song." "I sit without thoughts by the log-road, / hatching a new myth...," he writes. With that first issue Bly was hatching a new imagination.

Animals could play important roles as the shaman did his work. One animal in the cover image, as mentioned above, is the serpent, Jörmungand, the "most fearsome" serpent in Norse mythology.[72] He killed his victims by constriction, crushing them. Odin threw him into the sea. It may be of interest to note that, in the summer of 1960, Bly translated from Danish, *The Illustrated Book of Reptiles and Amphibians of the World* (by Hans Hvass). Bly told Hall: "they are pleased enough with the translation that they asked permission to put my name on the title page (by Robert Bly, the famous herpetologist!)... ."[73] So, he (sort of) knew snakes.

Here, then, is a snake story. Bly first notes the contrast between his experiences in graduate school and in college:

> We didn't attack the teacher this time; in general, the aggression went against each other.... I don't recall being aggressive myself, but perhaps my memory is bad. I do remember hearing around 1975 a story of my behavior in the Iowa workshop twenty years earlier. It seems that I regularly brought a snake to class with me in a gunnysack, and whenever someone began to criticize a poem of mine, I would take the snake out and lay it on the table.[74]

In fact, Robert and Carol had found two baby horned owls. They were intending to bring them back to the farm in Madison (where the owls, named Abelard and Heloise, lived for many years). But first, at Engle's request they brought them to his daughter's school to show. Somehow in the retelling the owls turned into snakes. The

71 Crossley-Holland, xxvi.

72 Ibid., 193.

73 RB to DH, 23 September 1960. The essay, "Blue Toads, Leaping Lizards, Dragon Smoke, the Reptile Brain, and Burrow-Crats: An Impressionistic Guide (with Thanks to Robert Bly, 'the Famous Herpetologist')" is forthcoming.

74 Dana, 39.

reason for the distortion was not lost on Bly: "By that time I had put out the magazine, so they were scared of me."[75]

It also happens that owls have an important role to play. *The Sixties* #4 (1960) opens with "The Swan" by the Mexican poet Enrique González Martínez, translated by Bly. The great Nicaraguan poet, Rubén Darío, founder of Modernismo, had used the swan as the emblem of his poetics. If *The Sixties* ever had a programmatic poem, this was it:

> Take this swan with puffy plumage, and wring his neck,
> Who gives his white touch to the blue of the fountain pool;
> He displays his elegance only, but does not understand
> The soul of creatures, or the voice of the silent fields.
>
> Keep away from all forms, and all styles of speaking
> That do not change quickly to follow the secret rhythms
> Of the life that is deepest...and adore life
> Intensely, and make life grasp your devotion.
>
> See the intelligent owl, how he lifts his wings
> Abandoning the Greek mountain, he leaves the shelter of Pallas,
> And finishes his silent moody flight on that tree...
>
> He does not have the elegance of the swan, but his troubled
> Eye, which pierces into the darkness, reads
> The mysterious book of the silences of night.

It is as if Martínez steals the owl of Athena, the manifestation of reason, and adapts it, as the bird of darkness, to the cause of the irrational, the unconscious, the new imagination.

Bly was intent on adopting the owl for *The Sixties*. He wrote Hall the following summer: "...we have a new subscription brochure complete with a new emblem! How do you like it—that old owl with his claws around a vulture? (That's me! The vulture is [John] Ciardi who has just eaten [Robert] Hillyer.) Do you think we should substi-

---

75 MG interview with RB, 31 July 2001.

tute it entirely for the horse and rider, or use both?"[76] Notice, by the way, Bly's identification with the owl. Yet Odin, whose dominance was already established, held on.

In an interview from 1971, we hear the wide range of Bly's cerebrations which would be manifest in *The Seventies*. For one thing, he speaks of "the interior animal life" as opposed to "the interior intellectual life," and of using animal imagery, as Lorca does, "to penetrate down into an evolutionary part of the mind." Meditation, Bly says, is an important factor, with its attention to breath. "After all, breath is....the one thing we can't stop.... Therefore it has a deeper evolutionary link than any other thing in our body."[77]

In this context we might also note Odin's own shape-shifting; for example, he changes into a snake and then an eagle in his quest for the mead of poetry. But Odin also likes disguises; he is a god of many faces.[78] Bly also wore many masks. Crunk was a *nom de guerre*, and Crunk's manner was such that attentive readers had little doubt of his true identity. But relatively few saw through the names Charles Reynolds, George Kresenky, and J.A. Cottonwood, poets and translators in *The Fifties* and *The Sixties*.

Using another shamanistic trait, the ability to win wisdom from the dead and communicate with the spirit world for the benefit of the community, Odin made journeys between worlds and eras. In the first issue, in the essay "Five Decades of Modern American Poetry," Bly notes the generation that appeared in the 1910s with Pound, Eliot, Moore, Jeffers, Williams, and, from Europe, Apollinaire, Ungaretti, Benn, Trakl, and others. He says: "These men carried with them, as we know, a new imagination, and with the imagination, a content, and with the content, a style....the new poetry appeared, and what I am wondering here is what happened to it." He means to reconnect with it, and to make it new, again.

At the end, Bly was seeking wisdom from antiquity. "Looking for Dragon Smoke" is the first of eight essays by Bly in *The Seventies*.

76 RB to DH, n.d. (July 1961). This was another drawing of Carol's, adapted from Dürer.

77 *San Francisco Book Review* 19 (April 1971).

78 They include Bolvert, Grimnir, Gagnard, and Harbard.

It begins, magnificently:

> In ancient times, in the "time of inspiration," the poet flew from one world to another, "riding on dragons," as the Chinese said. Isaiah rode on those dragons, so did Li Po and Pindar. They dragged behind them long tails of dragon smoke....
>
> This dragon smoke means that a leap has taken place in the poem. In many ancient works of art we notice a long floating leap at the center of the work. That leap can be described as a leap from the conscious to the unconscious and back again, a leap from the known part of the mind to the unknown part and back to the known.

He talks of Gilgamesh, and *The Odyssey*, and of how Christianity stifled "animal instincts" and the unconscious.

Stanley Plumly wrote: "*Seventies* 1 is incredible. It seems to me that it's as much a synthesis of our best poet-past as it is a definition of the shape of the future. I think your taste in poetry is sometimes quirky but I think you have the best instincts of anyone since Pound. And pardon my young opinions."[79]

There are so many polarities highlighted in the magazine: inward and outward, feeling and intellect, unconscious and conscious, the live world and the dead world. Wild association, leaping, was the way to travel between these worlds. Sometimes Odin set out riding on his horse. But here that horse has been transformed into a dragon.

The journeys between the worlds of North American poetry in the latter half of the twentieth century and those of Neruda, Vallejo, Lorca, Tranströmer, and many others, seems almost too obvious to mention. In the first issue, Bly says the new imagination is to be discovered through poets of other lands and languages. (Throughout the magazine's run we find poems translated from at least thirteen languages.) This new and sustained emphasis was invigorating. In 1961, Ted Hughes wrote from England, in admiration: "...this translation seems to me valuable beyond price.... I would like to see heavy doses of it coming out over here regularly—it's probably the only

79 SP to RB, 5 June 1972.

salvation, uproot a few of these oracular dry bodiless heads, & give the poets still in school a little courage."[80]

Bly's magazine and press became so identified with translation that some thought it excessive. LeRoi Jones called *The Sixties* "the most articulate spokesman" for the group of literary quarterlies "which publishes translations almost exclusively, or who like to hit you over the head with issues like, 'The New Poets of Wake Island,' suggesting, somehow, that there is no poetry, new or otherwise, in our motherland." Jones sees this, surprisingly, as colonialism.[81]

The critic Helen Vendler, on the other hand, was warmly affirmative. She wrote (with a nice Yeatsian reference) in 1973: "I heard you...10 or 11 years ago at Cornell. Like all scholars I am always somewhat appalled when my Catullus walks my way, but I would like to hear you read again."[82] A year later she added: "...I...feel bound by our mutual attachment to poetry to thank you for your magical translations of Rilke's *Sonnets to Orpheus* in *The Seventies* #1."[83] (In that issue, Bly writes ["Surrealism, Rilke, and Listening"]: "As Eliade noticed, Orpheus is an early shaman figure, who flies 'from one world to the next.'") After another year Vendler summarized: "I do think you are a super translator, & the cause of super translating in others.... I don't know how you get translations literal enough to be useful as a 'trot' to be at the same time so beautiful in themselves—it's a marvel."[84]

Let us conclude this section on Odin's shaman side at work with this comment of Carl Rakosi, after a reading in 1969: "Last night I would have been willing to cut open a bird and examine its entrails if you had so directed me, that's how powerful you were, dear shaman, in your long flowing serape from another age."[85] Bly had been looking the part since a trip to the Southwest in 1966, when he adopted

80 TH to RB, 24 April 1961.

81 Thus Jones entitled his review "The Colonial School of Melican Poetry (or, 'Aw, man, I read those poems before'," *Kulchur* 10.3 (Summer 1963), 83.

82 HV to RB, 1 September 1973.

83 HV to RB, 30 September 1974.

84 HV to RB, 19 September 1975.

85 CR to RB, 31 March 1969.

the Mexican serape as his dress at readings and other public appearances.

—As God of Poetry and Inspiration

A Norse myth tells us: "The blood [of the murdered Kvasir] and honey formed a sublime mead: whoever drank it became a poet or a wise man." Odin, in disguise, says, "I'm strong, very strong. I can take on the work of nine men." When he asks for a drink of mead but is refused, he says: "I may be strong.... But to be a poet: that's the finest calling." Finally, Odin gets possession of the mead. Thereupon, he drinks some of it himself. "And from time to time he offered a draught to...a man or two...; he offered them the gift of poetry."[86]

It was a Herculean labor to put out a magazine, especially given how much of the work Bly shouldered in his multifarious roles. He wrote, solicited, and gathered criticism, essays, reviews, parodies, satires, translations, quotations, etc. And the kinds of poems he was looking for were not plentiful; they did not (usually) grow on trees. Even when they did, they tended to be the product of a long and laborious process on Bly's part—planting the seeds, tending the soil, nourishing the new growth, fending off pests, pruning extensively, and waiting for the fruit to ripen. Also, as a figurehead for the new poetry, he had countless other duties. Bly wrote several major critical articles for other magazines during the 1960s; he was speaking up and out when and as needed, all over the place; and, of course, he was publishing books, including many of his own translations, thirteen in all, under the imprint of The Sixties (and later The Seventies) Press.

Friends like Simpson, Wright, and Hitchcock, who were enthusiastic about the magazine's goals and had visions of its full potential, urged Bly repeatedly to put it out more often. But the magazine, however seldom it appeared, was what it was—which, as it turns out, was enough, and more, for many poets in search of inspiration and example. They drank deeply of the mead which the magazine provided. Here are a few of their voices. Anne Sexton wrote:

86 Crossley-Holland, 27, 30, and 32.

> Are you Crunk? I like Crunk—he is changing my life, whoever he is.
>
> Your magazine is, for me, a work of immediate genius. At any rate, it changes me and I'm so God damn stubborn that few can even affect me—much less change my voice....
>
> I hate to show your magazine to anyone and let them in on such a marvelous secret.... You are the first new thing I have encountered since I began to write.[87]

Anselm Hollo said: "I knew that 'this is it,' that the *Fifties/Sixties* are truly part of 'it,' the ohsonecessary renaissance renewal and free flowering of poetry and life, the voyage to jungles and caves and to the eternal sea—.... Believe me: your magazine is...the very best of its kind I have seen for years."[88] A reader of *The Seventies* #1 called it: "...the most stimulating poetry experience I can remember in a long time—comparable in intensity and joy to reading Roethke's madhouse & love poems, Hart Crane's *The Bridge*, Ginsberg's "Kaddish," .... Your inspiration can give us all a shot in the arm."[89]

There was another, crucial reason that the magazine was so irregular—Bly was drinking mead himself, too. He may have had the strength of nine men, but he held the art of poetry in higher esteem. It was the private work on which all of his other work was based. Bly was engaged in an internal battle all during the life of the magazine. For example, as he writes in his journal in the early 1960s: "I think I have been mingling too much with the massive, turbid world—with the sour beehive.... Also with the magazine—I have participated too much...."[90] He needed to make time for all the inner work, the reading, solitude, and reflection that allowed him to write his own poems. In 1971 he writes to himself:

> What is there to do? Nothing! There are no letters that have to be written, no people that need to be chatted with, no rock that needs to be moved—let the rocks be—now for four days...

87 AS to RB, 30 January 1961.
88 AH to RB, 19 March 1960.
89 Gary Pacernik to RB, 29 June 1972.
90 RB journal, 23 August 1963.

> ten days...for this month take a vow, see no one, speak not a word that doesn't have to be spoken, forget the world and all the ants of God, walk at night, and let your feminine soul hover up toward the mad tree stars...see how many hours every day you can be alone.[91]

Thus he kept faithful to "the finest calling."

There are many wonderful poets in these pages, including: Hall, Snyder, Simpson, David Ignatow, Denise Levertov, Logan, Richard Hugo, Haines, Jerome Rothenberg, Thomas McGrath, Allen Ginsberg, Bill Knott, and Edson. I hold up for special attention: Wright's "Autumn Begins in Martins Ferry, Ohio" (*The Sixties* #6 [1962]); and Kinnell's "The Bear" (*The Sixties* #10 [1968]). But there are many of Bly's poems, too, including "Poem in Three Parts" (*The Fifties* #2 [1959]), and an excerpt from "Sleepers Joining Hands" (*The Seventies* #1 [1972]). Here is "Restless in the Fall Afternoon" (*The Sixties* #4 [1960]):

I.
I cannot wait for the night to come again,
And the huge stars to come—
All over the heavens! Bowls of cradles and black pools
And the blue to fade away.

II.
You must be alone six hours before you look at the stars—
Then coming out into the dark heavens
You will be like a drunkard returning to his table.

III.
There is a huge star that stands alone in the Western darkness:
Arcturus. When I read that the Arabs called it
The Keeper of Heaven, I felt a strange joy. I think
It was in the womb that I received
The thirst for the dark heavens.

Although I am not a poet, I know that thirst; I could get drunk on that mead.

---

91 RB journal, 10 June 1971.

III. The End

One person on whom the cover image of Odin was surely not lost was the Swedish poet Tomas Tranströmer. When Bly wrote that he was taking five of his poems, Tranströmer replied: "...to be published in *The Sixties* now seems to me to be a significantly greater honor, fully comparable to arriving at Valhalla and drinking beer with the great heroes."[92] He likely imagined Odin there, too, saying: "Welcome to Odin House!"

When the first issue of *The Seventies* appeared, in March 1972, no one, not even Bly himself, knew that it would be the last. And yet, Odin and his horse might have sensed that something was up. For just around the corner from them, on the back cover, were these words of Chögyam Trungpa (translated from the Tibetan):

> The Zen teacher hates the horse
> but the horse carries him.
> At the river both have to get into a boat.
> For crossing the mountains
> it's best just to carry an old stick.

Sleipnir, like Pegasus before him, was finally abandoned. But this wasn't the bitter end, the final destruction, Ragnarök (or *Götterdämmerung*). For the rider, now off his horse, there were new journeys ahead, across rivers and over mountains. And that is yet another story....

92 TT to RB, 20 July 1966.

BLY AND WRIGHT: A PASSIONATE POEM

By Anne Wright

When I was asked to speak at *Robert Bly in This World*, a conference held in Minneapolis during April of 2009, I was very happy to have an opportunity to honor Robert. Although he started out being James's friend, Robert has been my friend, too, since we first met in Minneapolis in the summer of 1967. The title of my talk, "Bly and Wright: A Passionate Poem," came from the chairman, Jim Lenfestey. At first I wasn't sure I liked that particular wording. However, after reading through the early correspondence between these two poets in preparation for this talk, I decided it was perfect.

* * *

On the afternoon of July 22, 1958 James Wright went to his mailbox at the University of Minnesota and found a copy of *The Fifties*. That moment changed his life.

He described his feelings in a letter that very day to Robert Bly, one of the editors of *The Fifties*.

> Dear Mr. Bly,
>
> This afternoon I walked over to the university...and picked up from the mailbox the copy of *The Fifties* which you were kind enough to send me. I am writing now to thank you.
>
> But the phrase "thank you" is too conventionally cold.
>
> Let me start again. I looked at the line on the inside of the front cover and was absolutely fixed with concentration for more than an hour, reading and rereading the magazine, wondering at the weirdness of it all.

The statement that had dazzled James was, "The editors of this magazine think that most of the poetry published in America today is too old-fashioned." Disturbed by the politeness of work in a recently published anthology, *New Poets of England and America*, Robert

Bly and William Duffy started a totally different type of literary magazine. Articles in the first issue stressed the need for American poets to work in a new style. As James had undergone many doubts about his own style of writing, the ideas he found expressed in *The Fifties* came at a perfect time for him.

James had found the first year of teaching in Minneapolis a huge change from his time as a Fulbright Scholar at the University of Vienna, back in 1952-53. In Austria he had immersed himself in the German language, poetry, music and the joy of writing poems in Viennese cafés. In Seattle, where he did graduate work at the University of Washington from 1953-57, he had been a prize pupil of Theodore Roethke. During that time his first book of poetry, *The Green Wall*, was about to be published. While he enjoyed teaching and the students at the University of Minnesota, he found the attitude of many colleagues difficult to understand especially when it came to his beloved Walt Whitman and the German poet Georg Trakl.

"I have an impossible time," he wrote to Robert, "even trying to get anyone to admit that Whitman existed, to find anyone at all—anyone at all—who even heard Trakl's name."

In the same first letter, he described the despair he felt about his own work. "I had just about decided to stop publishing any verse—to force myself to stop publishing, really—for at least a year or two, and maybe even more—to stop writing altogether...I deserted Whitman in order to write little tetrameter couplets."

That first letter of eight single-spaced typed pages was followed the next day by another long one. The contents of both letters were mildly hysterical and leapt from subject to subject: Ohio, Yeats, new poets whose work he thought Robert might like, poets of yesterday, today and maybe tomorrow, and, Lord help us, the role of iambic meter, a subject on which I will not dwell. What was very clear though was the relief and deep gratitude James felt after he read every page of that magazine. He described *The Fifties* as "funny, honest, deeply compassionate and intelligent."

Robert's reply, written on August 1st, also began with the formal "Dear Mr. Wright" but was far more organized and chock-o-block with opinions. Robert discussed the "new imagination," to use his term, the old style, poets from Homer to Karl Shapiro and, aha, meter, especially iambic.

Mr. Bly and Mr. Wright melted into Robert and Jim and their letters flowed like the Mississippi River. Georg Trakl became a first link in their friendship. James was overjoyed to find someone else in the USA who knew of Trakl. He wrote a carefully detailed description of how he had stumbled into the wrong classroom while in Vienna, where "a little Italian scholar named Susini was softly lecturing." Eugene Susini, according to Herb Lindenburger, a fellow Fulbright student, was a scholar serving as cultural officer with the French Embassy in Vienna. "Every afternoon," continued James, "at 3 o'clock, I think it was four days a week, I walked through that terrible cold and unheated winter city to hear Susini whisper in his beautiful, gentle liquid voice the poems of an Austrian...who had the grasp and shape of what you in your article called the new imagination."

Robert replied, "Your letter was interesting throughout, with the unforgettable scene in Austria like the notes of a flute."

Robert was quick to invite James and his family for a weekend visit to the Bly farm at the end of August. When it was over James wrote, "We all had the sensation of luminous space and kindness. I myself feel as the ripening orchard must have felt in the moonlight of late summer."

Letters from this intense time of correspondence were elegant, eloquent and frequent. There were many visits to the farm as well. James usually arrived alone with a briefcase bulging with books and copious drafts of poems, rather than a selection of shirts from Brooks Brothers.

Early in the correspondence James had sent Robert two poems with a request that he have a look at them when he had time. Robert's comments on the twenty- four lines of one poem were:

"Cannot take in the picture," "Too many thoughts," repeated twice, and "More concentration—but not excitement." A circle was drawn around six lines, accompanied by the word "*lovely*."

Those same six lines became the poem "In Fear of Harvests"

which was printed in the second copy of *The Fifties* side by side with another Wright poem, "In the Hard Sun." Robert seemed deeply impressed by that poem and wrote in a letter dated August 4, 1958:

> There is no question that you have within you the dark waters of a new life, and when I see the images in this poem, I see I have very little or nothing to teach you!
>
> The images are strong and firm and some like the tall ashes of loneliness perhaps the best line you have written. I'm glad if the articles helped with such a change but as they say around here "cow tracks in the pasture means cows only to somebody who has absolutely seen a cow."

Along with praise Robert offered advice. "Whatever explains too much, goes into too many details, weakens the poem and makes it sag like one of Dali's watches over a tree branch." Most of the ideas in that letter centered on the old style versus the new style, with the new style as winner.

The subject of iambic meter came up again, after James had read an essay by Robert on that subject and took it as a rejection of the meter. Robert wrote a strong, passionate response to his reaction on November 14, 1958. I regret there isn't time to read this letter in its entirety. In fact, to study all their letters from the early years would provide any reader with a splendid education. He began by writing:

> You seem to feel that I am moved by a grudge or hatred of iambic meter. But that's not true. I worked for three years, happily in nothing but iambic and I am to this day still writing in iambics.... I think the meter is graceful, precise and beautiful and in many ways. I love it.

He went on to say that his essay on iambics was "an attempt to say that we have overlooked the great element of poetry, such as the Greeks, Romans, Anglo Saxons have used—namely length of sound. However, my experience of spiritual adventures as I began to write in a meter of rhythm, with lengths of sound considered, led me to realize there are many things we haven't tried yet and later to thoughts of new subject matter and a new kind of imagination. However, none of these things, neither the thought of new subject matter nor the essay on sound, lead me to an absolute rejection of iambic meter, merely to the desire for something new."

James wrote a comment in the margin of that letter, which seems to me to be a true and heartfelt tribute.

> This letter has genuine human greatness in it. Robert Bly is a genius, possibly one or two of the really crucial poetic Geniuses of our century!

Added at the bottom of the last page was this resolution: "That was it! By God I'll try anything now!"

James continued to visit the farm where both Carol and Robert warmly welcomed him. He had a permanent room in the restored chicken house, one in which he was once locked until he finished a long overdue translation. The work he and Robert did was to culminate in the publication of several slim, beautiful books. In the fall of 1958 Robert planned to publish a series of five books that would contain selected poems by Neruda, Vallejo, Trakl, Jiménez, and Char. The Sixties Press did print *Twenty Poems of Georg Trakl* in 1961, *Twenty Poems of Cesar Vallejo* in 1962 and *Twenty Poems of Pablo Neruda* in 1967, with translations by James, John Knoepfle and Robert.

However, all was not sweet and peaceful. James chafed under some of Robert's suggestions and critical comments and did not take all of Robert's written pronouncements seriously. On a letter where Robert had written "We construct but the great poets are merely sensitive," James scribbled, "Explain—this sounds like a jellyfish."

These prickly feelings were nothing compared to what was happening in James's personal and academic life. Both his marriage and teaching career were under fire, coupled with serious emotional and alcohol-related problems. The farm became a haven, a sanctuary against the bitter and ugly attacks and a place where he felt wanted. James's letters are studded with remarks about the deep appreciation for what he described as a "beautiful, peaceful place."

To Carol Bly he wrote:

> I never go to the farm but what I feel a little less afraid of life and the less afraid I am the more marvelous I find life.

To Robert:

> I think your farm is the first such place I have ever really liked. It is beautifully mysterious and very much its own secret place.

Deeply depressed after the end of his first teaching year, he wrote Donald Hall claiming, "The summer had purged me, though I swear, by God, I think I would have perished without two or three instances of friends, one of them the correspondence of Robert Bly."

In the spring of 1961 he wrote Don this honest and splendid homage to the Bly farm.

> It is still morning...a spring sunlight over everything, the stones outside and the straw scattered in every direction outside the Blys' chicken house...I am here for nothing in particular. I arrived on Thursday evening, very late, in order to do nothing and be nothing in particular....
>
> Time and again during the last long winter I have been allowed to come here in order to gain a little necessary strength from the silence, the uncluttered solitude, the warmth of this chicken house where I have sat through some long afternoons either writing or doing nothing or being drunk, partly on wine and partly on things I have read and partly on nothing except the chance to drop my defense for a little while in a world which has come to seem to me increasingly desolate in those very places which I once considered the only meaningful things: the work for a living, the city I live in, my personal relations with other human beings outside my own skull and body, and my marriage....

I personally believe that the only respite in James's life at the time were his frequent visits to the Bly farm. The companionship, affection and respect he received from both Carol and Robert gave him the courage and will to survive whatever terrible experiences he had to endure, and created a lasting impact on his poetry.

In 1966 James received a Guggenheim grant and left Minnesota. In a letter written to Carol Bly that January, he assured her that he cared "very deeply for Minnesota itself, or at least its countryside and the farm which I love truly and freely and fully as any place on earth." Minneapolis, however, was another matter.

I met James in the spring of that year when he came to New York City to interview for a job in the English department at Hunter College. He was accepted and, once he settled into his new life, we became reacquainted. I began to hear about Robert during our first dinner together, as well as an abundance of stories about the farm, the Bly daughters Mary and Biddy, the chicken house, the stage in the barn where plays were given, David, the swayback palomino, Simon the big, shaggy dog, and sometimes, the translation work he and Robert had done. I was even with James at a florist shop when he sent flowers to Madison in celebration of Noah's birth. The stories never stopped.

James and I were married in the spring of 1967 and planned to visit "The Farm" that summer. Finally, at last I would see that heavenly place, meet all the Blys, and have a delayed honeymoon.

We flew to Minneapolis in August to stay with the poet Roland Flint and his family for a few days. Robert, who was on a fishing trip, would meet us there and drive us to the farm. My first glimpse of the tall Viking was watching him place a huge plastic bag of fish in Roland's freezer. When he saw us he gave a great shout of joy and hugged us both at the same time.

Robert and James talked non-stop on the drive to Madison. Robert, in his strong Minnesota accent, peppered his remarks with the query, "How does that grab you?" Carol and the children, still on a visit in Duluth, were not there to greet us, but Tim Baland, a young man who helped with *The Fifties*, was. I had a quick tour of the farmhouse, actually two houses built together, before we walked down a little hill to the schoolhouse where James and I would stay.

Robert had prepared this one-room schoolhouse especially for us. There was a beautiful old wooden bed with carved headboard against one wall and two armchairs and a writing table under the windows. He and Carol had bought the building at an auction and set it in a grove of trees not far from their house. Robert was particularly proud of the nearby, brand-new outhouse! He explained that he'd set three young visiting poets to work digging up the foundation, then added that they had left pretty soon after that.

Robert, Tim, and sometimes James worked on translations during the morning and early afternoon. Then we'd all drive into the town of Madison to buy groceries. After dinner we went for walks along the deserted highway.

"Come on Jim and Annie," Robert would say. "Let's lie down in the grass and listen for animals."

So, of course, we'd stretch out on in the tall grass and listen as Robert whispered about the owls, rabbits, or mice we might hear. However, the only sound was the hot summer breeze blowing through the fields of wheat. Years later, when I read through the early letters, I learned that the wind, particularly in autumn, meant a great deal to Robert. I think of these beautiful words from a passage in one of those letters as a prize of discovery.

> I can hear nothing today but the sound of the wind. That is my favorite sound—wind in the dead grass of fall or in the trees that are so agreeably settling down towards water and letting their leaves go, like people so old they have forgotten which of the young ones are theirs and which belong to others. I sit and listen to it for hours.

After Carol and the children came back, we went swimming at the town pool each afternoon with Mary and Biddy. Meal times were filled with good food, expansive talk and much laughter. The talk never stopped. There were heated discussions about the Vietnam War and the horrifying war policies of the Johnson administration. Various poets and their work were either praised or lamented, including those who were among the many visitors to the farm. Stories were told about *The Fifties*, including insulting letters to and from the editors. Sometimes Robert might reminisce about childhood on his father's farm or recent trips taken to Norway and England. He made some of his famous outrageous statements too, such as this description of another poet—"I think he is like an omelet made without eggs"—or this speculation: "The reason we have three different races on this planet is because each race came from a different place in outer space. Annie, how does that grab you?"

Those amazing evenings usually ended with someone reading poems and translations.

Other visitors came while we were there: Lois and David Budbill, the novelist Fred Manfred, who arrived with his own sleeping bag, and Hardie St. Martin, who came to stay for several weeks as a consultant for Spanish translations. James and I felt quite glum when our visit came to an end. "I feel so sad," was Robert's goodbye.

We could and did stay in touch. In the spring of 1968 the Bly family rented an apartment in New York for a few months, which gave all of us the chance to be together. We never knew whom we'd find sitting in their living room when we dropped by for the afternoon or dinner. Sometimes it was Louis Simpson or Paul Zweig. From time to time John Logan came in from Buffalo to see Robert or David Ignatow and his family might be there from Long Island.

That was also the year Robert won the National Book Award. We were in the audience to cheer and stamp when he read his acceptance speech. In fact we'd heard him practice it so much we knew it by heart.

James and I made one more visit to the farm in the spring of 1970. It was March and Madison, Minnesota seemed the coldest place I'd ever known! However, there was a brand-new fireplace in the living room and we practically lived next to that warmth. Mary and Biddy were in school now and Noah a four-year-old with flaming red hair and an awesome vocabulary. The schoolhouse had become a place of meditation for Robert, who kindly offered to set up the old wooden bed for us in the house should we want to recapture the atmosphere of our former honeymoon.

We continued to see Robert whenever he came to New York. He'd sweep into town dressed in his serape, accompanied by masks, musical instruments, a circle of followers and sometimes our Godchild

Mary. If he stayed with us, he always brought presents: a roast chicken, books, flowers, and once a pair of golden earrings for me. Those impromptu visits were a time of long conversations, high spirits and sharp wit. Each time we saw him, Robert presented us with dazzling ideas. He talked of Jung, the multitudinous levels of consciousness and his latest endeavor, the Great Mother Conference.

During the later years of their friendship, letters became shorter and less frequent. What had once been an avalanche of mail became a trickle. Sometimes Robert wrote and James didn't answer and sometimes James wrote and Robert didn't answer. The correspondence lessened but never stopped. Their lives were considerably different since the days when James went to the farm in need of quiet solitude. James's move to New York brought a greater distance between them than mere miles. Many of the ideas from the 50's and 60's that they had once shared and agreed upon had changed. In addition, James hesitated to send Robert his new work, perhaps in fear of strong criticism or disapproval, an action that must have been hurtful to Robert. However, this was a strong and steadfast friendship that could and would survive.

When James entered Mount Sinai Hospital with terminal cancer in 1980, Robert came to see him on a cold winter day. He entered the hospital room quietly and took James in his arms. Although James couldn't talk, he was able to respond to Robert with written comments on a yellow-lined legal pad. During that visit James was alert and responsive in a way he hadn't been for several months and would never be again. After Robert left, James wrote this note to me:

> I was afraid Robert was gone for good. I'm so relieved he's not. Today was a good day.

Robert has continued to be as good a friend to me as he was to James. I'm always delighted to receive one of his handwritten letters filled with news, a caustic comment or two and a touch of whimsy.

Last November I was in Minneapolis for a few days and had a lovely lunch with him, Ruth and Gioia Timpanelli. We toasted each other and Obama with Prosecco, Ruth's happy choice, and had the usual lively conversation one has with Robert. While I was here in November I read Robert's letters to James that are in the manuscript department of Andersen Library. I came across the last one, written on January 8th of 1980. I'm not sure I ever saw it before. I'd like to close by reading parts of that letter, which epitomizes so beautifully this splendid and unique friendship.

> Dear Jim,
>
> I was so shocked by your news that I was really stunned for several days; but it made me feel how frail we all are. How much the busy work of life hides that. And it brought our old friendship back to me in its zany form as well as its tender form....also the longing that has always run through our friendship to write more primarily or deeply. I still feel those currents very much....
>
> Well, I didn't mean to talk on and on but to send you my friendship, whose feelings have never faltered however annoyed I've been on little things, and my admiration and love. Our friendship and brotherhood has meant so much to me; I felt so lonely in the literary world until I met you, and you came out to the farm, and we had the chance to brood over horse-poems and Trakl-poems together.
>
> With much love,
> Robert

Yes, indeed: "*Bly and Wright: a Passionate Poem!*"

ANTONIO MACHADO'S EYEGLASSES: THE INFLUENCE OF ROBERT BLY'S TRANSLATIONS ON AMERICAN POETRY

By Ray Gonzalez

I want to begin by reading two poems by the great Spanish poet Antonio Machado, translated by Robert Bly.

THE CLOCK STRUCK TWELVE TIMES

The clock struck twelve times ... and it was a spade
knocked twelve times against the earth.
... "It's my turn!" I cried.... The silence
answered me: Do not be afraid.
You will never see the last drop fall
that now is trembling in the water clock.

You will still sleep many hours
here on the beach,
and one clear morning you will find
your boat tied to another shore.

THE WATER WHEEL

The afternoon arrived
mournful and dusty.

The water was composing
its countrified poem
in the buckets
of the lazy water wheel.

The mule was dreaming—
old and sad mule!
in time to the darkness
that was talking in the water.

The afternoon arrived
mournful and dusty.

I don't know which noble
and religious poet
joined the anguish
of the endless wheel

to the cheerful music
of the dreaming water,
and bandaged your eyes—
old and sad mule! ...

But it must have been a noble
and religious poet,
a heart made mature
by darkness and art.

I also want to quote Robert's introduction to his Machado translations in *The Winged Energy of Delight*: "Machado said that if we pay attention exclusively to the inner world, it will dissolve; if we pay attention exclusively to the outer world, it will dissolve. To create art, we have to stitch together both the inner and the outer worlds. How to do that? Machado concludes, Well, we could always use our eyes."

Over the decades, Robert Bly's translations have taught me to use my eyes as a poet as I gaze into my own life and, most importantly, into the lives of others. Bly's translations made me see how poetry destroys the introverted knot of mental speech and releases it as poetry that deals with the real world. It's why I put on Antonio Machado's eyeglasses to see the world beyond American borders and learn how various cultures redefined what a poem does centuries ago. I am not alone, of course, and new ways of seeing the world and using the poetic process were offered to American poets by Bly's translations of Pablo Neruda, Federico García Lorca, César Vallejo, Machado, Juan Ramón Jiménez, Vicente Aleixandre, George Trakl, Francis Ponge, Miguel Hernandez, Rolf Jacobsen and many others.

Bly has said that the translator has to find the words that will make the vision reappear whenever they are spoken.

In the work of these great poets, vision appears over and over and gives American poets the permission to do things in their work they had never done before because, as the great American poet Larry Levis once said about the Spanish poets, "It takes courage to see and grieve." Well, when the first translations of Neruda and Vallejo and Hernandez came out, U.S. poets did not know how to grieve and needed permission from somebody to step beyond what had come before. They thought they could see and the Beat poets of the fifties gave us one version of seeing, but no one was grieving and accepting that the real world had to be written about by going inside the dimensions of what we see, feel, and experience. The world poets in translation led us inward before letting us explode forward with visionary power. This forced many American poets to come to terms with their commitment to poetry and how they used it in their lives and how they lived their lives as poets. Through Bly's translations, we learned how to fuse reality with a deep imagination. This didn't happen overnight and didn't take place until Bly translated poets like Neruda, Vallejo, Tranströmer, and others.

These first translations of Lorca and Jiménez shocked American poets and forced them to set forth on a journey beyond the defensive language of U.S. literature and its traditions. Machado and Vicente Aleixandre pointed the way by showing us, as Bly did in *Leaping Poetry*, that the poet had to leap beyond one room of the psyche. American poets stayed in that one room for most of the 20th Century, until Neruda said, "It is only a deserted dining room, / and around it there are expanses, / sunken factories, pieces of timber / which I alone know, / because I am sad, and because I travel, / and I know the earth, and I am sad."

American poetry did not mature until its poets started reading and responding to poets from around the world, and Bly's translations were some of the first we came across in the sixties and seventies. His translations remain some of the most widely read and influential today but, in the sixties and seventies, when I first read Neruda and Vallejo in those early Beacon Press editions, I was stunned because these poets showed me that a poem was more powerful than I was. There went my ego! Neruda and Vallejo showed me that a poem was more powerful than its creator and that shook me because my American poetic education said the poet was everything. In high school, I was dumb enough to think only Americans wrote poetry. My public education implanted this ignorance. Robert Frost, Emily Dickinson, T.S. Eliot, and Walt Whitman were it, but they dwelled in that vast room where I was taught, and that American dwelling was my only world of poetry until Bly as translator expanded the house.

Spanish, South American, and European poets slapped us awake and showed us that the kaleidoscope of images we thought were serving our poetry could only go so far because American poets were not dealing with an inward reality, only an external one. Bly once said, "An image and a picture differ in that the image, being the natural speech of the imagination, cannot be drawn from or inserted back into the real world." ("A Wrong Turning in American Poetry") Before Neruda and Vallejo disturbed us and made us celebrate something besides ourselves, U.S. poets were busy trying to push themselves back into the real world by proclaiming that experimental poetry, formal confessions, and structured forms would open the way.

Again, when poets of my generation (I am 56 years old) opened their eyes to the fact other countries had an older, richer tradition of poetry than Americans did, it was shocking because world poets took poetry in strange new directions that challenged us as readers and writers, confronting us with the power to see things and find ways to enter what we saw. This changed our writing lives. We went beyond the groundbreaking obsessions of the Beat Poets, the careful steps of the Formalists and the New York School to create a new American poetry that freed the poet to write about worldly things while at the same time giving him or her new courage in dropping deeper into the poetic labyrinth of the soul; there he could take a risky look at the vulnerable self that had no choice but to go out into the larger world under new poetic terms. And it all began by seeing things because Neruda and Vallejo saw things by accepting the mind, the soul, the origins of language, the clear though constantly changing image in front of them, the hidden image behind them, and accepting the secret breathing force in all things. When those Beacon Press books first came out, Bly's work opened a whole new passage into poetic constructions. Poetry in English no longer needed an American guide map to become great poetry. The poets of the larger world crossed the country without a map long ago and it took a courageous translator to join them, transform their language, and reveal before an American poetic audience that didn't quite know we were hungry because we had been staring at our linguistic maps for too long.

Bly once said of Pablo Neruda, "Neruda has confidence in what is hidden." He said, "Moving under the earth, he knows everything from the bottom up (which is the right way to learn the nature of a thing) and therefore is never at a loss for its name." Bly also wrote, "... many critics in the United States insist the poem must be hard-bitten, impersonal, and rational, lest it lack sophistication." (*Neruda and Vallejo*) In the sixties and seventies, American poets were hidden in their own lives and did not know they were buried underground because American history and the literary canon had forbidden this kind of self-knowledge.

There are too many American poets to name who were influenced by this kind of poetry brought to them through Robert Bly's translations. Some of the key poets include James Wright, William Stafford, David Ignatow, Larry Levis, Richard Jones, William Matthews, Carolyn Forche, Robert Hass in his early work, Ai, Denis Johnson, Charles Wright, Adrienne Rich, James Galvin, Lorna de Cervantes, Joseph Stroud, Carolyn Kizer, Robert Wrigley, and too many others to list.

Robert Bly's translations taught American poets many things, but I have narrowed their eternal impact to what I feel are four important general areas of influence:

1. How to grieve—The Spanish and Latin American poets taught us how to climb into grief through imagery that changes the writer. In the work of these great poets, vision appears through immersion

in a state of being that fuses human desire with the natural powers of the earth. This way of seeing allows for emotion, and it gave American poets the permission to do things in their work they had never done before. Trakl, Rilke, Martinson, Jiménez showed poets how to accept "the spirit" inside poetic frameworks. Once this was done, American poets could cry and explode and celebrate and grieve because what they were seeing in themselves was a process of catching up with the rest of the world. So, the grief wasn't just from personal loss, but also from recognizing that poetry, sooner or later, will leave the poet behind as it goes out into the landscape of the psyche, the spirit, and its underground sources. Before Bly's translations, all U.S. poets could do was attempt to prop themselves up in a poem and hope to survive by the strict rules of American language. It wasn't proper to be emotional because the academy said, "Construct your poem, but stay away from the spirit of your words. We only want the mirror and not what molds the glass." The academy also said, "Never go under, into the body or mind, in order to breathe and see what is there and not there because those unconscious dimensions are the true nature of poetry."

2. How to enforce one's own solitude—By reading these translations, we began to learn how to see the various dimensions of our private lives and how our privacy cries out for the world while, at the same time, it wants to be left alone. Neruda, Lorca, and Machado gave American poets a fresh start in redefining sacred space. American poets were used to writing about their personal lives, their place, and their autobiographical wounds, but they didn't know how to express it in a way that invited the world to create new states of solitary existence through understanding the poetry of other cultures and nations. American poets were basically alone and didn't know it because they mistook solitude for isolation. This isolation meant U.S. poets didn't have to address the world or seek a sense of the larger self in and outside their solitude. Bly's translations of poets like Tomas Tranströmer revealed how the sustenance of solitude grew out of a more honest and visually curious poetry.

3. How to imagine the world beyond the personal self—Robert's translations of Francis Ponge are a good example of how the imagination melts out of the human cage to become something else and give life to all things. This life-giving force was one of the biggest lessons learned by American poets in the sixties and seventies because the Vietnam War, among several historical and cultural events, had shattered American culture. Bly's work in the prose poem and his translations of writers like Ponge came at a crucial moment because American poets needed to go beyond the personal self, in a shattered time, and discover how poetry brought all things to life. For American poets to give life to inanimate objects, or for them to ponder the idea that the subconscious life of things brings them closer to the mysteries of poetry, was something new to not only think about, but to experience because reading poets from other countries was a process of surrender.

In *Leaping Poetry*, Bly talks about how this power to give life to things often comes through leaping association in poetry. He says that the old American ways of poetry were moving down "old railroads of association" that had broken their tracks long ago. He writes that one thing "that has kept us from being aware of association as the core of a poem is the grudge American critics and university teachers have always had against surrealism." He also said, "American poetry faltered in the 40's and 50's.... if the Americans do not have European poets to refresh their sense of what association is, their work soon falls back to the boring associative tracks...."

4. The world poets taught us how to write a poetry that resides in two worlds—the world of the tragic American identity and the world of global sacrifice and redemption. For American poets to consider poetry as a political tool would mean they would have to divorce themselves from private ego and would not be able to raise their own flags over their limited audiences. When important books like *Poet in New York* by Federico García Lorca or Neruda's *Canto General* appeared, it was shocking to realize that the inner self was the most powerful weapon against injustice. If the Beats were trying to

address American cruelty in the fifties, repression and censorship still had their mighty cloaks. It took Bly's translations of Neruda, Lorca, and Jiménez to lift those clouds. Yet, American poets are still learning about the idea that a political stance can be taken without sacrificing the sanctity of poetic words.

In an interview, Bly once said, "[the] interior animal life cannot be expressed with images of ... curbs and broken bottles and the objects with which Williams hoped to express it.... It can't be expressed with abstract words, as many of the Black Mountain people hoped to express it." He goes on to say, "Lorca is always going into the animal imagery. It's the fact that the interior animal life, the inward animal life, can only be expressed in images that are live and that pick things up from evolution...." ("The Evolutionary Part of the Mind," *Talking All Morning*)

Here are two poems Bly translated which express that interior animal life. The first is by Lorca:

RUN-DOWN CHURCH
(Ballad of the First World War)

I had a son and his name was John.
I had a son.
He disappeared into the arches one Friday of All Souls.
I saw him playing on the highest steps of the Mass
throwing a little tin pail at the heart of the priest.
I knocked on the coffin. My son! My son! My son!
I drew out a chicken foot from behind the moon and then
I understood that my daughter was a fish
down which the carts vanish.
I had a daughter.
I had a fish dead under the ashes of the incense burner.
I had an ocean. Of what? Good Lord! An ocean!
I went up to ring the bells but the fruit was all wormy
and the blackened match-ends
were eating the spring wheat.
I saw a stork of alcohol you could see through
shaving the black heads of the dying soldiers
and I saw the rubber booths

where the goblets full of tears were whirling.
In the anemones of the offertory I will find you, my love!
when the priest with his strong arms raises up the mule and the ox
to scare the nighttime toads that roam in the icy landscapes of the
  chalice.
I had a son who was a giant,
but the dead are stronger and know how to gobble down pieces of the
  sky.
If my son had only been a bear,
I wouldn't fear the secrecy of the crocodiles
and I wouldn't have seen the ocean roped to the trees
to be raped and wounded by the mobs from the regiment.
If my son had only been a bear!
I'll roll myself in this rough canvas so as not to feel the chill of the
  mosses.
I know very well they will give me a sleeve or a necktie,
but in the innermost part of the Mass I'll smash the rudder and then
the insanity of the penguins and seagulls will come to the rock
and then they will make the people sleeping and the people singing on
  the street corners say:
he had a son.
A son! A son! A son
and it was no one else's, because it was his son!
His son! His son! His son!

And here is a poem by Miguel Hernandez:

"SITTING ON TOP OF CORPSES"

Sitting on top of corpses
fallen silent over the last two months,
I kiss empty shoes
and take hold wildly
of the heart's hand
and the soul that keeps it going.

I want my voice to climb mountains,
descend to earth, and give out thunder:
this is what my throat wants
from now on, and always has.

Come near to my loud voice,
nation of the same mother,
tree whose roots hold
me as in a jail.
I am here to love you,
I am here to fight for you,
with my mouth and blood
as with two faithful rifles.

If I came out of the dirt
and was born from a womb
with no luck and no money,
it was only that I might become
the nightingale of sadness,
an echo chamber for disaster,
that I could sing and keep singing
for the men who ought to hear it
everything that has to do with suffering,
with poverty, with earth.

Yesterday the people woke
naked, with nothing to pull on,
hungry, with nothing to eat,
and now another day has come
dangerous, as expected,
bloody, as expected.
In their hands, rifles
long to become lions
to finish off the animals
who have been so often animals.

Although you have so few weapons,
nation with a million strengths,
don't let your bones collapse:
as long as you have fists,
fingernails, spit, courage,
insides, guts, balls, and teeth,
attack those who would wound us.
Stiff as the stiff wind,
gentle as the gentle air,
kill those who kill,

loathe those who loathe
the peace inside you
and the womb of your women.
Don't let them stab you in the back;
live face to face and die
with your chest open to the bullets
and wide as the walls.

I sing with a griever's voice,
my people, for all your heroes,
your anxieties like mine,
your setbacks whose tears were drawn
from the same metal as mine,
suffering of the same mettle,
your thinking and my brain,
your courage and my blood,
your anguish and my honors,
all made of the same timber.
To me this life is like
a rampart in front of emptiness.

I am here in order to live
as long as my soul is alive,
and I am here to die
when that time comes,
deep in the roots of the nation,
as I will be and always have been.
Life is a lot of hard gulps,
but death is only one.

We read these translations and were taught to write a new kind of poetry after encountering Bly's Neruda, Lorca, Vallejo, Machado, Jiménez, Aleixandre, Trakl, Hernandez, Jacobsen, Ponge, and others. Reading Bly's translations gave American poets a fresh start with their own language and their way of relating experience, imagery, voice, and vision, discovering there were many hidden layers of poetic awareness yet to be learned. As a translator, Bly didn't simply settle for bringing a Spanish or Swedish poem into English; he insisted on making a Neruda or Machado or Tranströmer poem into a vessel of human experience beyond the origins of language and personal triumph. This vessel contained universal truth stripped of national boundaries and also was filled with a deep hole of shock—that magnet where American poets in the sixties and seventies looked down the well and realized they had to fall in to get to the other side of the world. They fell in when poetry in translation became an eye-opener, a savior, and a gift. They dropped into the well of the unconscious when Bly's translations were new, joyful, disturbing, and caused a celebratory anxiety among American poets. By the end of the sixties and through the seventies, it was a time to change American poetry and these translations spoke to every poet who was wandering blind through America.

Again, the only way to get there and finally take a good look was by writing a more adventurous, risk-taking kind of poetry that was absent from U.S. literature when Bly introduced his first translations of Neruda and Vallejo. Quite often this experience of finding the vessel and jumping in encompassed the body and the mind and forced American poets to go beyond old notions that the "American Me" was everything in poetry. As Robert Hass once wrote in an essay on Tomas Tranströmer, Robert Bly has "a hunger for excited states of mind."

Well, an excited mind is going to turn on itself, its person, its imaginative soul, and the world, and is going to push the poet into starting over by falling in the hole of the imagination and excavating underground layers of language that were there all his or her life. It took reading Lorca, Jiménez, Ekelöf, and Rilke to recognize that what the world sees through poetry is ancient and new and can never be confined to one country and its tragic cultural vision that replays its tragedies, over and over again, and often expresses them in the same kind of poetry. Through translation, the excited and magnetic states of the mind and of seeing drew American poets in fresh directions and made them do something in their poems, instead of merely thinking about it on the page.

In *Leaping Poetry*, Bly writes, "Mere mechanical pulling of images out of memory stores will not produce leaping poetry; and that is possibly why so much mechanical surrealist poetry fails.... leaping poetry probably cannot be written without great spiritual energy." Pablo Neruda gave me spiritual energy. Federico García Lorca sang about my poetic energy. César Vallejo destroyed my ego and I felt my spirit as I read his poems for the first time decades ago. Critics can write about this forever, but when Bly's first translations came out, American poets had very little spirit. The Beats had it, but their autobiographical demons tied them down. The New York School had it, but museums framed their energy for them. The American spirit was confined to the U.S., and it existed on the black-and-white plane of confessing how terrible we felt without really exploring the magical powers of pain and tragedy and how they were connecting threads to other worlds that contained fresh poems bridging and leaping between our sadness, our educational system, and the way we were taught to write. Pablo Neruda taught me to write. César Vallejo taught me to recite. Miguel Hernandez taught me to hurt and be lifted beyond that hurting through writing a poem. In the end, it took a risky spiritual energy to go past the one-dimensional "I'm so sorry" stage I was in as a poet in my twenties. After reading Neruda and Lorca for the first time in the old Beacon Press books, I woke up and many of my poetry colleagues woke up and pointed to these books and poems and reached out to each other.

In the end, Robert Bly's translations, regardless of the poet he is translating, fill me with desire. These translations create a marriage between Lorca's *duende*—that dark force of sudden creative expression and the American need to desire things. Each time I read Pablo Neruda or Tomas Tranströmer, I desire things. As a poet, I want something, don't always have to know what it is, though I see what I want through this writing that does not come from American shores. I emphasize this to remind everyone that to read a translation, on one level, means to borrow the initial vision and experience of the poet and redefine it in a second arrival of language. Well, when Bly's translations appeared decades ago, American poetry was already set in its ways, though there were fractured schools of poetic thought from West Coast to East Coast and everyone assumed

Robert Lowell's wild hair was going to make him confess and dominate American poetry. Bly's translations of Spanish, Latin American, and European poets complicated the situation but gave U.S. poets a chance to breathe and gaze upon new sets of wild hair. Bly's work with world poetry made us educate ourselves again by writing and, yes, it involved imitation, leaping, dreaming, failing, succeeding, and closing and opening our eyes to a larger world that, finally, after years of American poets stalking the hallways of public schools, was actually inviting them to leave the hallway and come outside where the ocean was crashing against the black rocks of Isla Negra.

Bly once wrote of César Vallejo, "[His] wildness and savagery rest on a clear compassion for others." (*Neruda and Vallejo*) Bly's translations taught me compassion through poetry and seeing and this encounter with compassion and the visionary self is something the best American poets are constantly exploring and have been exploring since the early days of one of Robert Bly's greatest accomplishments—translating the world.

SO MUCH HAPPENS WHEN NO ONE IS WATCHING

By Daniel Deardorff

In *Leaping Poetry*, his seminal work on associativity, Robert Bly posits: "[I]t *is possible that rapid association is a form of content.*"[1] The question before us then is: "What might that content be?" There are three things involved in making an associative leap: a place to leap from, a place to leap to, and most importantly, that space which "no one is watching," the distance in-between. Bly suggests that the in-between, the liminal space of the leap, provides a mysterious kind of content. The invisible and spacious reaches in Bly's poetry and prose are the focus of this essay. There are two poems that I know of, "Four Ways of Knowledge"[2] and "Testifying to the Night,"[3] in which Bly calls our attention to the many things that happen "when no one is watching." Pointing toward that which must remain outside our conscious awareness is like Lao Tzu saying that "knowing with not-knowing is best." Connecting "what happens when no one is watching" to the emphasis on associativity, we notice a similar invitation to consider the unconscious space behind the associative image. There is a great distance, swiftly traversed, between the philosopher and the predator in the line: "Plato wrote by the light from sharks' teeth."[4]

So many strange, unpredictable, and inexplicable things happen in the poems of Robert Bly; especially when we speak them aloud, it isn't necessary, or even desirable, to understand everything that happens—we aren't really meant to—the important thing is to *feel* the many hidden currents moving through one's body. Later it might be good to do a little research and learn that, on February 16, 1600,

---

1 Robert Bly, *Leaping Poetry: An Idea with Poems and Translations* (Boston: A Seventies Press Book, Beacon Press, 1990), p. 14.

2 "Four Ways of Knowledge," Robert Bly, *Selected Poems* (New York: Harper & Row, 1986), p. 164

3 "Testifying to the Night," Robert Bly, *The Night Abraham Called to the Stars* (New York: HarperCollins, 2001), p. 83.

4 "Monet's Haystacks," *The Night Abraham Called to the Stars*, p. 15.

the Inquisitors burned Giordano Bruno at the stake for the crime of heresy. However, for the moment it's better to simply sense:

> ... it was when
> He first saw the print of the sparrow's foot in the mud
> That Giordano Bruno knew that the world was on fire.[5]

Bly the poet tells us that fire is both divine and dangerous, and that it's possible for a human being to apprehend the radiant glory of creation by looking down at something small, alive, muddy, or even broken.

One key to entering the vast spaces in Bly's thought is understanding something I've called "associative alacrity"—the adroit capacity to form unexpected correlations. In the modern world this capacity has been so repressed that it's hard to work out any sense of it. In Norse mythology there is an ash tree that connects many worlds. This "World Tree," called Yggdrasil, presents a complex image that works like this: at the top is the solar bird, the great eagle; at the bottom is the old lunar serpent. The third thing, which connects this opposition, is something much less grand, a squirrel. Leaping from branch to root, the acrobat squirrel carries messages between the extremities. The furry mammal presents the limbic capacity to bridge the contradictions without reconciliation. The squirrel is the embodiment of the leaping consciousness.

Many of Bly's most inscrutable leaps are on a level akin to Blake's *Marriage of Heaven and Hell.* On one hand, Bly offers us "the glory of ruin,"[6] and on the other hand, "the old inn of desire."[7] These two images are taken, here, as the clashing rocks through which to steer our course into the leaping alacrity of Bly's poiesis. They represent two contrary streams of apprehension—ascent and descent, transcendence and immanence, spirit and flesh—contraries that run through the life and work of Robert Bly. Theologically, transcendence is the

5 "Giordano Bruno and the Muddy Footprint," *The Night Abraham Called to the Stars*, p. 7.

6 "Eudalia and Plato," *The Night Abraham Called to the Stars*, p. 21.

7 "There Are So Many Platos," Robert Bly, *My Sentence Was a Thousand Years of Joy* (New York: HarperCollins, 2005) p. 13.

belief that all matter is fallen, whereas the opposing belief in immanence says that matter is filled with god. In Bly there is no argument, the spiritual longing to ascend is counterbalanced by the soul's need to descend.

It is not my purpose to examine the personal life of Robert Bly. However, speaking of this man as my "teacher," it is difficult to separate his work from his presence; moreover, the power of Bly's work often lies in the fact that his writing is *lived*—we can feel the breath and blood spent on the images and sounds. This particular quality of Bly is best described in the words of Federico García Lorca: "[I]t is not a question of ability or aptitude but a matter of possessing an authentic living style; that is to say of blood, of culture most ancient, of creation in act."[8] Let us say, then, that to have an "authentic living style" has more to do with showing one's defects than with being lofty:

> Eudalia will not allow Plato to come near
> The Garden of Lovers because Eudalia knows
> He, being lofty, is afraid of the glory of ruin.[9]

To reach for glory in art often invites the ever-lurking danger of an inflated buoyancy or lofty optimism; so in the pursuit of fullness we forget the value of emptiness. Whether we see the glass as half empty or half full may depend on our willingness to love that which disappears. So Bly asks:

> ... Friend, tell me what to do,
> Since I am a man in love with the setting stars.[10]

To love the setting stars means finding "the glory of ruin"; it requires us to admit that the world is filled with sorrow, decay, farewells, grief,

8 Federico García Lorca, "The Havana Lectures," trans. Stella Rodriquez, *The Rag and Bone Shop of the Heart: Poems for Men*, eds. Robert Bly, James Hillman, and Michael Meade (New York: HarperCollins) p. 165.

9 "Eudalia and Plato," *The Night Abraham Called to the Stars*, p. 21.

10 "The Night Abraham Called to the Stars," *The Night Abraham Called to the Stars*, p. 1

death and yet, with a badger's ferocity, prizing open a hole or crack, disclosing the immanent glory and divine fire hidden in all things—while, on the other hand, "living in the old inn of desire" means refusing to deny the pleasure and joy in the earthly and homely life of the body. It's as if Bly leads us into a muddy hole where, astonished, we discover the entire Milky Way and all the burning heavens!

Leaping in this manner, the poems of Robert Bly refuse to turn away from Heaven, and at once, stubbornly refuse to renounce the earthly life. "In a great ancient or modern poem, the considerable distance between the associations, the distance the spark has to leap, gives the lines their bottomless feeling, their space."[11] The relationships formed by these leaps are not linear—they are not stops along some rational railway, or some predictable system of linked facts—they are images or feelings related by something inexplicable and mysterious. In this kind of association the distance, the *interval* of the leap, provides verticality and depth, a kind of bottomless content which functions as what Lawrence Hatab has called "mythic disclosure": it does not explain things but "presents an intelligible picture of the lived world and the form of human involvement with the lived world."[12]

> In ancient times, in the "time of inspiration," the poet flew from one world to another, "riding on dragons," as the Chinese said. Isaiah rode on those dragons, so did Li Po and Pindar. They dragged behind them long tails of dragon smoke. Some of that dragon smoke still boils out of Beowulf. ... This dragon smoke means that a leap has taken place in the poem.[13]

Dragon smoke tells us that some subterranean or chthonic energy has erupted skyward and grown wings. Bly's understanding of such "leaps" in poetry is profoundly expanded in his determination to use mythic stories as portals through which to "think" about relevant sociological and psychological issues in an associative manner:

---

11 Robert Bly, *Leaping Poetry: An Idea with Poems and Translations*, p. 4.

12 Lawrence J. Hatab, *Myth and Philosophy: A Contest of Truths* (La Salle, Illinois: Open Court, 1990) p. 14.

13 Robert Bly, *Leaping Poetry: An Idea with Poems and Translations*, p. 1.

> The associative paths ... allow us to leap from one part of the brain to another and lay out their contraries. Moreover it's possible that what we call "mythology" deals precisely with these abrupt juxtapositions.... using what Joseph Campbell called "mythological thinking," it moves the energy along a spectrum—either up or down. [It] can awaken the "lost music," walk on the sea, cross the river from instinct to spirit.[14]

Bly's thinking is filled with the vital relationship of myth and poetry. Rather than falling into the typical mythologist's trap of comparative, oppositional, adversarial, "either-or" thought, he clearly appreciates that entering myth involves something more than cognition:

> The images the old stories give—stealing the key from under the mother's pillow, picking up a golden feather fallen from the burning breast of the Firebird, finding the Wild Man under the lake water, following the tracks of one's own wound through the forest and finding that it resembles the tracks of a god—these are meant to be taken slowly into the body. They continue to unfold, once taken in.[15]

Joseph Campbell's notion of "mythological thinking" was developed further by Bly in his suggestion that the interval of the leap provides content. The greater the distance of the leap, the more intensely we feel something we do not actually see.

It is in the interval of the leap that "so much happens when no one is watching" and this is related to Richard Schechner's idea that certain rituals require "selective inattention." He says: "Selective inattention allows patterns of the whole to be visible, patterns that otherwise would be burned out of consciousness by a too intense concentration."[16]

---

14 Robert Bly, "Poetry and the Three Brains," *American Poetry: Wildness and Domesticity* (New York: Harper & Row, 190), p. 62.

15 Robert Bly, *Iron John: A Book About Men* (Reading, Massachusetts: Addison-Wesley, 1990), p. ix.

16 Richard Schechner, *Performance Theory* (New York: Routledge, 1977) p. 202.

Again, "so much happens when no one is watching." These patterns are felt but remain inexplicable. Indicative language cannot convey them; poetry, myth, and dance are loved by the gods because they connect humans to the experience of Mystery:

> The first experience ... is interior. When the poet realizes for the first time ... when he touches for the first time, something far inside him. It's connected with what the ancients called The Mysteries, and its wrong to talk of it very much.... Then there's the second necessary stage which I don't see described very much, but which I would call something like cunning. And cunning involves the person rearranging his life in such a way that he can feel the first experience again.[17]

This first experience is one of interiority and connection to Mystery, which entails something that cannot be explained but may be implicated. This experience is not one of conformity—what Joseph Campbell called the mythos of the village—but an experience that requires solitude, the "left hand path," the departure into the mythos of the forest. In Bly's language the two streams of village and forest are "wildness and domesticity." The "Mystery" Bly speaks of is related to Campbell's first function of myth: "The first function of a living mythology, the properly religious function ... is to waken and maintain in the individual an experience of awe, humility, and respect in recognition of that ultimate mystery, transcending names and forms ... "[18] Holding an experience of "transcending names and forms" goes against the expectations of social conformity, and is, to say the very least, quite difficult. So, Bly offers us a second crucial stage to the first experience: *cunning*. If one is to cultivate solitude and yet remain connected to the human community, a one-sided naïveté will not suffice. As Bly declares:

> To those who want me to change, I say, "I will

17 Robert Bly, *Talking All Morning* (Ann Arbor: the University of Michigan Press, 1980), pp. 174-75.

18 Joseph Campbell, *Creative Mythology* (New York: Penguin Arkana, 1968) p. 609.

> Never stop traveling that road which connects
> Socrates to the turtle, and Falstaff to the Baal Shem."[19]

Here upon the road of wild association—the incalculable distance between solitude *and* community, between cunning *and* grace—is the crucial leap that has helped redirect and inform my own struggle with the separateness and isolation of being Other.

Polio visited me as an infant, bequeathing an inability to walk, a life-long need for a wheelchair, a body-shape quite different from the norm, and the challenge to negotiate the social ignominy of fear, assumption, ostracism, and condescension. For me, Bly's work opened an extraordinary possibility: that by "following the tracks of one's own wound through the forest and finding that it resembles the tracks of a god" we might discover that what happened to us, our circumstance, is something much, much more than merely personal. Trying to understand what happened to *me*, led through the forest of story, to an understanding of what happened to *us*—I became a part of culture, *a storyteller*. It was a journey from isolation to solitude—and as Bly has said, "[I]t was first in solitude that I really felt affection for the human community."[20]

Bly's devotion to the human community is not born of a desire to be recognized as a bona fide member of the social structure, but rather, to be an advocate and bringer of culture. But what, you say, is the difference? James Hillman gives us a clue:

> By becoming more civilized tamed, mannered, adapted, and participatory do we therefore become more cultured? If civilization requires cohesive structures of architecture, engineering, law, government, education, finance, supply and distribution in short bureaucracies of maintenance to name but a few of the institutions that support civilization ... where does culture figure in, if at all? ... Culture seems to be beyond rational control of civilization.[21]

---

19 "Listening to the Sitar Before Dawn," *My Sentence Was a Thousand Years of Joy* p. 7.

20 Robert Bly, *Talking All Morning*, p. 10.

21 "City, Soul and Myth," James Hillman, online, PDF downloaded Oct. 1, 2010, http://www.cityandsoul.org/index.php?option=com_content&task=view&id=5&Itemid=6

Culture is to society as Soul is to Body. Robert Bly as a poet and a teacher is surely a champion of culture.

* * *

Bly has written two poems which describe negotiating and enduring the lived experience of this opposition. The first "A Godwit" deals with the exigencies that one is compelled to endure in the separate circumstance of being misfit. In this poem, he observes a flock until he notices one different and particular bird:

> One godwit, not as plump as the others, stands balanced on one leg, the other drawn up. My breath pauses as I notice that the foot is missing, and in fact the whole leg below the knee is gone. When he hops, his isolated knee bends like the other one; his single foot kicks a little sand away with each step. Feeding and hopping, he comes up near one of the plump ones, and with a swift motion, perfectly in rhythm, bites him in the ass. He then hops out of the flock and feeds alone.
>
> It took me so long to notice that one bird was not a real member of the flock; the flock moves continually, striding or flying. Sometimes the flock strides away and leaves him; at other times feeds around him. The flock rises once more and flies toward the sea where the packed sand shines. The bird with one leg rises with them, but turns in the air, his long wings tipping among the winds, and lands at his old place to feed alone.[22]

In the second poem, "Warning to the Reader," we learn something about the common errors involved with negotiating freedom of choice:

> Sometimes farm granaries become especially beautiful when all the oats or wheat are gone, and wind has swept the rough floor clean. Standing inside, we see around us, coming in through the cracks between shrunken wall boards, bands or strips of sunlight. So in a poem about imprisonment, one sees a little light.
>
> But how many birds have died trapped in these granaries. The bird, seeing the bands of light, flutters up the walls

22 "A Godwit," Robert Bly, *What Have I Ever Lost By Dying?: Collected Prose Poems* (New York: HarperCollins, 1992) p. 45 .

> and falls back again and again. The way out is where the rats enter and leave; but the rat's hole is low to the floor. Writers, be careful then by showing the sunlight on the walls not to promise the anxious and panicky blackbirds a way out!
>
> I say to the reader, beware. Readers who love poems of light may sit hunched in the corner with nothing in their gizzard for four days, light failing, the eyes glazed.... They may end as a mound of feathers and a skull on the open boardwood floor....[23]

The choice to take the rat's way is uncivilized and unpopular; hence, it requires cunning. Moreover, in both situations—that of the one-leggéd bird, and being trapped in the empty granary—there is a danger of succumbing to the bitterness of isolation. To cultivate the "ass-biting" energy of the godwit, and the willingness to take the dark roads of the rat, is counterbalanced by the challenge to hold a generative connection to culture and community. To do this, one must be mature enough to hold paradox—to place great value on "what happens when no one is watching."

In many old Russian stories, the darkly divine grandmother, Baba Yaga, asks us her ritual question: "Did you come here by compulsion? Or of your own free will?" If we say "compulsion," she cuts off our head, but if we say "free will," she also cuts off our head. This is because she represents the world's longing for mature human beings; she requires us to be true to our nature, which is complex. As Bly explains:

> We could say that Baba Yaga's area is the territory of truth. The difficulty lies in how to say the truth about complicated things, which is essential if you plan to survive her world. ... We can even sense in her question a quandary around our birth. "Did you choose your parents, or did someone else arrange it?" She never ate Robert Frost, because he gave a complicated answer to that question in his poem "The Lovely Shall Be Choosers."[24]

---

23 "Warning to the Reader," Robert Bly, *Eating the Honey of Words* (HarperFlamingo, 1999) p. 104.

24 Robert Bly and Marion Woodman, *The Maiden King: The Reunion of Masculine and Feminine* (New York: Henry Holt and Company, 1998) pp. 54-5.

Baba Yaga disdains a halfhearted answer, and so she challenges us to think with some cunning leaps that can hold free will and compulsion in a generative tension. So Bly, seeing the one-sidedness of the "panicky blackbirds" trapped in the granary, asks us to look down. By holding the great spaces between ascending and descending, community and solitude, Robert Bly has opened many doors and windows into living a wholehearted life; as he says:

> It's all right to praise the raven's dark feet,
> And the crows settling down at dusk in the oak,
> For setting stars always predict the stars that rise.[25]

Holding descent and ascent together is an old idea, which Bly describes as "verticality": "The higher the spirit goes the more deeply the soul sinks down."[26]

This capacity to hold concurrent yet conflicting values runs the full course of Bly's work; he has been touching the heavens while directing our gaze downward for many years. The setting stars and the sparrow's footprint beckon us to the rat's way. Here, in the end as in the beginning, Bly takes the lesser-known road, not that of the gentle biblical dove, but the carrion crow of Sumer; for the adrift and starry-eyed optimist, the downward gaze holds great promise:

> On the third day the crow shall fly;
> The crow, the crow, the spider-colored crow,
> The crow shall find new mud to walk upon.[27]

---

25 "Giordano Bruno and the Muddy Footprint," *The Night Abraham Called to the Stars* p. 7.

26 Robert Bly, *The Sibling Society* (Reading, Massachusetts: Addison-Wesley Publishing Company, 1996) p. 212.

27 "Where We Must Look for Help," Robert Bly, *Selected Poems* (New York: Harper & Row, 1986) p. 10.

SMALL ENGINE REPAIR: THIRTY-FIVE YEARS OF THE ANNUAL CONFERENCE ON THE GREAT MOTHER AND THE NEW FATHER, ORGANIZED BY ROBERT BLY

A Personal Account by John Rosenwald (with help from Jean D'Amico, Fran Quinn, Andrew Dick, Ann Arbor, and others)

It's a big name for a small organization that has had a longer life than anyone might have imagined. It all started in 1975 with Robert Bly. In the early 70s Bly often gave poetry readings that lasted three or four hours, moving from a monster-masked chant of the Campbell's soup jingle while he charged through the middle of the audience, to a Shakespearean sonnet accompanied by the dulcimer, to a falsetto recitation of his own anti-Vietnam War poem "Counting Small-Boned Bodies," this time in the mask of a shriveled scraggly haired crone, to psychological observations based on his study of Carl Gustav Jung, to love poems or verses expressing his own loneliness: "like a man trying to cover a whole double bed" ["The Hockey Poem," *Eating the Honey of Words*, p. 97].

At a reading in Denver Peter Martin heard Bly discuss Erich Neumann's concept of matriarchal societies and fantasize about gathering a group of people somewhere in the wilderness for a week or so to share poems, art, personal visions, and study of Jungian archetypes. Inspired by the notion, Martin drove to Bly's home in Minnesota and offered to help realize the fantasy. Bly responded: "If you'll do the organizational work, I'll recruit participants and teach."

By spring 1975 a bright red and yellow poster announced the Annual Conference on the Mother. In a letter to the Colorado Council on the Arts, Bly outlined some of his interests: Jung's discovery of a "matriarchal layer" in the mind, Robert Ornstein's left brain/right brain research, a longing for "the return of the Mother" as reflected in "changes in music, dress, and literature in the last few years in America" [letter to Barbara McLaughlin and Robert Sheets, 17 Feb, 75, University of Minnesota Archives]. At the conference Neumann's book *The Great Mother*, writings by Joseph Campbell and by Jung's associate Marie-Louise von Franz would provide material for discussion, as would Homer's *Odyssey* and the poet Rainer Maria Rilke, whose prose had deeply influenced Bly and whose poems he was translating. In addition to considering the implications of possible historical matriarchies, Bly focused on Jung's complex vision of humans, comprising four functions–intellect, emotion, sensation, intuition–as well as male and female elements, *animus* and *anima* respectively, and a darker, wilder side, the *shadow*.

I first heard about the conference early that spring. I was teaching in Massachusetts, working regularly with Fran Quinn, a leader of the Worcester County Poetry Association and Bly's unofficial agent for readings throughout New England. A few months later four of us–Quinn, Mary Fell, Ann Arbor, and I–piled into Quinn's Matador and headed for Colorado. In the rear window we taped a sign, "To the Mother or Bust."

As he traveled the country doing readings, Bly informally but effectively advertised the conference and recruited staff. He invited the North Carolina artist Rita Shumaker to teach drawing, the Charleston artist, educator, and dancer Ann Igoe to offer classes on movement, the Cincinnati symphony and choral director Robert Sadin to discuss music. These invitations often came casually, the result of meeting someone after a performance. Peter Martin meanwhile had located a site, a private camp in Conifer, Colorado, thirty miles southwest of Denver.

We gathered in early June. Accommodations remained simple: shared cabins, no heat, plain food. Shortly after we arrived it snowed. We held sessions in the round central building, with Bly talking, others listening and offering their own opinions. All of us assumed we would be part of all sessions. It didn't matter whether in the outside world we were poets or painters or dancers or psychologists. We danced, drew, joined in the discussion of poetry. Bly, not a skilled dancer, not remarkably comfortable in his body, did warm-ups with the rest of us. "Squeeze your ani," Ann Igoe would chant.

I can't remember if we began already that first year completing a tale told only partially by Bly and then acted out at night by numerous small groups, each adding its own imaginative interpretation to the mix, transforming bodies into trees, oceans, witches, queens. Soon, however, this type of inclusionary skit formed one core of conference activity.

The mailing list developed after the first conference includes fifty names. I remember the number of those who stayed the full ten days as about thirty-five. Each of us paid $100, all expenses included. At the end of the week, according to a request for funds sent out a month later, the conference "ran a deficit of $800" [letter to participants from Peter Martin, 1 July 1975].

As in any small community, tensions sometimes arose. One centered on the notion of the Mother. By 1975 the country had engaged a new wave of feminism in academic and non-academic circles. Neumann's exploration of possible woman-centered cultures paralleled this movement. Some participants asserted the conference emphasized historical matriarchies and male interpretation of Jungian archetypes more than the Great Mother herself or human manifestations of womanhood. Although the reading list prepared by those who attended included numerous works by women, Bly clearly remained the central figure, the organizer; Peter Martin served as administrator; Neumann, Ornstein, Bachofen, and perhaps more subtly Joseph Campbell functioned as prime theoreticians.

Gender politics, however, did not dominate the ten days together. In the middle of the week, responding to heightening tensions, we gathered on a hillside, where each participant volunteered his or her impressions of and concerns about the conference: Food. The snow. Lack of privacy. Near the end of the session, one participant stood up and attacked the group as a whole. Not for its lack of artistic or intellectual commitment, not for the style of its poetry, but because, he said, you are "the cheapest motherfuckers I've ever seen. Your cameras are trash, your sleeping bags are old, you're not carrying any cash. My buddy and I came here to rip you off. You ain't got shit. We paid our way in and we're gonna lose money. We're outta here." And with that, the two of them mounted their motorcycle and disappeared.

Despite our apparent poverty, something amazing happened within these ten days: We became a community. Even the snow contributed to the sense of isolation and commitment and intensity and freshness. A few of us transformed a small cabin into a zendo, a space for meditation. We moved our bodies in new ways, saw the world slightly differently. One afternoon an artist who called himself Peter Papoofnik held a seminar on negative space. Stretching rope between trees, outlining the mountains in front of us, using whatever was at hand to fill in the spaces, teaching us to see perspective, foreground, middleground, background, he slowly created his virtual canvas. Only when he had finished did we realize he had used mostly his own clothes as props, and that now he was standing naked in front of us, transformed into a portion of his own work of art. It was, after all, the seventies.

The intensity had other effects as well. During one breakfast two participants, strangers to each other the week before, burst into the dining room to announce they were leaving immediately to get married in Indiana. "Don't do it," shouted Bly. But Ivana Spalatin, a Serbo-Croatian lover of love, leapt up to spritz them with the rose perfume she carried in her bosom, urging the rest of us, "We take up a collection for their flight, no?" Even as they informed us of their decision, however, it became clear the two lovers had not yet discovered all they might need to know about each other. "But I don't fly," said the male. "Fine, we'll drive," his fiancée responded. "Now, let's eat before we go. You do eat meat, don't you?"

In a letter written a decade later, Bly looked back at this first conference: "When we started years ago, it was as if everyone with a motorcycle or a ponytail was your family. How quickly that changed" [Bly, letter to Arbor and Rosenwald, 6 July 1996]. Moments of humor and pathos aside, the conference had, for many of us, accomplished a great deal. We had explored interdisciplinary dimensions of our lives and of our arts. We had engaged in intense, substantial conversations about gender, Jungian psychology, Rilke, our relationships to others and to ourselves. We had made new acquaintances and even friends. As the conference concluded we talked about repeating the experience. A number of us, including Fran Quinn, Ann Arbor, and myself, offered to help if Peter Martin needed assistance the following year.

I remember clearly driving to that first conference. I remember arriving and remember being there. I don't recall leaving. Maybe I never did.

Over the next eleven months those of us who attended this first gathering spread the word about its successor. We had agreed it would be valuable not to return to the same site but to move the conference around the country. Peter Martin located Camp Widjiwagen near the Canadian border. By now the poster read *Annual Conference on the Great Mother, organized by Robert Bly and Peter Martin*. The mailing list for 1976 includes more than eighty names. Logistics were terrible; the nearest airport was Duluth, much too far away for commercial needs or for convenient pickup of participants and teachers. But the site, located near a sparkling Minnesota lake, was spectacular, feeding our Jungian desire for sensate as well as emotional or intellectual stimulation and satisfaction. By the shore sat a sauna. We used it so much that the camp's entire summer supply of sauna firewood disappeared within ten days.

Many of the same teachers and participants returned: Bly of course, and Shumaker, Igoe, and others. The Minneota, Minnesota poet Bill Holm showed up and taught us music, making his huge Icelandic hands dance across the keys of his tiny clavichord. Daniela Gioseffi demonstrated the art of bellydancing. Coleman Barks came for the first time; Bly introduced him to translations of Jelaluddin Rumi, asking the poet from Georgia to "release...them from their cages" [Barks, personal communication], thereby transforming not only Barks' life but also the landscape of American poetry.

Etheridge Knight joined us as well. Knight's impact was huge. I recall no persons of color at the first conference. Knight changed that. His booming voice as he read "Ilu, the Talking Drum"; his streetsmarts as he did the dozens on "I Sing of Shine"; his life as a Korean War vet, junkie, ex-con; his physicality, his presence as a street singer, his commitment to the oral tradition, all made his weight felt. Even in comical ways. Not all participants were Finn-friendly, not all experienced sauna users. When Ann Igoe, the dancer, who had grown up in rural South Carolina but married into big-city Charleston, ventured down to the sauna for the first time she wore a discreet swim suit; ladies did not sit naked in public, even in a sauna, even in the dark. Knight also was not conversant with saunas, but he had no such compunctions. As this large midwestern black man sat down next to this slim southern white woman, the magic of bodily response was inevitable. Sensate, indeed. Soon Knight, following the lead of others and sensitive to the immediate circumstances, lunged out of the small steamy space and plunged into the freezing lake, shouting, "I'm goin' to the water. I'm goin' to the water."

The physical world manifested itself in other ways as well. Isa Drennin discussed the Sufi tradition, but even better, in the evening, Andy Dick instructed us in Sufi-dancing, spinning us around, our eyes linked with those of another person, until a balance of Jungian sensate, intellectual, emotional, and even intuitive functions appeared not only possible but also immediate and actual.

One characteristic that has helped the conference survive probably emerged during the first session but certainly contributed to the second: a pleasure in self-deprecation, the ability to laugh at ourselves. At one of these early gatherings the Massachusetts poet Tomas O'Leary recreated Bly's poem, "Tongues Whirling," which starts, "You open your mouth, I put my tongue in / and this wild universe thing begins" [*Jumping Out of Bed*, unpaginated]. O'Leary, swinging his long arms, bowing and bending across the floor in a limber-limbed version of Bly's tentative dance steps, began: "I stick my nose into your eye and this weird thing happens." The group loved it. More significantly, Bly loved it. Though the implicit critique of Bly's deep imagism and quasi-romantic language was real, the effect remained not negative but appreciative. This self-deprecation would serve the conference well in years to come, often in the form of "The Players," a cluster of participants who at an evening performance satirize the week's events.

O'Leary in a long "evaluative report on The Second Annual Conference" identified the fundamental "task of the conference" as a need "to generate a dialogue which would stress the common evolution of members of both sexes, and at the same time cast some light on the societal perversions that have divided men and women and caused them to distort their basic sexuality" [O'Leary, p. 4]. He praised the presence of the many teachers, but also emphasized "all of us (including Bly...) participated both as teachers *and* students" [p. 8]. O'Leary would identify "our basic energy" as "sexual" [p. 18] and commented explicitly on the contrast and perhaps conflicts experienced within both the group and individuals as a result of dealing with an imbalance of Jungian and other forces:

> So off we went around the floor of the lodge of Camp Widjiwagen (owned and operated by St. Paul's Y.M.C.A.), sophisticated pagans throwing our bodies into a frenzy of fertility, invoking the blessings of the Great Mother to ourselves and to the fruit of our wombs, and all this under the warm and WASPish visage of a framed, unblinking Jesus Christ, whose mild gaze travelled the length of the lodge apparently fixed in contemplation of what hung there on the opposite wall: the hairy hide of a big black bear.... As we danced–jabbered, sang, socialized, improvised, ate, drank–in the great lodge (between those ever-present figures of Christ and the bear) we were nurturing some trust towards the darkness in our minds. [pp. 22, 26]

Not all dimensions of the second conference went smoothly. Another concern surfaced when this "darkness," the shadow side of Jungian thought, appeared in a late evening dance that some felt threatened to become, using Bly's later terminology, more filled with destructive savagery than creative wildness. The logistical difficulties of feeding, housing, and scheduling a large group of artists without a firm organizational structure had also become apparent. Dissatisfaction over food, and eventually over finances, surfaced as well, leading to a confrontation between Peter Martin and others, and to an eventual decision to place some participant control over Martin's use of funds. By the next spring he would argue that though volunteer efforts greatly assisted his work, the conference should hire him, and him alone, to run it. Despite these difficulties, however, as the second session ended, it was clear we would try to do it again.

For some of us a week in summer did not satisfy our needs. Following the 1976 conference, pleased with the combination of Jungian thought and actual performance of the arts–dance, music, mask-making, drama–three of us, Andy Dick, Ann Arbor, and I, asked Bly if he would be willing to join a small cluster of conference participants for a weekend and explore with the general public the ideas and practices we had been investigating in relative isolation. For three of the next four years the Great Mother Travelling Troupe barnstormed the Midwest. In the spring of 1977 we did a single workshop and performance in Madison, Wisconsin. More than twenty of us gathered, borrowed costumes from the Beloit College theater collection, rehearsed briefly, and then, the next day, performed what might best be described as Jungian vaudeville. In 1978 we grew more ambitious. Using a Celtic tale as a base, Bly wrote a playlet, "The Thornbush Cockgiant," which we performed in three locations with Andy Dick as a young boy searching for his magic piston rings, Bly as the Giant, with Julia Hainline, Ann Igoe, and numerous others in supporting roles. Improvisational Jung delighted some of our audiences but profoundly distressed others, who wanted polish rather than exploration. In 1980 many of the same group, now joined by the poet Connie Martin, ran at Beloit College a three-day workshop on oral performance of poetry, funded by the National Endowment for the Arts. As they relate to the Mother Conference as a whole, the significance of these experiments lay 1) in the desire to make available to a larger community the joys and insights we were discovering in our isolated summer experiences, 2) the willingness of Robert Bly to expose himself to the rigors and probable failures of improvisational theater, 3) the desire of some conference participants (especially the mask-maker Pat Apatovsky) to explore transforming members of the community into something like a permanent theater company, and 4) the power of these annual gatherings over the lives of many of us.

For 1977 Fran Quinn located a site on Sebago Lake, initiating the relationship to Maine that remains strong to this day. During these thirty-five years, the state has hosted more than a dozen conferences, first at Luther Gulick, later at Camp Kiev on Lake Damariscotta. In the late 1990s Robert Bly and others even contemplated purchasing land and buildings in Maine as a permanent Great Mother Conference location.

Perhaps partially in response to increasing sensitivity about gender issues, the conference poster for 1977 expanded its scope, announcing The Third Annual Conference on the Great Mother and the New Father, organized by Robert Bly, Peter Martin, and Elsa Wycisk. True, Elsa Wycisk played some role, and Peter Martin retained his position as primary administrator, but others, notably Fran Quinn, had begun to do the bulk of the work.

By now food had assumed a larger role in conference planning. In Colorado we ate simply and well, but did not pay much attention to the needs of vegetarians. At the first Minnesota session conflicts between Peter Martin and the hired kitchen staff threatened the future of the conference, and near the end, an altercation led to a rapid change in personnel. By the time we gathered in Maine, Jamie Stunkard had emerged as camp cook; he would exert a powerful influence on the group during the next few years through the quiet force of his personality.

As we concluded the third conference, praising teachers, leaders, and organizers, our applause rang loudest for the cook. Furthermore, with Jamie had arrived his cousin Marcus Wise, who, when not working in the kitchen, practiced on the Indian drums we soon learned to call *tabla*. In addition, Wise had introduced David Whetstone, a young musician/composer who was developing his skills on the *sitar*. Robert Bly had already shown his willingness to explore the combination of poetry and music in experiments with the dulcimer. Now he recognized the possibility of collaboration with Wise and Whetstone, combining their music with his new translations of the medieval poets Rumi, Kabir, and Mirabai. The Boston-area journalist Shepherd Bliss observed that Bly was "quite excited by the opportunity to read the Hindu poems accompanied by such Indian sounds. He commented that it allows his ego to withdraw, as the music filled the empty spaces between the lines" [Bliss, manuscript #1, p. 12]. Thus began an interaction which has provided a central element both of conference life and of external concerts ever since.

The conference was already no longer solely in the hands of Peter Martin. Fran Quinn did the set up work and some of the correspondence. Jamie Stunkard had control of the kitchen. Jean D'Amico, another of the Worcester set, had begun helping with various business matters. Ann Arbor and I, living in Maine, handled much of what might be called local arrangements, including sleeping at night with all the registration money, maybe $6,000, tucked into the bottom of our purple sleeping bags. Martin's recommendation for a centralized administrative structure had not proved acceptable. Collectively we handled such organizational matters as best we could without worrying too much about hierarchies or formal procedures. By current standards our fiscal responsibilities remained astonishingly small. Total budget for all expenses lay under $20,000. At the Luther Gulick site we paid $5 per person per day for housing, $2.50 per day for food. We rented camps during the first week in June, before schools let out, during the period owners performed annual maintenance and trained their staffs. Facilities, however, remained primitive: outhouses, minimal showers, cabins without heat or electricity. During that first Maine conference rain fell non-stop; we huddled around the small fireplaces in a few cabins. Only on the last day did the skies clear; we immediately organized a sun worship ritual on the red clay dance area outside the meeting hall.

In drafts of his essays Shepherd Bliss evaluated what he had experienced at his first Bly conference. He praised the event as a whole, commenting on some elements that had been transformative for him personally, such as Stunkard's vegetarian and locally based menu. He responded strongly and positively to Bly, to Rita Shumaker, whose "quiet voice would enter the large lodge with a clarity of understanding and practice of Jung" [Bliss, Draft #1, p. 6], to Howard Norman for taking to heart and recreating traditional Cree stories. Bliss also presented Bly's list of what needed to happen next: greater emphasis on women, more physical work, less passive acceptance of presented material, less technology. Perhaps Bliss' two most trenchant observations had to do first with Etheridge Knight's insistence on the political realm and his critique of the predominantly interior searching, and second with the masculinization of The Mother, for Bliss observed a positive response to what he considered "rapid and aggressive" male behavior. As illustrative of one dimension of the gender tensions, Bliss quoted a brief conversation between Jamie Stunkard and Asta Bowen:

> *Asta*: The Mother Conference is actually a father thing. The mother appears only when we return home. Such conferences are a father form.
>
> *Jamie*: But isn't there a mother within the father, which comes out at the conference?
>
> *Asta*: Well, yes. This conference was not cold and sterile, as are so many others.
>
> *Jamie*: The conference was an implantation, which grows when fertilized upon returning home.
>
> *Asta*: But that is still a father thing. The nurturing comes later.
>
> [Bliss, Draft #2, p. 6]

Others shared Bliss's concern about the role of women at the conference. Mary Fell, who had expressed her frustration at the lack of female-centered knowledge following the first gathering, attended the third, but expressed her dissatisfaction in a letter explicitly criticizing the language proposed for the fourth conference poster. She attacked not only the failure to address directly feminism and male growth but also the conference's implicit apolitical focus on "private consciousness" [Fell, letter 7 March 1978].

In 1978 the group met again in Minnesota, with Rita Shumaker joining Robert Bly as the announced organizers, and Peter Martin now listed as "Conference Secretary," for his vision of how to run our annual session clearly had become increasingly at odds with the reality of workload, finances, and personal responsibility. By the end of this second Widjiwagen gathering he had fundamentally removed himself from the organizational structure.

The following year we moved for the first time to the west coast to a camp located by David Seal and Connie Martin on Tanglewood

Island in Puget Sound. Then in 1980 we returned to Luther Gulick. During these first six years patterns emerged that have characterized the conference ever since. Finances remained delicate. In my recollection and according to my sketchy records, during those years the conference experienced regular shortfalls; Robert Bly made up the deficit at times either by working without pay or by actually contributing cash at the end of sessions.

In a desire to make the experience available to more participants we had insisted on moving the conference around the country, though the return to Minnesota and Maine laid the foundation for greater geographic stability ahead. Tensions emerging at nearly every early session led to what became the "fifth day ritual," time out for expressing concerns about all elements of community life, facilitated after the third year by passing a kitchen pot, until all who wished to had voiced their complaints. From the beginning, scheduling remained chaotic, intense, and uncertain. To deal with individual needs in a large community we created small groups, sometimes assigned, more often random or self-selected. In these clusters newcomers could express their mystification at various rituals; old-timers could try to explain the history of the conference and the impact of that history on its procedures. Sometimes these groups formed the basis for fairy tale completion or for the assignment of camp chores.

As exemplified by Jamie Stunkard's attempt to provide through a sense of responsibility and his vegetarian menu the most integrated approach to food the conference had yet known, a philosophical and pragmatic commitment to work and self-support underlay many of the early years. Money was tight; we needed to do everything as frugally as possible. Many of us also rejected emphatically the notion of conference participants as somehow separate from conference staff. Bly himself, as Bliss had observed, wanted the group to do more physical labor. In those years all attending had work duty: garbage removal, meal set up, outhouse cleaning, dishwashing, scheduling. During the second session at Luther Gulick in 1980 we made a deeper commitment. In exchange for the pleasure of sharing their camp for ten days, we offered the owners a workday to complete a major project of their choosing. What we negotiated was building/repairing a stone wall, highly labor-intensive and therefore a low priority for the camp owners, but a relatively easy task for 100+ able-bodied participants.

Concern about the role of women both as subject and as leaders of the conference led to what I'd describe as a search by Robert Bly for a woman who would match or parallel his own intelligence, charisma, flexibility, imagination, and curiosity. Although powerful women played a major role in the group from the beginning, both as teachers and as participants, none quite matched Bly's areas of strength. Rita Shumaker and Ann Igoe, brilliant teachers and strong personalities, did not possess the outspoken verbal power to share his stage. Gioia Timpanelli and Robert Bly traveled for years telling stories together, and their superb work formed an important center at the conference, but Gioia showed little interest in assuming responsibility for organizational or administrative matters. Alice Howell, crone and wise astrologer, in a sense interviewed for the position for two or three years. For the third conference Bly invited Daniela Gioseffi, the writer and bellydancer, to teach, but the level of her work struck many as inadequate for our purposes. Over the years perhaps the only woman who paralleled Bly was Marion Woodman, fully his equal as scholar, storyteller, intellectual, and Jungian, *and* his match as well in approach and demeanor. Their telling the Maiden King story at the twenty-fifth conference in 1999 on Orcas Island remains a high point of the conference.

Even before Marion Woodman, however, perhaps the first time a woman poet both challenged and met Bly as an equal occurred in 1979, when Connie Martin introduced to the group her long poem "Woodwork." Strong enough to earn her living as a carpenter, imaginative enough to inspire her fellow participants, disciplined enough to assume organizational responsibilities, Martin became a central figure; by 1980 she shared credit with Bly on the conference poster. Not surprisingly for a group interested in Jung, some of our explorations during early sessions dealt with dreamwork. For me the most evocative evidence of Connie Martin's contribution occurred on Tanglewood when she enlisted a large group of women to enact one of her own dreams, sending some to gallop across a large field while others formed a visual boundary, a "house of women" she named it, for the ocean cliff behind them. The drama itself suggested power, but also the sense that at this instant the conference belonged to and had clearly focused on the world of women.

A general concern with religion and spirituality represents another characteristic of the group during these early years. Following the first Maine gathering in 1977 Shepherd Bliss interviewed many participants for his essays. I remember being surprised when he asked if religion formed the conference core. For me religion did not hold the center; instead the arts and psychology did, with cross-disciplinary experience essential to all the explorations we undertook. With his question, however, Bliss compelled me, as an atheist, to see the conference through eyes radically different than my own.

So did Joseph Campbell.

Campbell had served as a focal point for the conference since its inception. Had Robert Bly had his way, I suspect the teaching staff would initially have included Campbell and Marie-Louise von Franz. Age, at least in the case of von Franz, made their participation implausible, as did financial considerations. In 1980, however, Campbell agreed to teach a single day at the Luther Gulick site. By luck I had the task of driving Bly to the airport to pick up the noted mythologist. As we drove back to camp, Campbell outlined his schedule: First talk from 4:00 till 5:15, second 5:15 till 6. Did we eat supper? Third, on the Grail, immediately after supper. Fourth, at 8. By the time he had reached the middle of the night, for his discussion of Tarot symbolism, even Bly, famous for his long readings and seemingly indefatigable energy, seemed tired. "I'll need a morning nap from 3 till 4:30," Campbell added, "but then we should be ready for some work on meditation practices." When either Bly or I suggested this program might demand too much of his audience, Campbell offered a simple response: "You asked me to come for a day. Last I looked, a day contains twenty-four hours. I believe in giving value for my fee."

Of the many extraordinary talks I've heard over these thirty-five years, the ones I wish most I had recorded remain those by this brilliant scholar/writer. His subject, though always particular, became, though never explicitly, generally religious as well. I learned this the hard way. As I drove Bly and Campbell back to the airport after his twenty-four-hour marathon, I ventured to question him from my stance as atheist. Glancing in the rearview mirror, I commented over my shoulder, "It seems you believe in God." From the backseat came the thunderous reply, "What do you think I've been talking about the past twenty-four hours!"

Then silence.The religious dimension of the conference remained usually subtle, always eclectic, rarely arcane. Bly had been studying with a Tibetan teacher, and by the third conference sat meditation at 6:30 each morning, inviting those interested to join him. Although he chanted in Sanskrit he also soon attempted to make the language appropriate to our own world. Seeking to capture the sounds of the original, he transformed the traditional "Om Mani Padme Hum" into "Black Dog Take Me Home." During these meditation sessions Bly shared what he had learned from his studies of Buddhism; especially instructive for me remains the Hindu notion of Vajra energy, the knife that cuts through bureaucracies, unnecessary indecision, and other nonsense.

The presence of Joseph Campbell exemplifies another element that at times has dominated conference discussions and planning. Campbell was obviously an outsider, brought in for one day, neither then nor ever to become a member of the community. Bly understandably wished to include as teachers people he admired, who stimulated him, who could enlighten him as well as us. At the same time, the emerging tradition of participant performances, the skill level of those who had been part of the group from the beginning, and the general democratic impulse of most teachers and participants meant that many wished to reserve time for presentations either prepared in advance or emerging, like the fairy-tale conclusions or like Connie Martin's dream, during the conference itself. As the number in attendance grew, and the number of former participants and teachers invited to give brief performances increased, opportunities for participant-centered activities diminished. Sometimes invited guests integrated effectively into the community, as the Traveling Jewish Theater did in 1980. Sometimes teachers stressed the need for participant public presentations, as the poet Naomi Shihab Nye later did during her years at the conference. Joseph Campbell, in his second (and last) visit, spoke at length with participants and worked closely with his small group. So did William Stafford. But sometimes invited speakers saw themselves as gurus, chose not to mix with ordinary participants, ate by themselves. In addition, as Robert Bly grew older, his need for rest and privacy increased, so that understandably he, but consequently and unfortunately also some teachers, grew more isolated from other members of the community.

As the conference approached its tenth birthday, we needed to change if we were to survive. Finances remained questionable. We needed to focus more explicitly on different topics if we wished to draw new participants and attract old-timers to return. In response to Bly's shifting interests and to the danger of death by paralysis, posters for the eighth and ninth gatherings advertised not the Annual Conference on the Great Mother and the New Father, but instead, "A Conference on Form." The first of these, in 1982, took the group to California for the first time.

Meeting the needs of teachers and participants has demanded an immense workload for those involved in creating, running, and then closing a ten-day conference. For starters, negotiating with Robert Bly is always challenging, always interesting, and always exhausting. He has strong opinions (often, as he used to say proudly during his three-hour readings, 84% wrong), and respects co-workers most if they stand up and face directly his hurricane of words and ideas. At the same time he remains unfailingly gracious and generous to those who work with and for him. The influence he exerts on many of us complicates this relationship further. If we learn from him and from the conference more generally, then to put these ideas into practice demands its own time, so much time that we can no longer easily return to the conference itself. Various organizers, not surprisingly, have experienced burnout or have taken a break from the conference to do what Bly in *Iron John* called "ashes work."

At times Robert Bly has also wanted a break. He maintains a deep commitment to writing, translating, editing, public readings; his wife, his children; houses and small cabins; his community; his circle of private friends. These, plus his deep distrust of academic institutions and insistence on innovation/discovery, might have made him at times willing to let go of the Great Mother Conference or GMC as we often label it. Taking a stance that relates to his refusal to accept public money for his magazine *The Sixties* during the Vietnam War, he has insisted since the beginning that we not accept government or foundation funds. As he said once in an interview, accepting such support would introduce "too much of a father influence" [Bly, *Talking All Morning*, p. 216]; this desire for independence has further compounded his relationship to conference finances, for in the early years, at least, his own limited resources constituted the emergency fund. At the same time the conference has served as extended family for him as well as for others. And to a certain extent Bly integrated his own family into the GMC. His two sons Noah and Micah attended regularly during the 1970s and 80s, with Noah's entrepreneurial instincts–selling candy bars brought from town to sugar-starved young adults at elevated prices–at least superficially in conflict with the quasi-official minimalist eco-friendly conference vision. And, starting in 1980, Ruth Bly, Robert's second wife, also has played a role, often a significant one, serving at times as teacher, ritual leader, and sage.

After the second session on form, held at Widjiwagen in 1983, the conference returned to Maine in 1984, and returned as well to a theme that paralleled the tensions some felt concerning the organizational principles and practices that had emerged. This tenth gathering identified itself as a conference on form *and* spontaneity. Continuing the ritual of moving around the country, we went back to California in 1985. Following this 11th conference, Bly decided he would not participate the next year as primary teacher and so the

12th conference took place over seven days, not the traditional ten, and centered "itself around creativity. That is, actually writing poems, painting pictures, composing dance pieces and making and performing music" [Conference poster, 1986].

Whether or not in response to this new vision, one less dependent than in previous sessions on the presence of Bly as leader, the two years following the 12th gathering presented a transition time that threatened to end the conference. In 1987 Bly decided he did not wish to participate at all, so a cluster of conference regulars took two steps that in the long run not only permitted a truncated gathering that summer but also insured the future of the conference. With Bly's blessing or at least acquiescence, Jean D'Amico and Andy Dick began the process of systematizing procedures so that burnout of individuals would not mean collapse of the conference itself; Dick, who now identified himself as Andrew, finally codified these procedures into a written text, *The GreenBook*, which despite debate concerning its use and influence remains the primary written authority on all conference matters.

Though the nomenclature is deliberately different, the structure created for itself by the conference resembles that of a small college. *Greyhairs* resemble the board of trustees, with overall responsibility/liability but few day-to-day tasks. *Convenors* function as the administration, the three of them doing everything from hiring cooks to negotiating the daily event schedule. This structure on the surface freed Bly from most administrative responsibility, though his charisma and contacts meant that the greyhairs and convenors had to work closely with him on the annual theme, teachers, and tone. In addition, in order to stabilize the conference in its financial dealings, D'Amico, Dick, and others registered the organization as a nonprofit corporation, Tor Gul, Inc., thereby insulating the conference as an idea from the fiscal vagaries of any individual annual meeting. To some, those who worked on this systematizing may seem to have compromised the initial free-flowing spirit of the conference, or imposed "form" on "spontaneity." *The GreenBook* takes a clear stance on such issues: "The Conference has been run differently over the years:

from reeling like a sailor on leave, to a very tightly run ship.... Organization and spontaneity should be present at every Conference–it's a delicate balance. Certain things should be well organized.... But, we shouldn't organize the **Juice** out of the Conference" [1991 version, p. 50].

Following these structural changes the conference has continued in a fairly regular fashion. Perhaps it would help to summarize some trends rather than focus on particular conferences. First, true to our initial instinct we retained some movement around the country: conferences in California again, Wisconsin, Washington State again, Montana. Yet the difficulty of locating appropriate sites–campgrounds with physical facilities for one hundred fifty people, tolerant of alcohol, occasional nudity, strong language, alternative political expression–remains substantial, "one of the biggest hassles in organizing the Conference," as *The GreenBook* points out [1991 version, p. 16].

Second, a cluster of continuing participants, many of whom have regularly held positions as greyhairs and/or convenors, has aged. A few couples, faithful participants since the early years, have had a strong positive and yet (in the best sense of the word) conservative impact on the continuation of the group. Robert and Ruth Bly obviously fall into this category. And the continuing involvement of some teachers, especially Rita Shumaker and Ann Igoe, even after they have ceased to teach regularly, has also proved beneficial.

The aging of this core group has probably influenced the conference in both obvious and subtle ways. Some of the frenetic sexual energy that Tomas O'Leary identified as characteristic of early gatherings seems to have diminished (though my aging perspective may mislead me on this point, and one of my correspondents assures me that the conference *eros* remains healthy!). The desire for creature comforts such as flush toilets, hot showers, beds not cots, professional food service has played a larger role in recent years. Our sleeping bags, cameras, and cars are no longer so cheap as at the first conference. A sense of the history of the GMC has at times enabled these grey- (and now white-) hairs to identify potential trouble spots and avert disasters. Robert Bly's comment about ponytails and motorcycles quoted earlier went on to claim: "How swiftly television broke up the real family. How dangerous it is to live without a family larger than that in your own house.... faithfulness has come to be the sort of virtue I once imagined free thought to be" [Bly, letter to Arbor and Rosenwald, 6 July 1996].

The stabilizing of the conference structure has surely had an impact on what we do and how we do it. In recent years the pattern of a conference or of a conference day has become predictable: breakfast; morning sessions led by Bly and invited guest teachers; lunch; small group meetings; workshops in drawing, pottery, poetry writing, drumming, dance; quiet time; gathering for dinner, often with a shared blessing led by a member of the community; dinner itself; evening performances by guest artists or by the satirical Players; more music and dance. Although unlike Joseph Campbell we don't officially go straight through the night, we have always held once a year a very early morning session of small poems spoken by heart and accompanied by David Whetstone and Marcus Wise. In recent years we've celebrated the end of the conference with a banquet involving elaborate decoration and numerous toasts and roasts.

Despite an increasing sense of continuity, history, and structure, powerful individual forces have often either interrupted the pattern or at least modified it. In the mid-1990s the native Canadians Shirley Cull and Mel Chartrand changed the tone of our gatherings with their meticulous attention to meditation, stress-relief, and natural history. Rachael Resch, Toni Zuper, and others tried to mitigate what they perceived as an exaggerated focus on the brain by holding yoga sessions early each morning. Ruth Bly initiated a workshop that enabled participants to trace their dreams through a single night. Her interest in ritual and even more acutely the presence of Martín Prechtel centered attention on ritual process, and in Prechtel's case the power of initiation rites of the Guatemalan and Mayan cultures that adopted him. In recent years perhaps the two strongest new influences have come from Caroline Casey and Doug von Koss. Casey, with her irreverent wit, trenchant political commentary, and serious study of astrology has become a mainstay at morning sessions. Even earlier arrives the joy of working with von Koss. At 6:30 each morning he creates what he calls a "failure-free zone" for the celebration of Buddhist, Hindu, Jewish, Christian, African-American, and secular poems and songs, sometimes in eight-part harmony.

Over the past thirty-five years, though new faces and ideas continue to stimulate and inspire the group, the Great Mother Conference has managed to create a sense of continuity that appeals to both old-timers and newcomers, those we call nubies. Continuity of staff, participants, location, schedule, structure, size, and even finances enables the organization to survive without abandoning the wildness that helped create it. Yes, money remains tight, but the conference has found ways to support itself and to succeed. We operate a book store; record and sell discs containing most sessions; run near the end of each conference a silent auction with craftwork, first editions, memorabilia–treasures to take home but with a cut to reduce conference expenses. After years of paying rather minimal attention to the numerous visual artists in residence, the conference accepted Rita Shumaker's suggestion that we open a gallery during the latter part of the week, with work for sale and again a portion for the conference itself. Though full cost for the seven days currently stands at $850, we have tried to keep fees reasonably low, and have managed through the generosity of many participants to provide a limited number of scholarships and work-study positions so that those with fewer financial reserves, whether young or old, can afford to attend.

Even with continuation and perhaps what some would see as success, numerous issues remain, including several that have played a role at the GMC since the beginning. The question of gender remains significant. It is important to note that Robert Bly's initial impulse towards both the conference and the materials we have studied over the years came from his concern about gender issues. The success of *Iron John* and the popular recognition/fame/notoriety that book brought him have led some to assume mistakenly that Bly's primary interest has been in masculinity. With his omnivorous hunger Bly remains simply and profoundly committed to exploring how gender works and how men and women act and interact. During the height of the *Iron John* years, yes, we met at times as separate groups, men together and women together. Most of the time, however, we have held only integrated sessions. That said, the concerns voiced early by Mary Fell, Shepherd Bliss, and Bly himself remain an issue.

A second issue that remains delicate involves a continuing struggle between emphasis on a participatory conference and what seems essentially a star system. As early as the sixth conference a participant named David Robinson articulated at great length in a letter to Connie Martin this sense of the danger of abandoning the collaborative elements of early conferences.

> One of the things that I really like about the conference is...the value that it places on people being open with each other.... But, it seems as though we are not to apply a similar kind of openness to the organization of the conference itself. [There is a choice between] two extremes. If the choice is minimal feedback, I think these are the implications. The structure is fairly tight. There are "teachers" and there are "students".... Students come to take courses...BUT they are NOT encouraged or even permitted to assume responsibility for what is going on around them.... If the choice is significant feedback, then things become in some ways more difficult. The people who come to the conference can see themselves as being part of a community.... [and] will arrive at its purpose collaboratively.
>
> [Letter to Connie Martin, Rosenwald, Arbor, 5 October 1980]

Conference organizers have attempted to find ways around this divide, encouraging a open poetry reading "salon" at which anyone who wishes to read a poem may do so and scheduling "blank time" for those who desire to attempt more elaborate projects, but these are essentially band-aids on a larger conceptual disagreement on what the conference represents. The question remains significant, partly for theoretical reasons, partly because as Robert Bly gets older and has less immediate responsibility for determining the larger program, any hope of continuation for the conference will depend upon its becoming again participant-based, as it was that one year, the 13th, that Bly chose not to attend.

In recent years decisions about teachers have occasionally exacerbated the issue of participants/invited guests. Major teachers included older white men whose explorations interested and influenced Robert Bly. What Bly sees and uses as metaphor, however, they have at times presented as science material based on research that failed to meet any reasonable standard. A number of participants have taken Bly to task for focusing significant time and attention on such work. This situation has numerous facets: the question of Bly's leadership within the conference, his aging, our need for his prestige and brilliance to attract truly significant guest teachers, the limitations of other participants including greyhairs, whitehairs, and convenors, financial constraints, and general conference bias.

Conference bias works two ways. The inception of the Great Mother Conference as Jung-centered, Bly's notoriety as supposed leader of the supposed "men's movement," individual preferences, all contribute to the willingness of potential teachers and participants to join us. At the same time, a general reluctance to deal with science and Bly's general opposition to academia have also limited the range of the conference. Although, for example, we have had numerous medical doctors as participants, I cannot recall a single time that material from the world of medicine has become a focal point. Science more generally has attracted occasional interest. During the third conference Charlie Smith ran a workshop on scientific developments, especially the implications for "masculine" thought of anti-Aristotelian aspects of twentieth-century physics. The Berkeley geologist Fred Berry has perhaps made the most significant scientific contribution to the GMC, especially in the late 90s when he gave one of the most stunning talks ever given at the conference, a high-speed, highly humorous, challenging description of the Irish origin of the Maine soil on which we stood. Such attention to science, however, remains rare.

A third concern includes religion. Bly's antagonism towards academia at times has a parallel in his relationship towards dogma or organized religion. At the same time, much of his vision connects directly to elements of the Lutheran culture of his childhood environment: "I was brought up in the patriarchy of the Middle West. I was a Lutheran besides; and then I went to college" [*Talking All Morning*, p. 214]. I remember a small group of participants who, following the first conference in 1975, joined Bly at an autumn event at Augustana College. The evening reading was classic Bly: masks, music, poetry, political commentary. In those years no one else *performed* poetry in that way. The next morning, however, Bly led a class at the Lutheran hour of eight o'clock. As he entered the room in his long black woolen coat and talked to the students about the discipline of writing poems, the need for commitment, the power of language, the importance of political stances, one could see him posting on a door in Wittenberg his manifesto, like those delivered early in his career to the editor of the *New York Times Book Review* or the chairman of the National Endowment for the Arts. In the "evaluative report," written in 1976, Tomas O'Leary had already pointed out "the enigmatic priesthood of our main man in the Mother, Robert Bly" [O'Leary, p. 30]. And yet O'Leary goes on to praise Bly as leader, to cite an appreciative comment concerning the "impersonal energy of Robert Bly" [p. 31]. Bly's commitment to diversity, to exploration of religious and spiritual principles from traditional Christianity to Daoism to Buddhism reflects the intensity and intelligence of his search.

A fourth area of concern involves the relation between attendance and work within the conference structure. This connects to the shift from a participant-centered organization. In the early years we collectively did most of the clean-up, organized the food supply, attempted to offer a workday. Perhaps for some paying participants, this system seemed like an interruption of a holiday. For the convenors it certainly meant additional supervisory responsibility and occasionally real grief. Bly, however, initially wanted the conference to include physical labor, some "ashes work." Abandonment of this principle offends those who regret the division between physical and mental labor, who insist that ecological responsibility depends upon personal involvement in the heating, eating, cleaning aspects of daily life. The move to create and then increase work-study positions and the offering of scholarships, though laudable attempts to increase participation by those with less disposable income than others, has in a sense also contributed to this class divide.

Mentioning such work-study opportunities returns the discussion to finances, always a concern for the Great Mother Conference. A conflict exists between opening the conference to more participants (especially those who pay full fare) and keeping it small enough to insure a feeling of community. So do struggles between Bly's spontaneous invitations to artists he meets and the attempts by greyhairs and convenors to balance the budget, even though *The GreenBook* makes it clear that unauthorized extemporaneous offers come out of Bly's own pocket.

The issue of finances raises the even more substantial question of ownership. As the group working on *The GreenBook* debated this topic in the mid-1980s they asserted emphatically that the Annual Conference on the Great Mother and the New Father does not belong to those who organize and run it. Nor, they claimed, does it belong to Robert Bly, though they recognized that without Bly the conference would never have existed and would be challenged to survive. Nor, they finally understood, does it belong to the participants. Instead, it is "its own beast" cooked of various ingredients "till done to taste" [1991 version, p. 49]. What must be said, and it remains high praise, is that thirty-five years later, the conference survives.

Not only survives. Thrives. After this many years, can we identify particular contributions by the Annual Conference on the Great Mother and the New Father to our culture as a whole and to us as individual participants? Let me suggest some accomplishments:

First, we exist as a community. To be sure it's a physical community only for a few days each year, but through phone calls, email messages, our newsletter the *Crow*, its on-line version the *ecrow*, letters, songs, poems sent, visits made, it has become a community. And, at least in its physical form, it is more than a community; it's a village. For a week or more we mostly abandon our reliance on automobiles, television, and (until the arrival of ubiquitous cellphones and wifi) on electronic communication as well. Special pleasures inhere in walking the path between one cabin and another, between the meeting hall and the dining room, between the lake and the library. This touch of communal life becomes metaphor for a larger sense of community towards which many of us strive on a local, national, and international level.

For its days together this community is based not upon money but upon the flow of ideas and, even more, of art. Painting, dance, and poetry form the currency of this gathering. From the beginning our experiment has been multidisciplinary. This art-centered community thrives on diversity, on a combining of the arts in ways that have encouraged our growth as individuals as well as artists. When the conference began, Robert Bly was already doing more in most readings than any other poet I had had the privilege to see. In movement sessions with Ann Igoe, however, Bly may have achieved a greater level of comfort in his stage presence, working like all the rest of us at squeezing our ani. Collaborating with Wise and Whetstone has taken him further as well, as have his explorations with other musicians who have graced the conference.

We have long struggled about whether and how to share our collective personal conference experiences with an outside world. The celebration, in public and in print, of *Robert Bly in this World*, organized by the University of Minnesota Libraries in April 2009, and in particular the invitation to me to attempt a history of the conference represent a rare opportunity to take the GMC on the road, as we did in a very different format with the Great Mother Travelling Troupe so many years ago.

We have kept our arts "unplugged." Within the conference almost all work has been live: an oral literature, whether recited poems, or traditional stories told to the community by Gioia Timpanelli, Marion Woodman, Bly, and many others. The radical conservatism of our commitment to living and breathing art forms remains a central commitment of both Bly and the conference. Even the topics announced year-by-year share this deep reliance and indebtedness to tradition, but traditions often neglected by mainstream media or university academics. The breadth of our exploration parallels and relates directly to the breadth of Bly's poetic curiosity, his continual search for what lives and lasts among poets around the world, usually sensed by his antennae long before others have gained familiarity with these authors, whether contemporaries such as Harry Martinson, Vicente Aleixandre, Neruda, or the old ones, Kabir, Mirabai, Hafez, and of course Rumi. Who has done more than Bly to expand the poetries available to our mostly monolingual citizens? As a conference we participants have drunk from the well of Robert Bly's curiosity and courage.

These artistic endeavors have often involved risk. Daring to dance when we feel we have no body. Daring to sing at 6:30 a.m. when we feel we have no voice. Daring, as Bly did, to bring the manuscript of his book *The Sibling Society* to the group as a whole and ask for comments. And getting them, not least from some of the younger participants, who told him directly that his comments about them and their predilections (their music, their clothes) remained ill informed and insulting. At which point Bly made a date for the next day to sit down with the younger set at lunch and to listen.

Despite continuing conflict and concern about gender issues, the conference has boldly kept that topic on the table during most of its thirty-five years. Bly's interest in Jung and Neumann provoked an expansion, not a restriction, of discussion about male and female existence. That exploration has had its impact on us as individuals and as members of this community. Surely the creation of friendships forms one of the most powerful accomplishments of the conference, friendships within *and* across gender, age, race, class, national, and religious lines. As a group we have collectively provided support by and for each other, whether in success or in distress. When necessary we've created healing rituals for those who have lost lovers, children, friends, parents, themselves.

It is this healing that I turn to last. For it is this healing that provides the title for these comments and recollections: Small Engine Repair. Those of us who work at institutions of higher education sometimes need to offer rationale for our attendance at an organization with such a strange name, devoted to such strange topics, and with such strange procedures. Such institutions have difficulty recognizing the advantage of the life Robert Bly urges at the end of "I Came Out of the Mother Naked," one dedicated to "the parts that grow far from the centers of ambition" [*Sleepers Joining Hands*, p. 50]. "Did you give a paper?" an administrator asks. "Were you a section leader? A panel discussant? Will they publish the proceedings?" In the early years of the conference, Ivana Spalatin, dear Ivana, that lover of love, now nearly blind and house bound, but then teaching at some of the most callously bureaucratic institutions of higher learning, could endure only so many such questions before she discovered an Ivana answer. When asked what kind of conference she had attended, what the topic had been, she learned to say, "Small engine repair. A conference on small engine repair." That, she said, always shut them up. And each time she would tell the story she would reach up with her right hand, tapping that small engine, the heart.

LIST OF SOURCES CITED

Bliss, Shepherd, "Balancing Feminine & Masculine: The Mother Conference in Maine," *East/West*, Vol. 8, No. 2 (February 1978).

Bliss, Shepherd, "Carnival of creativity spring from Great Mother Conference," *Equinox: Independent Feminist Newspaper For Women Everywhere* (August/September 1977).

Bliss, Shepherd, "The Great Mother Conference," (unpublished duplicated typescript, "First Draft: Criticisms Requested," 18 pp., identified as in this essay as "Bliss, Draft #1," dated in accompanying letter June 22, 1977).

Bliss, Shepherd, "The Great Mother Conference," (unpublished duplicated typescript, "Draft: Criticisms Solicited," 23 pp., identified as in this essay as "Bliss, Draft #2," dated in accompanying letter August 16, 1977).

Bly, Robert, "About the Conference on the Mother: An Interview with Bill Siemering, in *Talking All Morning* (Ann Arbor: University of Michigan Press, 1980).

Bly, Robert, *Eating the Honey of Words: New and Selected Poems* (New York, NY: HarperCollins, 1999).

Bly, Robert, *Iron John: A Book About Men* (New York, NY: Addison-

Wesley, 1990).

Bly, Robert, Letter to Barbara McLaughlin and Robert Sheets, Colorado Council on the Arts (unpublished typed/signed correspondence, two pages, dated 17 Feb, 75, Bly Archives, University of Minnesota Libraries).

Bly, Robert, Letter to John Rosenwald and Ann Arbor (unpublished typed/signed correspondence, one page, dated July 6, 1996).

Bly, Robert, "Tongues Whirling," *Jumping Out of Bed: Poems by Robert Bly / Woodcuts by Wang Hui-ming* (Barre, MA: Barre Publishers, 1973).

Bly, Robert, *Sleepers Joining Hands* (New York: Harper & Row, 1973).

Fell, Mary, Letter "To Mother Conference Participants" (unpublished duplicated typescript, 3 pp., dated March 7, 1978).

Martin, Peter, Letter (unpublished duplicated typescript, one page, date July 1, 1975).

O'Leary, Tomas, "PRACTICAL EXERCISES TOWARDS A MODERN MYTH (an evaluative report on The Second Annual Conference on the Great Mother)" (unpublished duplicated typescript, 37 pp., 1976).

Poster for Robert Bly's Twelfth Annual Conference of the Great Mother and the New Father, 1986.

Robinson, David, Letter addressed to Connie [Martin] (unpublished duplicated letter, 3pp., dated October 1, 1980), attached to letter for John [Rosenwald] and Ann [Arbor] (unpublished typed letter, 1 p., dated October 5, 1980).

The GreenBook (unpublished digital and printed document of The Annual Conference on the Great Mother and the New Father, 1991 edition, 51 pp.).

Author's note: My apologies to those many friends and conference participants who remain here nameless, despite their substantial contributions to the GMC. I will gladly provide an electronic copy of an expanded version of this essay upon request to rosey@beloit.edu.

NOTES AND PIECES ON SPEAKING POEMS AND STORIES, LEARNING BY HEART

By Gioia Timpanelli

The community flowers when the poem is spoken in the ancient way – that is, with full sound, with conviction, and with the knowledge that the emotions are not private to the person speaking them.

—Robert Bly

Respect for the folk tale and its spoken tradition was significantly missing at the time I began telling stories. The old stories showed ways of living in the world, reflecting central concerns reborn in the 60s that reflected values in every part of the natural indigenous world. Nature and stories, place and humans: as an artist this was my nexus. Coming from a spoken and literary tradition where reciting poetry and telling stories were both part of my family's everyday life, I began telling stories on my Educational Television series *Stories from My House* in the 1960s. I was surprised that "Tales from Viet Nam," one of the 30 programs, and the series itself each won an Emmy citation for content and "compelling storytelling format." The programs mixed written stories and world folk tales. I loved producing and broadcasting these educational television series in literature, but when I first told stories in public with a group of people, I knew that the stories had to be told communally. I could find no better art at the time than retelling in an extempore way perennial folk stories with small, spontaneous poems in them that had an urgency and relevance to contemporary life. The old stories had something enduring in them, and my telling was of the moment. These old stories were not fleeting stories that Columcille of Iona warned against, but rather the enduring stories that he urged us to keep. The marketplace had a great many stories about accumulation and wealth, while the folk tales talked abut the human propensity to fall asleep and to find what was missing in life. At the assembly of Druim-Cetta in 580, St. Columcille of Iona spoke against disassembling the Bards. Keep the Bards among you, said Columcille, for it's better to pay for the enduring story rather than the fleeting one. Hearing the old, I was always interested in bringing in a new art.

Although coming from different traditions, Robert Bly and I met in 1977 with a number of serious values in common. We both had a great respect for the spoken tradition, the marginal and unfashionable in modern society, peace, the underdog, the soul and spirit. (I'm sure Robert would make a better list here). These stories and the way of speaking poems were great treasures from our illiterate ancestors from all cultures. All this and more made it imperative to sing them back.

We were not interested in teaching concepts but in poems and stories which were by their nature expressed in analogies, clustering of analogies, metaphors and images. The oral tradition still looks at analogies as having life in them; whereas the "generalized" word, i.e., the "concept," gathers live qualities and brings it into the area of "dead concept," which stops thinking so there is no longer a live situation. And there was another thing: we each had missed this communal sound bringing in the heart's affections.

While looking in the poetry section at the Elliott Bay Books in Seattle I found this note, written by one of the booksellers, taped to the Bly poetry shelf:

> I had the good fortune
> of seeing Robert Bly
> last year at the Theodore
> Roethke Memorial Poetry
> Reading. Bly completely
> astounded me. He read
> and recited Roethke, his
> own and others' work
> with so much heart
> often stopping 4 lines
> into a poem to say "Can
> you feel that, listen..."
> and he would start all
> over again so we

could feel it with him.
Read Bly.... Read
Bly out loud, and
FEEL IT!

JW

Keats had written in a letter (April 21, 1819) to his brother and sister-in-law, "The common cognomen of this world among the misguided and superstitious is 'a vale of tears'.... Call the world if you Please 'The vale of Soul-making.'"

We hoped to bring the joy of spoken poetry and old stories meant to nourish the soul, a theme not mentioned often in the prevalent market culture.

For a number of years (1977-1993), Robert Bly and I went criss-crossing the country giving performances and leading workshops on poetry and stories at the invitation of art and educational centers, universities, colleges, C. G. Jung centers, libraries, large and small foundations, giving performances of (speaking) poetry and (telling) stories on Friday evenings and then leading a workshop on Saturday and Sunday on a theme we had chosen. We worked where we were invited, and following the images in stories and the emotions found in the spoken and written poems, we encouraged lively discussions. The performance on Friday night and the spontaneous poems and stories during the workshops were all material learned "by heart." Speech and literature were our starting points. I think we were trying to find the "universe of words inside" so that we could give the experience of speaking emotion from the communal voices of poems and stories where the experience has been sung and recorded.

We worked this way about a third of the time, and the rest individually with the same form, teaching our own individual work on poetry and stories in themed performances and workshops. Everywhere we went singly or together, we hoped to create a respect and a real interest in reviving the oral tradition, bringing it back into general acceptance. We often met the same groups of people in places we came back to again and again, gaining a community for poetry and stories. People brought opinions, reflections, and good discussions of poems and tales. How many poems or stories do you know "by heart"? When you have learned poems and stories by heart, you do not need paper or a mechanical device; nothing you hold, paper or computer, separates you from the poem or story. It's there even when the electricity fails or some louts are trying to make you and your neighbors learn their language and forget your own language and stories, a pernicious result of power moves everywhere.

As I wrote in an essay in the collection, *Sacred Stories*, "The old folk tales especially have a sneaky logic found in poetry, metaphor, and dreams. We can be thankful that they are not given to large statements on meaning, for like the heart to whom they constantly speak, they prefer experience to discussion, unity to separation. Everything in them has weight, even a feather flying here and there. They live in the particular while trying to talk politely about everybody. Full of lively images, these old tales carry with them the magic of the world."

The Story of the Indian Bird

Once there was a merchant who caught a wild bird and put it in a cage. It was a large cage in a large room. Each day the bird was given fresh water and seeds. Time passed. One day when the man was passing the cage the bird said to him, Man, will you let me go free? No, no said the man. Then please when you go to the forest where you caught me, will you tell the free birds that I am still alive? Yes, I will do that, said the man, and thought to himself, I didn't know that birds were so sensitive. After some months the merchant went back to India on business and as he was walking in the same forest he noticed the same kind of wild birds as his own and called out to one, Listen, I caught your relative but do not worry, he is alive in my house in a cage with plenty of seeds and good water. But as soon as he said this, one of the birds fell dead from the tree. Oh, how awful, said the man, I didn't know my words were so powerful. When he finished his business he returned home. Weeks passed. One day he went into the room with the cage, and the bird said, Merchant, did you see my friends and relatives? Yes, I did, but I have bad news for you. Even though I told

> them that you were alive in a large cage and had plenty of seeds and water, immediately after I said this one of your relatives fell off the branch—dead. Oh, no, said the bird falling off his perch lying dead at the bottom of the cage. Look at what I have caused, said the man, but since this bird was so special I will bury it properly. He opened the cage door, picked up the little bird and placed it on the sill of an open window, thinking to pick it up later and bury it in the garden. But when the man walked off, the bird righted himself around and flew away saying, I knew those birds would have good advice for me.

The last line of this story always gets people to laugh. The caged bird is freed. The Merchant was fooled as we were, but unlike him we are relieved to know the bird is alive and free, both conditions close to our own hearts. One of the surprises of the story is that you don't ever really know where the teaching is coming from; it can even come by way of an enemy. We might also think we understand one thing the story is saying: the collective wisdom of the tribe might know how to save us. Well, that may be generally true, but these stories are not about a single saying as are fables which teach simple morals, but instead give us, individually and communally, things to think about for a long time. They are not about Meaning or Doctrines. The system of apprenticeship relied on learning by doing, learning by eventually understanding what the master crafts man or woman teaches, by individually gained experience. In this case the enemy himself brought the message back by describing what he saw. The caged bird learns from an image, a gesture, an action. Words alone would not have gotten the message across. A manual or written doctrine would not have helped, but a ruse, playing dead, an old trick of nature, got the message across. The Merchant has forgotten "playing dead," the hidden truth—the answer to the bird's dilemma. As a well-known Hindu teacher said, *all stories are ultimately about consciousness;* and it is only when the listener is able to understand the next level of consciousness that the teaching comes. The Merchant knows what is useful to him and what is not. What isn't useful is left abandoned to go its own way. What can he do with a dead bird? (And who hasn't waited out or temporarily escaped dead systems, caged places, bad situations, by being "not present, not useful, not visible"?) Could it also be that playing dead is known and transmitted from experience to experience? Can we learn from the one who knows the larger, whole situation and offers a solution that allows the other to learn from it?

Dante wrote in *La Vita Nuova*, "*...esperienza che intender non la puo chi non la prova.*" You can't completely understand what you haven't experienced. The understanding that comes from experience doesn't come from the intellect or the emotions or history or cultural know-how. There is something in our experience that can go beyond our usual ways of knowing. But once you have experienced something, even if you forget it (so many stories and poems are about falling asleep or forgetting), you have been changed in a place that can't be explained completely. You have learned something that works between doing and knowing, that shows a new possibility. Sometimes, like experience, the old stories are about ways of seeing. There is no system; it wouldn't really help. To understand an experience you have to understand the other as well as yourself. In the end, it depends on knowing the situation and for this *way* you need the knowledge of the whole experience.

Ultimately, what one gains from a complete understanding of experience is not a continual memory of the cage or the blow to the head, but the knowledge of pain and the value of freedom, for others as well as oneself.

Lately a certain kind of folk story has been appearing in my life. I first heard and later read an instance of this sort of story in Ballaghaderreen, Ireland, and since I once stayed in that town and have relatives through marriage there, it caught me. There are examples of its kind in ancient texts and modern fiction, but the reason a story catches you is almost always personal. Here's a synopsis of what happens:

> Once there was a poor and generous old man from Ballaghaderreen who has a dream. In it he is told to make a journey at the end of which he will find a pot of gold. In this case the old man

> has to leave Balla and travel a good way to Dublin and there, when he crosses one of the bridges over the River Liffey, he will find a pub, and there he will find his treasure. The old man follows the dream map and when he sees the pub that was in his dream he looks around but there's no place he can dig for a hidden treasure, so he stands beside the door and waits. He waits all day and at nightfall the publican comes out and asks,
>
> What are you standing here for all day long?
>
> I had a dream that told me to come here.
>
> A dream? I think you must be a daft old man to follow dreams. I, myself, had a dream a month ago and it told me to go to some poor old sod's cottage on the crossroads from French Park to Ballaghaderreen and if I did, I would find a pot of gold in his front yard. Do you think I would go traipsing all over the countryside because of a dream? It's cold. You should go home.
>
> Indeed I should and will, said the old man.
>
> And when he got home he dug in his front yard and found the treasure and wasn't he himself and all the others the better for it. And if he hasn't given it all away we might share a bit with them.

Now this old folk story has in it that tricky logic. In the last month, I found two people I had lost by way of this kind of crooked story. But then what is meant by the word "dream" or "pot of gold," for that matter?

In the spring of 1977 I was telling stories at the Spoleto Festival and a man in the audience came up to me and said, There's a conference in Maine organized by a poet, Robert Bly, and he would love your stories. If you have time to tell stories there, I'll call him tonight. It just happened that I had read an article by him on a Jungian subject in *The American Poetry Review* which started me reading Jung and also I remembered right then that years before I had been doing research at the Donnell Library for my television series on poetry when I happened to see a poster in the lobby for a poetry reading – it was almost over but I slipped in and listened. Robert was speaking, not reading in the flat, close-to-the-page "poetic voice" that was popular in some American circles at the time. I liked that in speaking his poems he was like those of us who started the story revival trying to bring back the experience and joy of the oral tradition. I felt I owed him two "thanks," so I went to Maine and told stories at his poetry conference.

We soon were getting requests for our collaborative work. We both worked on our own as before, Robert giving poetry readings and workshops, I giving storytelling evenings and workshops. While our own individual work took most of our time, the collaboration became a part of what we did. We began as colleagues who admired each other's work and maybe we were even surprised that there were two of us doing the same work in different arts. We helped each other by bringing in insights: when one of us was bringing in intuitive possibilities the other was giving examples of particulars and so on. We aimed at balance. Remembering the joy I felt in art history classes and because I had been collecting slides and using them in my own workshops on the Greek myths and Chinese and Zen stories, I brought my slides for mythic images into our collaborations (always when we taught Greek stories and the medieval Wild Man and Wild Woman).

Working with poetry, fairy tales, and mythic images is a way of working with a respectful communal distance to speak of close realities. We spoke of the inner person (Boehme) and the outer one. We paid attention to images and analogies as having life in them. (We stayed away from concepts, which tend to deaden language.) Images and analogies are more interested in variety, speaking of the spirit and the possibilities of a soulful life.

From starting out as respectful, polite colleagues we became respectful, polite friends. I have been told many times that people were happy to see a man and a woman as colleagues who, respectful of differences and agreements, recited poetry and told stories in tandem. Robert was the best man at our wedding (Ken and I married in '81), and I went to Robert and Ruth Counsel's wedding. Ruth and I became best friends. Now the four of us are family friends, and it started by chance or because the four of us believe you should pay attention to most old stories and surely pay very close attention to all dreams.

Here is a Haphazard List of Bly & Timpanelli Performances and Workshops from a box of flyers from circa 1982-84 that I had saved. Robert and I worked together mainly from 1977-91. There are many more boxes, but time has spared us further listings.

—*Heart Movement and Soul Movement: Myth, Story and Poem in the years 1100-1200 in Northern and Southern Europe*, (Interface Foundation) Boston, MA. With Robert Bly, Joseph Campbell, Gioia Timpanelli, June 4, 5, 6. Out of the period 1100-1200 AD in northern and southern Europe came highly creative painting, sculpture, music and dance. Intense religious life was also evident, with the myth of the Grail spreading rapidly over Europe. These events indicate a strong movement of heart and soul during the century.

—*An Evening of Love Stories and Poems in Performance*, April 8, Mundelein College, and April 9, 10, "*The Wild Man and the Wild Woman*," two-day workshop (C. G. Jung Center Evanston, IL).

—*Poems and Stories*, Friday evening Robert Bly & Gioia Timpanelli, *Celebrating the Coming of Winter* (New School for Social Research and the C. G. Jung Foundation for Analytical Psychology, NYC).

—*Fairy Tales* (course 3612-0) seminar. A workshop dealing with relationships between women and men; some investigation of the use of love language in the spiritual quest. (The New School & C. G. Jung Foundation)

—*An Evening with Robert Bly and Gioia Timpanelli: Uniting Two Ancient Arts of Poetry and Storytelling*, at Luther Burbank Center for the Arts, June 7, 1987. Gift-giving is the theme of the first half of the program. In the second half, Gioia and Robert will come into contemporary places with personal stories and poems.

—*Irish Folktales and The Poetry of W. B. Yeats* (Tony Joseph Associates). A week-long workshop on stories and poems.

—*Leaving Symbols and Approaching the Universe*, Friday performance and Saturday seminar (New School for Social Research), Fall 1982.

—*The Animals, Our Souls and Theirs* with Robert Bly, James Hillman and Gioia Timpanelli. Harvard Science Center (Interface Foundation, Boston, MA). Seeing animals in dreams poems and stories.

—*Poems and Stories in Celebration of Winter*, Friday, Oct. 30, 1981 (New School for Social Research). Part I, The Gathering and the Coming In; Part II, Spiritual Awakening (Marcus Wise on Tabla and David Whetstone on sitar playing classical ragas from North India).

—*The Wild Man and The Wild Woman*, (Interface, Boston) with Robert Bly and Gioia Timpanelli. In any given century there are certain energies that drop out of the conscious mind or survive in a form so occluded that they lose their availability. The "Wild Man" and the "Wild Woman" energies are two of those. Slides from Medieval art will be part of the workshop presentation.

—*Poetry and Stories on a medieval theme*, St. Paul's Church, London.

—*Poems and Stories* by Robert Bly and Gioia Timpanelli (The Poetry Cooperative), Druid Theatre, Dublin, July 28.

—*Healing, Poetry and Fairy Tales*, Robert Bly and Gioia Timpanelli (Wellspring Los Angeles, CA), April13, 14, 1981.

—*Tales from the Hearth: An evening of Poems & Stories* with Robert Bly and Gioia Timpanelli. Feb. 22, First United Methodist Church (Resource Institute, Elliott Bay Book Co. Seattle Storyteller Guild, and others) Saturday Workshop with Gioia Timpanelli: *The Folktale as a Child of Place.*

—*Magical Storytelling* with Robert Bly, Gioia Timpanelli & Steve Sanfield, music by Marina Bokelman (American Victorian Museum, Nevada City, CA).

—*An Evening of Poems and Stories and Two Workshops*, January 8, 9, 10 with Bly & Timpanelli (Fountain Street Church), Grand Rapids, MI.

—*An Evening of Poems and Stories to Celebrate the American Landscape* with Robert Bly & Gioia Timpanelli, November 23 (Interface, Boston).

—*Sacred Stories: Healing in the Imaginative Realm* (Common Boundary Conference, Arlington, VA), November 8-10, 1991, with Maya Angelou, Robert Bly, Matthew Fox, Natalie Goldberg, Senator Albert Gore, Jr., Sam Keen, Babatunde Olatunji & Gioia Timpanelli.

—*Psychology: With/Without Soul?* (The Society for Jungian/Archetypal Psychology and the Center for Continuing Education of the University of Notre Dame) with R. Bly, R. Stein, D. Miller, R. Sardello, Alice O. Howell, Howard McConeghey, T. Kapacinskas and G. Timpanelli.

—*Poems and Stories* with Robert Bly and Gioia Timpanelli (Art Institute of Chicago), Oct. 2-4, Performance and Workshop.

—*An Evening of Poetry and Storytelling* with Robert Bly & Gioia Timpanelli (The Open Center, NYC), Bly reciting from his Selected Works and Timpanelli stories of 40s in Brooklyn in Italian and Jewish neighborhood.

—*An Evening of Poems and Stories and a workshop on Archetypes* (C. G. Jung Society in San Francisco) with Bly and Timpanelli.

—*Robert Bly and Gioia Timpanelli: Wolfram von Eschenbach's Parzival, Story and Commentaries*. Film for series on Public Television: one-hour film presentation shown on Canadian Public Broadcasting and PBS throughout Canada and the USA.

Robert kept notebooks so he has, I suspect, some of this written down. I have no recording of all those told stories. Like my Great Grandmother who told them before me, the stories were passed on naturally in the telling and now in the same way, I pass them on. Very moved by the sense and form of the old stories, I have been writing and publishing fiction. Writing his poems and translating many poets that he has loved, Robert has changed American culture and given it a great gift.

Why did we do all of this work, Robert?
Because we loved it.
And that was / is so.

A LITTLE BOOK PROJECT WITH ROBERT BLY

By William Booth

I have a forty-year-old reel-to-reel audio tape of the first Robert Bly reading I ever heard. It was a reading not to be lost or forgotten. "Poetry reading" seemed an inadequate term to suggest the intensity of that event at a community college in Santa Rosa, California in 1969. Robert Bly was brassy, tender, funny, moving, and then, with his anti-war poems, deeply disturbing. The poems ranged from Issa's to Russell Edson's before Robert read "The Teeth Mother Naked at Last," his great anti-Vietnam War poem that was still evolving each time he read it.

> Eight hundred steel pellets fly through the vegetable walls.
> The six-hour infant puts his fists instinctively to his eyes to keep
>   out the light.
> But the room explodes,
> the children explode.
> Blood leaps on the vegetable walls.

If we couldn't be poets, we teachers thought as we left the reading, we at least needed to be better teachers, striving to move our students as Robert Bly had moved us.

In the more casual moments of his reading, Robert had said a little about living in Minnesota, with a fascinating image, for Californians, of digging a trench through the snow to his writing shack and having to roof it over with boards so that it wouldn't fill up with more snow. The picture stuck with me, though I had no idea that it had a connection with my future.

About three and a half years later I left teaching because of deteriorating eyesight. My wife and I bought a business, a small lakeshore resort, in the state where there are ten or fifteen thousand lakes and a lot of Norway pines and tall spruces, Minnesota. Weeks after we moved from California, we found that we had landed on a shore of the very lake where Robert Bly and Bill Duffy had worked on issues of *The Fifties* and *The Sixties*, collecting poems and essays and sending out scathing and amusing rejection slips from a shoreline cabin.

When Robert got word from Santa Rosa that a Californian who had liked one of his poetry readings had taken over a little resort on his favorite north woods lake, he made the long drive up from Madison, in the southwest corner of the state, and stayed a few days. And for years after, Cry of the Loon Lodge was a sort of writing retreat for Robert, as he would work on poems in a chilly cabin in the off-season and often join our family for supper. Our five kids loved his stories and the fried chicken he cooked on a very hot skillet, the linoleum floor in the kitchen getting slippery with grease.

I was no longer reading print but listening to books and magazines on audio cassettes. Robert brought up tapes by the carton of his readings and seminars, rich fare for a listener sitting near a wood stove through winter days in the north woods. As tapes kept coming, I edited some audio programs for Ally Press and Sound Horizons. Roger Easson, a Blake scholar, Bly fan, and assiduous collector of Robert's work, hoped that some presentations could be adapted for print and get into the little magazine he helped edit, *Raccoon* from St. Luke's Press in Memphis. Most of Robert's readings, diverse in material, loose in structure, full of spontaneous commentary and interaction with the audience, did not lend themselves to print form. A few readings on the human shadow were exceptions, especially two substantial presentations at a conference in San Francisco in 1983 that were not only clear and vivid in their shadow imagery but almost essay-like in structure.

The shadow can be a shadowy concept, and complex. In the introduction to the shadow book I quote the Jungian analyst Marie-Louise von Franz and C. G. Jung himself on the shadow, and both definitions are relatively abstract. But Robert's original talk started out vividly and swiftly with images of a child as a 360-degree personality, a living globe of energy, soon to lose its wholeness as parts of the personality our parents disapprove of ("It's not nice to try and kill your brother!") are stuffed into the long bag we drag behind us. Robert's image of ourselves at twenty was "a thin slice of the globe of energy that once radiated in all directions."

Not only the aliveness of the metaphors in Robert's recorded San Francisco talk on the shadow, but the careful structure apparent in headings like "Five Stages in Exiling, Hunting, and Retrieving the Shadow," made Roger Easson at St. Luke's Press and me think this material had to be preserved between the covers of a book and reach a much larger audience. Besides the San Francisco presentation, there was an earlier studio reading of poems selected around the shadow theme, and a powerful essay Robert had published on Wallace Stevens and the shadow. We could address some of the questions raised and not answered in the collected material with a question-and-answer interview. So we had more material than *Raccoon* magazine knew what to do with in its 48-page format. In the end, the *Raccoon* editors expanded the issue to 60 pages and omitted the Stevens essay.

Robert gave his blessing to a project that would take a lot of his time for revisions and that would not bring in a dime unless it went beyond the *Raccoon* special edition stage. My job, for starters, was simply to transcribe the material from audio tapes, go from the spoken word to the printed word, always with a worry about what was being lost in the process. Technology that was brand-new to me, a partially sighted person, let me do what would have been impossible only three or four years earlier. I had a new computer created for low-vision users and a closed circuit TV magnifier that, when I put a typescript with Robert's squiggly hand-written corrections and changes under the camera, threw an image of a small section of the page onto a 17-inch monitor, magnified up to 60 times.

So I typed the recorded programs, supplying punctuation and paragraphing, cutting out the "ums" and the coughs, the rapid "you unnerstan' me what I'm saying," the obvious repetitions, usually (not always) resisting the temptation to sneak in a tiny, brilliant revision. I would make editorial comments about possible cuts or changes that Robert comfortably accepted or ignored. And I would send the clean printout to Robert by snail mail—no e-mail then in the 80's, at least not for either him or me. The printout would come back with hand-squiggled revisions above lined-out sentences, but often the nature of Robert's revisions could not be described as "polishing" or "refining." In my own revisions I hoped to lose as little as possible of what I had sweated to create. But Robert, with rushes of creative energy, would sometimes only glance at the page as I had typed it (and as he had revised it, and as I had retyped it) with fresh suggestions, and he would simply come at the idea with new images, new syntax, a whole new draft of a paragraph or page. It was as if, in his creativity, he were saying, "I'm not afraid to lose the page, to kill this paragraph, because it will be born again."

The freshly revised chapter would arrive in the mail, and it was time to put the corrected typescript under the CCTV camera and try to make out Robert's very appealing, regular, finely curved handwriting, anything but messy or careless, an art form in itself, but sometimes more artistic than legible, and make a new clean typescript, with new suggestions. Days later the pages would come back, often with no fewer line-outs, fresh paste-ups of old and new, and new squiggles than in the first revision. Some chapters of the book were revised five times. As was our recorded interview.

The interview that became a chapter titled "Honoring the Shadow" was a kind of collaboration in clarifying ideas and filling gaps in the other chapters. Robert Bly is not only a great talker but a creatively attentive listener, often seeming to understand your assertion or your question better than you yourself. So my brief questions were answered by Robert with responses that were completely in tune with the question and often presented as coherent oral paragraphs.

After typescripts had gone back and forth between us for some months, we had a finished copy to send to St. Luke's Press and *Raccoon* magazine, along with a title. That title, *A Little Book on the Human Shadow*, was strictly Robert's idea, and I loved his reason for the choice. He liked the humor of it. A vast subject, the human shadow, and a very small book.

We asked for red ink, I can't recall why, on the cover of the book that came out from St. Luke's Press. The cover was handsomely designed, with no indication that the little book was an issue of *Raccoon*. The traumatic surprise for me was that the text of the book as well as the cover was printed in red ink. A little misunderstanding. My shock and dismay had to do with the unconventionality in ink color that seemed to carry a mysterious message about the shadow but was in fact just a mistake. Robert took the mistake with complete equanimity. There were later printings from St. Luke's Press that were black, not red.

And then Robert's publisher, HarperCollins, took the book from St. Luke's Press and brought out a hardcover edition of *A Little Book on the Human Shadow* in 1988, adding the essay on Wallace Stevens that *Raccoon* couldn't afford to include. It has not been out of print since, has sold 103,000 copies, and has been translated into German, Dutch, and Spanish.

Something of the book's influence can be seen in the record of other published shadow books before and after 1988. The best online list of shadow titles I found included only one predating Robert Bly's book, *The Shadow and Evil in Fairy Tales* by Marie-Louise von Franz, 1971. The other books, at least a half-dozen of them, all coming after the *Little Book*, invariably acknowledge Robert Bly's influence, may carry an essay or introduction by him, and sometimes come close to plagiarizing his words.

Robert did a reading on the shadow in 1991 in New York City that I edited for Sound Horizons, published as a two-cassette set, *The Human Shadow*, in which he said something that hadn't appeared in other shadow programs. He told his listeners, "Imagine we're in a living room, and as in any living room, lots of things will be said that aren't true. So you pick and choose." He added later, "Some say the shadow makes up our dreams at night. That's a good one to think about. Who knows if it's true?" I like these disclaimers. They invite us to stay open to ideas in the book that might trigger resistance. However stark and apparently simple some of the shadow metaphors are, the accumulated metaphors are numerous and complex, and their relation to our experience is complex. We can open our minds and hearts and senses to what goes on in a talk on the shadow and a book on the shadow, take in what resonates with us, just as we do in a Robert Bly poetry reading, without getting stuck on what stumps us or arouses our skepticism. The shadow is a rich metaphor, "a good one to think about."

I should mention in closing that there is a big book on the human shadow. It is called *Iron John*, by Robert Bly.

PRAISING THE SOUL IN WOMEN AND MEN: ROBERT BLY AND THE MEN'S MOVEMENT

By Thomas R. Smith

Nineteen-ninety, the watershed year for the mythopoetic men's movement in the US, was also, not coincidentally, the year that rocketed Robert Bly, along with his best-selling book *Iron John*, to media celebrity.

Interviewing Bly in the October 1990 *New Age Journal*, Jeff Wagenheim asked a question apparently puzzling many: Why a *poet* leading this men's movement, and not a politician, say, or a sports hero?

Deflecting emphasis from himself, Bly responded, "One reason poetry is at the center is because the language that men use to communicate with each other has gotten very damaged."[1] Bly's answer, though utterly consistent with his lifelong role as a defender of the beauty, depth, and nourishing power of language, effectively sidestepped the question, Why *this* poet? In this essay, I will suggest an answer to that question.

1.

While Robert Bly has generally insisted that his work with men is psychological rather than political in nature, his first major pronouncement on gender matters originated, somewhat ironically, in one of his most political moments. During the Vietnam War, Bly composed his furious anti-war poem "The Teeth Mother Naked at Last," often improvising before live audiences passages of the poem later transcribed from tape and folded into the finished version, first published by City Lights in 1970.

Clearly "The Teeth Mother" required some explaining for the uninitiated, and one imagines Bly hoping to head a few of those questions off at the pass when he reprinted his great jeremiad in *Sleepers Joining Hands* in 1973. In that volume, "The Teeth Mother" strategically precedes a lengthy essay, "I Came Out of the Mother Naked," in which Bly elaborates on the Jungian underpinnings of his poem. Drawing heavily on Erich Neumann's study of the goddess archetype, *The Great Mother*, Bly lays out a highly poetic interpretation of Neumann's ideas so as to illuminate the figure of the "Teeth Mother," in Neumann's schema one of the goddess's destructive aspects. Bly viewed the Vietnam War as 1960s America's introduction to the dismembering fury of that aspect of the goddess, standing for

> numbness, paralysis, catatonia, being totally spaced out, the psyche torn to bits, arms and legs thrown all over. America's fate is to face this Mother before other industrial nations.... My Lai is part way down; hard drugs that leave the boy-man permanently "stoned" are among the weapons of this Mother.[2]

And yet Bly's impulse, despite his knowledge of the darker potential of the Great Mother, was to embrace and affirm her values. Later in the essay, he says, "All my clumsy prose amounts to is praise of the feminine soul, whether that soul appears in men or women." He adds, "The masculine soul ... also needs praise, but I am not doing that here."[3]

Indeed the Seventies were, for Bly, mainly a time of "praising the feminine soul." During that decade, inspired by Joseph Campbell, he began working into his poetry readings brilliant commentary on fairy tales, which he included among the highest intellectual achievements of the vanished "Mother civilization" pre-dating patriarchy. At the farthest extreme of this arc, Bly would ask the men as a group to leave his readings, preferring to address only the women.

Remarks Bly made to *East West Journal* in August, 1976 testify to the speed with which his thought on gender matters was evolving. Asked about his efforts to "recognize the repressed feminine side," Bly responded:

> During the sixties, women began to have more confidence in the dignity and energy of their consciousness, and males began to feel that their consciousness had built-in destructive elements. Many writers wrote from that point of view. But there is some sort of mistake in the terms, since it involves preference. It virtually prevents one from praising male consciousness. I feel the seventies will need to do that.[4]

Foreshadowing his work with men in the coming decade, Bly continues: "I think it is a good time for both men and women to develop the ability to begin movements, not follow them...."[5]

Bly's celebration of matriarchal values, rooted also in his reading of the Swiss anthropologist Bachofen's *Mother Right* (1861), found a festive communal expression in the creation of the Conference on the Great Mother, which has continued to meet annually since 1975. Emphasizing the "ecstatic" side of the Great Mother, the conference has brought together original, independent artists and thinkers, collectively constituting one of the notable underground streams in American culture in the past half-century. In 1981, heralding the shift in attention from feminine to masculine consciousness, Bly accepted an invitation from the Lama commune in Taos, New Mexico to teach a group of about forty men.

2.

In opening himself to the possibility of teaching men, Bly also signaled a willingness to engage his own neglected or unexamined masculinity. His 1981 collection, *The Man in the Black Coat Turns*, articulates this change, not only in its title image but in poems such as "The Prodigal Son," "The Grief of Men," and "Fifty Males Sitting Together." The latter, a meditation on Bly's own isolation as a self-described "mother's son," was subsequently adopted as a key text by the nascent men's movement.

Soon other opportunities for teaching men arose. In California, the first Mendocino Men's Conference in 1983 became the prototype of the gatherings for which Bly was to become famous: a mix of inspired teaching by Bly, psychologist James Hillman, storyteller Michael Meade, and others, home-grown ritual addressing American men's lack of initiatory experiences, and alternately exuberant and tearful self-discovery.

Bly's decade of teaching and organizing such groups became the testing ground for his best-selling book-length essay, *Iron John*. In fact, Bly had chosen to teach the titular Grimm Brothers tale at his very first men's workshop for the Lama commune, one of a handful in the Grimms' collection he had identified as specific to the problem of male initiation. Bly's exploration of the "Iron John" story took a giant step toward the book it would eventually become in an interview, "What Men Really Want," conducted by Keith Thompson for *New Age Journal* in March, 1982. That interview probably did more than any other single source to alert American men to the potential of Bly's new concentration on masculinity. In the proliferating men's groups of the 1980s, new men would typically preface their introductions with the sentence, "I'm here because of the *New Age Journal* interview."

Minnesota understandably became an epicenter of the new men's work, as Bly, responding to local demand, agreed to lead the first Mendocino-style conference to be held in northern Minnesota in September, 1984. The flier for that gathering reads in part:

> This conference, and others held in different parts of the country, are tentative explorations toward what a men's conference might be, now, in this decade. Some of the questions asked are: What does the mythological world mean now for men? Why are so few men's relationships with women working? Why do so few men have deep male friendships? Is that connected with anger at our father? How is the wild man developed inside? What do men dance about?

The 1984 conference directly inspired the formation of the Minnesota Men's Council, which met monthly into the mid-1990s at the YMCA on the University of Minnesota campus in Minneapolis. In 1987, Paul Feroe, who operated his Ally Press as a comprehensive clearing house for Bly's work, published *The Pillow and the Key*, an essay worked up from the Thompson interview, the first chapter of Bly's prose masterwork. A second chapter and chapbook, *When a Hair Turns Gold*, followed in 1989.

Toward the end of this decade of ferment, Bly used the Twin Cities men's community as a sounding board for his work in progress. Fifty or sixty men would converge on the University Y on a Sunday evening to hear a new chapter and then respond. Bly has always demanded forthrightness of his audience, and these men, despite their admiration for Bly and his project, could be bluntly critical. Bly took it in stride, duly noting remarks that seemed to him on-target, whether positive or negative. I think we all left those sessions feeling that our intelligence had been exercised, honed, and privileged by this sharing.

3.

In many ways, the five years on either side of 1990's publication of *Iron John* were the golden age of men's work in Minnesota and perhaps in the United States as a whole. At the time I was helping to edit a small men's literary journal, *Inroads*, and had many vigorous, sometimes heated discussions with fellow editors, John Lang, Anthony Signorelli, and Jonathan Stensland, over whether the media attention sure to result from the impending publication of *Iron John* was an altogether good thing. We and many groups like ours around the country had up until that point been able to conduct a disciplined exploration of masculinity on our own terms with a minimum of outside scrutiny and judgment. During that time, we were effectively invisible to mainstream society and appropriately esoteric. We harbored serious doubts that a psychologically unsophisticated America could do anything but mock a men's movement based on poetry, storytelling, and Jungian psychology, and we were right to be wary, as subsequent events proved.

In January 1990, a Bill Moyers public TV special, *A Gathering of Men*, gave Bly's mythopoetic men's work its first big splash of national exposure. Moyers's presentation, interspersing thoughtful interview footage with scenes from a large workshop for men in Austin, Texas, effectively balanced Bly's private and public sides. Almost immediately, the Moyers program took its place alongside the *New Age Journal* interview as a major recruiting instrument for the new movement. The Moyers special also helped whet the reading public's appetite for Bly's forthcoming book.

The first hardcover copies of *Iron John* appeared in bookstores in early October, 1990. From our perspective twenty years on, it's difficult to recall the explosive power of this arrival. For a generation of confused and father-hungry men, *Iron John* signaled the beginning of a process of self-reclamation that would have far-reaching effects on our lives and the lives of our spouses, lovers, sons, and daughters. And for a multitude of women nervous about this whole enterprise of men redefining masculinity, it served to manifest extremes of fear and loathing as well.

In the Grimm Brothers tale for which Bly titled his book, a boy discovers, in the person of a "wild man" covered with rust-colored hair at the bottom of a pond, a powerful teacher. In emphasizing the tempering of a modern man's psyche through acknowledgment of grief over the absence of the "wild man" in his life, *Iron John* proposed an alternative to the stoicism of traditional masculinity. Beneath the colorful mix of poetry, mythology, psychology, and social commentary lay a brooding conviction that the emotional isolation and violence of American men masks a hunger for fathering and male mentoring, a hunger heightened in a time of multiplying divorce rates and single-parent households.

I remember, reading *Iron John* for the first time, my admiration at how Bly had unified all those disparate ruminations previewed piecemeal in interviews, chapbooks and critiques at the Y. The sturdily handsome volume somehow made coherent that far-flung speculation and debate, and did so in a way that felt both organic and constructed, familiar and startling. Breaking the Grimm Brothers' story down into eight thematic stages, Bly applied literary, psychological and mythological understanding to each, in a dazzling display of intellectual dexterity. *Iron John* represents Bly at the peak of his associative and intuitive power, adroitly weaving the varied threads of his learning into a rich tapestry. In *Iron John*, Bly really does give readers his all as a poet and thinker.

It would be wrong to pass this point in our reflections without backing the superlatives with some samples of *Iron John*'s prose. Here is Bly in his mythological vein, reminiscent of "I Came Out of the Mother Naked":

> Water in symbolic systems does not stand for spiritual or metaphysical impulses (which are better suggested by air or fire) but earthy and natural life. Water belongs to lowly circumstances, ground life, birth from the womb, descent from the eternal realm to the watery earth, where we take on a body composed mostly of water. When our mythology opens again to welcome women into sky-heaven and men into earth-water, then the genders will not seem so far apart. White men will feel it more natural, then, for them to protect earth, as the native American men have always felt it right to do.[6]

Bly could be equally effective in relating to the concrete details of ordinary life a son's need to be physically near his father:

> Now, standing next to the father, as they repair arrowheads, or repair plows, or wash pistons in gasoline, or care for birthing animals, the son's body has the chance to retune. Slowly, over months or years, that son's body-strings begin to resonate to the harsh, sometimes demanding, testily humorous, irreverent, impatient, opinionated, forward-driving, silence-loving older masculine body. Both male and female cells carry marvelous music, but the son needs to resonate to the masculine frequency as well as to the female frequency.[7]

And this passage about the symbolic interior place we keep for our father gives a taste of Bly's genius for the poetic image as well as his zany wit:

> ... What sort of room have we made up for him? If we have the grudging, stingy respect for him suggested by ... the sitcoms, the chances are the room will be in a run-down neighborhood, with sagging door, plastic curtains, a smelly refrigerator with rotten food in it. The demons of suspicion, we can be sure, have visited this place. They throw out the sofa one day without opening the windows. They put up paintings of Pinochet and Jesse Helms, and tie little black dogs to the radiator.[8]

4.

It needs to be said that the country we live in now is vastly different from the one in which *Iron John* was published. Only three months after the appearance of *Iron John*, President George H. W. Bush launched the first US war against Iraq. This attack portended a return to a more macho, aggressive approach to foreign policy abandoned more than a decade earlier by Jimmy Carter who endured the Iran hostage crisis without resorting to warfare.

Against this backdrop of events, the men's movement inevitably took on a hawkish complexion in the eyes of some. In particular, Bly's praise of the internal Warrior (ultimately a figure symbolizing firmness of character rather than a literal soldier) alarmed well-meaning feminists and anti-militarists unable or unwilling to follow Bly's metaphorical thinking. This reaction reached its nadir in Sharon Doubiago's attack in the March/April 1992 Ms.:

> *Iron John* is so badly written, so inflammatory, and of such potential and outright treachery as to have, if not exactly unleashed the barely contained Mass Murderer in us, been a statement of his validity.[9]

"*Iron John*," Doubiago concluded angrily, "is our Desert Storm book."[10]

A poet herself, Doubiago was indulging in hyperbole as rash and inflammatory as any of Bly's more reckless pronouncements. One can imagine how Doubiago, who was living in Paris at the time, might have conflated from a distance the energy of the men's movement with that of the first President Bush's war. Less forgivable was her failure to factor in Bly's well-known anti-war activism, constant throughout his public life as a poet. During the first Gulf War, Bly interviewed, lectured and wrote tirelessly in opposition to the US battering of Iraq. Ironically, at the time Doubiago was preparing her salvo, an ABC TV crew sent to film a Minneapolis men's gathering with Bly and storyteller Michael Meade received in the bargain three hours of uncompromising condemnation of America's popular war.

None of this footage was aired. Somewhere in the vaults of ABC, one of Bly's finest, most courageous anti-war pronouncements has languished these past two decades, along with, as it happens, an eloquently impassioned call for peace by Bly's wife, psychotherapist and writer Ruth Bly.

Not all feminists felt threatened by Bly's work with men and mythology. Molly Layton, a therapist quoted in the May/June 1990 *The Family Therapy Networker*, sounded a moderating note:

> Before Robert Bly got into all this stuff around men, he did a lot of investigating into the female within himself.... In my mind, Bly has really paid his dues in being able, at this point, to proceed dialectically into this focus on men.[11]

In one of the most insightful articles of that period, Don Shewey reminded *Village Voice* readers of a confrontational appearance on CNN in which Bly had called an atrocity from the Iraq war "our My Lai": "The interviewer changed the subject. 'Are you going to let that lie on the floor between us?' Bly asked. She said, 'Yes.'"[12]

Shewey further noted that the press's coverage of the men's movement repeated "a pattern recognizable from the trivializing coverage—not so long ago—of feminism as a movement of 'libbers' and 'bra-burners,' of man-haters and ugly women."[13]

5.

From this moment forward, Bly became a polarizing figure on the American literary and cultural scene; residues of resentment and distortion of his men's work persist to the present day. None, not even his friends and colleagues, seemed able to agree on the value of Bly's work with men. On the one hand, Bly's frequent cohort, the Jungian psychologist Robert Moore could assert, "When the cultural and intellectual history of our time is written, Robert will be recognized as the catalyst for sweeping cultural revolution."[14] On the other side, Bly's old political activist friend, Michael True, dismissing *Iron John* as "a file folder of sometimes interesting, mostly nutty ideas,"[15] could call on Bly to "return to his proper work, as poet and critic, in the years ahead."[16]

But spiritual gold, and plenty of it, remained in that mine, and Bly was not about to walk away from the men's work. Navigating such antipodal assessments with determined panache and a healthily cheerful disregard for his critics, Bly stuck with the men's work long after the media, in its short attention span, had zeroed in on other targets. Although Bly went on to write two other volumes of prose aimed at a mass audience, it might be argued that the true sequel to *Iron John* came not in printed form but in the prolific live workshop recordings of those years. Originally released on audio tape, these presentations, sometimes in collaboration with James Hillman and Michael Meade, proceeded in rapid-fire succession from publishers such as Ally Press, Oral Traditions, Sound Horizons, and Sounds True. The titles—*The Human Shadow, Men and the Life of Desire, What Stories Do We Need?, The Inner King and Queen*, and many more—only begin to suggest the breadth and depth of Bly's subject matter. A master of "composing on the tongue," Bly has left from that period an unparalleled spoken word archive, now little known, ripe for rediscovery.

Despite bitterly hostile attacks, Bly, along with Hillman and Meade, continued to fill lecture halls and retreat centers well into the mid-1990s. Underlining the importance of poetry as an essential inner resource for men, the three co-edited a massive poetry anthology, *The Rag and Bone Shop of the Heart: Poems for Men*, perhaps the best poetry anthology of any kind in its decade.

Yet during the public flourishing of the mythopoetic men's movement, Bly harbored an ambivalence toward the work and his role in it. There has always been an element in Bly's thought on men (often detectable in *Iron John*) of a personal need generalized and amplified as a statement of collective need. It seems likely, in fact, that Bly's men's work may have originated in part as a way of dealing with a mid-life crisis, or facing more directly the emotional legacy of a kind and upstanding but alcoholic father. Bly told Clarissa Pinkola Estés in a 1991 interview that he'd at first thought, "My male side was developed, and my feminine side was not developed.... [But] what I developed is the *shallow* form of the masculine, and what I need now is to develop the *deeper* form of the masculine...."[17]

Although Bly's personal search for a viable masculinity struck a resonant common note in millions of American men, Bly found himself internally divided in his relationship with his emerging mass audience. What, for instance, did Bly have personally to do with the grinning, bare-chested CEO holding a toddler in one arm and a conga drum in the other appearing on the cover of *Newsweek* on June 24, 1991? Perhaps no one was more surprised than Bly himself at *Iron John*'s lightning ascendance. In *Esquire* in October, 1991, Bly maintained caution: "A movement implies a doctrine. I just say something is stirring."[18]

Bly's doubts about a men's mass movement came to a head in his much-publicized refusal to participate in what was billed as "the First International Men's Conference" in Austin, Texas, in 1991, ostensibly on grounds that it was too soon to "centralize." Bly told the Minneapolis *Star Tribune*, "I think it is time for continued work at a local level, in small groups of men, in prisons, in schools, in hundreds of cities and towns. I believe in many small streams instead of one river."[19]

Bly's avoidance of the Austin event no doubt owed in part to anger over organizer Marvin Allen's decision to allow ABC's "20/20" to film for television one of his "Wild Man Weekends," drawing public ridicule to men at their most vulnerable. Bly also hated the appropriation of his term "wild man." Overall, his suspicion of mass movements was genuine and well-founded, heightened by the runaway speed at which the whole business seemed to be moving.

As with Marvin Allen's perceived rip-off of the "wild man," Bly voiced serious reservations over the directions in which others carried his ideas in those years of intense activity. He has sometimes been territorially critical, for example, of the New Warriors, one of the more durable organizations to come out of the 90s men's work. The Promise Keepers, a conservative evangelical Christian movement of the mid-1990s capable of packing sports arenas, co-opted trappings of the mythopoetic men's movement, but, as Bly noted in *The Sibling Society*, "The Promise Keepers seem to suggest that men can throw out all the work that women have done in the last thirty years."[20] Though he admired the Promise Keepers' attempts at conscientious fathering, he ultimately viewed them as "literalists," prevented by their religious fundamentalism from dealing effectively with the dark side of their "missionary movement," which, unlike the Jung-based men's work, admitted of no "shadow."

6.

By the time *The Sibling Society* was published in 1996, Bly had begun calling the branch of the men's movement with which he'd become associated the "expressive men's movement." The coinage "mythopoetic" had always whiffed of the inaccurate and vague, and Bly's re-labeling located the work squarely within the domain of art and verbal eloquence.

However, "The expressive men's movement," Bly wrote in *The Sibling Society*, "...is not expressive enough." He continues in this important critique:

> Its stories are tuned primarily to the Anglo-Saxon world, and only in the last three or four years has it succeeded in attracting men from the black and Hispanic communities, who are in many ways more expressive than white men. The expressive men's movement tries to make shame among men conscious, just as one wing of the women's movement has tried to make women's anger conscious.... anger brings one more quickly into political battles than shame does. The expressive men's movement has been slow in asking for political change and developing enough clarity so that the program they stand for can be apprehended even by the media.[21]

At this time Bly had already made significant headway in bringing outstanding teachers of color to leadership roles in his men's gatherings, including the Mayan writer and healer Martín Prechtel, the black poet and publisher Haki Madhubuti, the African ritualist Malidoma Somé, and Guatemalan percussionist Miguel Rivera, to name only a few. In its early years the mythopoetic/expressive men's movement had been glaringly white in complexion. Widely published photographs of Bly knock-off gatherings with their corny tribalism did nothing to dispel the image of privileged white men as Indian wanna-be's pilfering the spiritual treasures of already materially plundered cultures.

Bly first invited Haki Madhubuti to teach at a historic men's conference in Buffalo Gap, West Virginia, in May, 1991. A conscious early attempt at broadening the racial scope of the men's work, Buffalo Gap brought black and white men together in equal numbers for a week. Among the black men attending Buffalo Gap was Malidoma Somé, who had both graduated the Sorbonne and undergone traditional men's initiation in his native Burkina Faso. Subsequently, Malidoma became an indispensable teacher at Bly's men's events.

With the arrival of these non-white teachers who retained living roots in traditional indigenous cultures, the tone and character of the men's work underwent a gradual but profound shift. While the early conferences had been primarily psychological in nature, weighted toward discussion and analysis, in the mid-90s an experiential element took on new prominence, as participants began to put into practice what they'd only talked about previously. This added dimension of indigenous ritual moved Bly's work with men even farther beyond the ken of mainstream media and society.

As the 90s wear on, one can detect a shift in Bly's involvement in the men's work and in gender issues as a whole; his interest in specifically men's issues plateaus by mid-decade, and then begins a process of falling off. Even in his chapter on men and women in *The Sibling Society*, one senses a degree of detachment, even a pulling back. Of course Bly has always "walked swiftly" through the stages of his life and thought, but there is something else going on here as well.

At the height of *Iron John*'s popularity, an interview with Clarissa Pinkola Estés (whose *Women Who Run with the Wolves*, 1992, is the nearest thing we have to an *Iron John* for women) in *Bloomsbury Review* should have given pause to some of Bly's feminist detractors. Referring to his position circa the 1970s, Estés asks Bly whether he still "believes in" a "return to the matriarchies." Replying in the affirmative, Bly amplifies, "There are ways to look at how matriarchy and 'men's work' go together. One is that the patriarchy has not only damaged the women, it's damaged the men deeply. I think the feminists haven't been entirely aware how much it's damaged men."[22]

The whole interview implicitly rebukes those who would accuse Bly of being an unreconstructed male chauvinist. It also confirms that Bly's men's work was in no way intended to repudiate his earlier championing of the feminine. In the 1973 essay, Bly wrote: "[In the matriarchies] each man was once with the Mother—having gone out into masculine consciousness, a man's job is to return."[23] Bly's collaborative book with Marion Woodman, *The Maiden King: The Reunion of Masculine and Feminine* (1998), further enacts his continued fidelity to the arc or path he'd described nearly thirty years before. Certainly that volume as a whole reflects Bly's long-standing fascination with the matriarchies more than it does his interest in men's consciousness. One might deduce from *The Maiden King* that Bly has come full circle, or at least around to a position on the spiral similar to his pre-1981 thinking.

Among the issues "not addressed in *Iron John*," says Bly, "is this noisy literalism that now characterizes the struggle between the ready-made masculine and the ready-made feminine." He continues:

> The masculine side of young men may find itself deeply at home with the masculine, or it may not. Probably not. And with its overemphasis on sports and financial success, our culture gives very little help to the feminine side of men. Thus, the masculine in young men may know almost nothing about the feminine, particularly its depth and fierceness.[24]

7.

With the coming of the new millennium, the issues that powered *Iron John* and the mythopoetic/expressive men's movement seem to have faded from public consciousness. One can be forgiven nostalgia for the quickly passing moment when it appeared that American society might be ready to take a step toward a more European-flavored psychological sophistication, a time when books exploring the meaning of fairy tales could crack the best seller lists. As a mass movement, the men's work enjoyed its allotted 15 minutes of fame, before sinking, far from unscathed by media savaging, into its former obscurity.

This has occurred not at all to the displeasure of the powers-that-be. The largely unseen manipulators of the military-industrial economy would far rather American men occupy their waking hours with a struggle for basic survival than inner study that might lead to unpredictable or radical change in the social order. Bly has frequently chastised the corporate mentality for its hostility to inner values. In a *Paris Review* interview, he quoted as example a Dewar's ad ("You don't need to beat a drum or hug a tree to be a man.") and remarked: "The corporate world dares to say to young men, knowing how much young men want to be men, that the only requirement for manhood is to become an alcoholic. That's disgusting. It's a tiny indication of the ammunition aimed at men who try to learn to talk or to feel."[25]

In the spring of 2000, the Minneapolis *Star Tribune* asked Bly to propose activities for a national day for boys equivalent to Take Our Daughters to Work Day. Bly suggested that fathers take their sons to the library and show them the books they love. Noting that women have often been excluded from the work world, Bly said, "I think it's just as likely now that men will be shut out of the inward world, the literature world."[26]

Though this may strike some as a descent from the more dynamic intensities of *Iron John*, it is consistent with everything Bly has been saying about gender since the 1970s. In *Iron John*, Bly argued, against the prevailing feminist position, that, despite obvious gender inequalities, the word "patriarchy" does not accurately describe our present situation. A true patriarchy, he contended, honors the interior mythological personages of "the Sacred King and Queen." We now have no such common psychic figures:

> The death of the Sacred King and Queen means that we live now in a system of industrial domination, which is not patriarchy. The system we live in gives no honor to the male mode of feeling nor

> to the female mode of feeling. The system of industrial domination determines how things go with us in the world of resources, values, and allegiances; what animals live and what animals die; how children are treated. And in the mode of industrial domination there is neither king nor queen.[27]

Though Bly's words here bode ominously for the fate of everything he has striven to achieve in his explorations of masculine consciousness, the last word has not yet been written on these matters. The mythopoetic/expressive men's movement in fact continues, though in reduced numbers, in various parts of the country, not least in Minnesota where Bly's annual conference has persisted for over a quarter century. Though Bly writes and speaks less of men's issues, he has added terms to the discussion that have become a permanent feature of the ongoing debate. It seems to me entirely possible that the near future may witness a revival of the concerns that brought the men's work to national prominence in the early 1990s, a period which arrived, like the present moment, as the hangover to another disastrous right-wing binge in America.

Clearly we, as a nation, are now in what Bly terms in *Iron John* an "ashes" period, in which events call us down from the heights of self-deceiving hubris to confront the realities of life "on the ground." Whatever viable seeds the 1990s men's work has produced, their intellectual DNA will bear strong traces of the work Bly and his collaborators have accomplished. Younger teachers like Daniel Deardorff and Martin Shaw show the readiness and energy to carry the mythopoetic work to a new generation. Gifted established teachers such as John Lee, Robert Moore, and Doug Von Koss, in addition to those named earlier, continue to make valuable contributions. The conditions making *Iron John* necessary have not gone away. As more wounded men return from our imperial wars and more men on the home front face the crisis of meaning and self-esteem resulting from unemployment, the hungers that drove men to *Iron John* in 1990 will rage perhaps even more desperately than before. And some of these men will surely find illumination, encouragement, and a measure of healing in Bly's writings. *Iron John*'s effect on the masses of men will naturally be more modest and less visible than twenty years ago in the salad days of *Iron John*. But perhaps that is finally to the good. In one of the more perceptive reviews of *Iron John*, the Denver poet Phil Woods wrote: "I found it best to enjoy Bly's book on aesthetic grounds, to let it nurture like water, retaining my capacity for discernment rather than intoxication. *Iron John* is not fuel for ideology, but for inner alchemy."[28]

These days Robert Bly is again less polemicist and more poet. But poetry, lest we forget the obvious, has always been a crucial element in his work with men and women. As he told *New Age Journal* in 1990: "All poetry was originally love poems, and poetry is still a way of appreciating the universe. The part of American men that's been most damaged is the lover."[29] In his poetry, which he is still writing, Bly is very much the "lover," working his unique "inner alchemy" for the good of the many or the few.

A Personal Coda

Throughout this sketchy backward glance at a fertile, underappreciated moment in our cultural history, I have tried to be fair while knowing full well that I could never be objective about any of it. For I myself am one of the beneficiaries of the mythopoetic/expressive men's work circa 1985-1995, the golden decade of that effort, which I have traced in this essay.

My life today is immeasurably better for having been there to do the work with other confused men of my generation. Vocation, relationship, and spiritual practice would, for me, be poorer without it. I especially owe a personal debt to Robert Bly for the role his men's work played in repairing my relationship with my father, a repair that ultimately allowed me to face his death with renewed love and dissipated rancor over the injurious battling that had marred and defined our relationship into my thirties. I know that I am only one of a multitude who can cite the same debt of gratitude to Robert. The men's work opened me, before it was too late, to a late-coming sympathy for my father and an appreciation of his struggles as a man. Though he never belonged to a men's association more esoteric than the Lion's Club, he acquired some measure of respect and perhaps even pride for the explorations I selectively reported to him, though he never understood them and never read or met Robert Bly. Robert's work with men finally allowed me to reconcile differences with my father and arrive at a more affectionate understanding of him while he was still alive and an absence of corrosive regret after he was gone. For that in itself, Robert would have earned my eternal thanks.

In concluding, I want to turn attention back to Robert's poetry, without which we would not have known him as a half-reluctant leader of this strange, unwieldy, and wonderful, if not movement, then "stirring" of men. In doing so, I wish to emphasize once more the inner necessity that has driven the ultimately coherent arc of Robert's work with both genders, praising the soul in both women and men. Here is "A Man Writes to a Part of Himself" from Robert's first book of poems, *Silence in the Snowy Fields*, from 1962, more than a decade before he began in earnest his adventures in the mysteries of mythology and gender. I believe it contains in seed form the whole development of my theme.

What cave are you in, hiding, rained on?
Like a wife, starving, without care,
Water dripping from your head, bent
Over ground corn ...

    You raise your face into the rain
That drives over the valley—
Forgive me, your husband,
On the streets of a distant city, laughing,
With many appointments,
Though at night going also
To a bare room, a room of poverty,
To sleep among a bare pitcher and basin
In a room with no heat—

    Which of us two then is the worse off?
And how did this separation come about?

NOTES

1 "The Secret Life of Men," interview with Jeff Wagenheim, *New Age Journal*, October, 1990, p. 43.

2 Robert Bly, "I Came Out of the Mother Naked," *Sleepers Joining Hands*, Harper & Row, 1973, p. 41.

3 Ibid., p. 49.

4 "About Gurus, Grounding Yourself in the Western Tradition, and Thinking for Yourself," interview with Sherman Goldman, *East West Journal*, August, 1976, p. 15.

5 Ibid., p, 15.

6 Robert Bly, *Iron John: A Book About Men*, Addison-Wesley, 1990, pp. 43-44.

7 Ibid., p. 94.

8 Ibid., p. 118.

9 Sharon Doubiago, "'Enemy of the Mother': A Feminist Response to the Men's Movement," *Ms.*, March/April, 1992, p. 82.

10 Ibid., p. 82.

11 R. Todd Erkel, "The Birth of a Movement," *The Family Therapy Networker*, May/June, 1990. p. 34.

12 Don Shewey, "Town Meeting in the Hearts of Men," *The Village Voice*, February 11, 1992, p. 46.

13 Ibid., p. 46.

14 Robert Moore, "Robert Bly and True Greatness: Some Musings from the Study of Leadership in Human Culture, *Walking Swiftly: Writings and Images on the Occasion of Robert Bly's 65th Birthday*, ed. Thomas R. Smith, Ally Press, 1992, p. 217.

15 Michael True, "Celebrating Robert Bly, But Taking Him to Task as Well, *Walking Swiftly: Writings and Images on the Occasion of Robert Bly's 65th Birthday*, ed. Thomas R. Smith, Ally Press, 1992, p. 237.

16 Ibid., p. 238.

17 "The Man in the Black Coat Turns: A Discussion with Robert Bly," interview with Clarissa Pinkola Estés, *The Bloomsbury Review*, Jan./Feb., 1991, p. 12.

18 Charles Gaines, "Robert Bly, Wild Thing," *Esquire*, October,

1991, p. 127.

19 Kim Ode, "Robert Bly: A Man Rethinks His Role," *Minneapolis Star Tribune*, "First Sunday Section," February 2, 1992, p. 8.

20 Robert Bly, *The Sibling Society*, Addison-Wesley, 1996, p. 179.

21 Ibid., pp. 178-9.

22 "The Man in the Black Coat Turns: A Discussion with Robert Bly," p. 12.

23 Robert Bly, "I Came Out of the Mother Naked," p. 29.

24 Robert Bly, *The Maiden King: The Reunion of Masculine and Feminine*, with Marion Woodman, Henry Holt and Company, 1998, p xvii.

25 "The Art of Poetry LXXIX," Interview with Francis Quinn, *The Paris Review*, #154, Spring, 2000, p. 68.

26 H. J. Cummins, "From BOYS to MEN," *Star Tribune*, April 27, 2000, p. 1E.

27 Robert Bly, *Iron John: A Book About Men*, p. 98.

28 Phil Woods, review of *Iron John: A Book About Men*, *The Bloomsbury Review*, Jan./Feb., 1991, p. 13.

29 "The Secret Life of Men," *New Age Journal*, p. 44.

ROBERT BLY: STILL TAKING ON THE WOR(L)D

By Victoria Frenkel Harris

"It is difficult
to get the news from poems
yet men die miserably every day
for lack
of what is found there."
—William Carlos Williams, from. *Asphdodel That Greeny Flower*

If, as I believe, poetry attends most copiously to the word's affect, the need for poetry is never more vital than it is now. This is the time to analyze the way language determines reality, and realize that our attention to language has global consequences. While this world cannot possibly be understood in all its complexities, the language that informs us 24/7 needs a perspicacious audience. Personal, national, and multicultural issues are deeply intertwined in Robert Bly's attention to the ethical dimension of human relationships. While silence and solitude remain important to Bly, it is through language that he connects to the world—"We are bees ... our honey is language" ("Words Rising," *Black Coat* 43). A social critic, poet, and philosopher, Bly strives to make us understand the inextricable link between human consciousness and national sentiment. These poems of the world that always are interconnected to the inner world of the speaker reveal what Robert Duncan describes as responsibility: "Responsibility is to keep / the ability to respond" ("The Law I Love Is Major Mover," quoted in Hass). Such ability, furthermore, requires a qualitative character of consciousness and implies process, what in German is termed *erlebnis*, the world as a current of consciousness that cannot be halted or measured by either categorical logic or predetermination. It takes resolution and stamina to resist being overwhelmed by a staggering amount of information and spectacle dispersed through media 24/ 7 and to take heed of the power, source, and motives behind the flood of facile phrases that now obscure urgent complex global issues.

It is with breadth, compassion, and passion that Robert Bly has been taking on the world with words. It is our responsibility, likewise, to resist letting our worlds be framed, letting ourselves be "leveled," as Bly characterizes it in *Sibling Society*, by continual, widespread controlled information. "Each of us," Bly states, "has to take the responsibility for the continuation of discipline and fineness that was once the responsibility of the people ....We have to choose" and remain visible as adults capable of resisting the hold of mass society (*Sibling Society*, 235). Such a leveling process may not seem insurmountable once we take note of the impact made by one individual whose poetry diverges from mainstream locution in often unsettling ways.

The quality of *erlebnis* reverberates throughout Bly's career, indefatigably devoted to justice and freedom, through a use of language that forcefully and effectively inveighs against all forms of subjugation. Time and time again, Bly exposes programmatic agendas and instrumental thinking that eclipse humanitarian sentiment. My total respect for and complete endorsement of Bly's efforts and injunctions makes it incumbent upon me to follow his lead with references to current examples that attest to the inherent force of language and the concomitant need to rally against instrumental language that seems to be used for ruthless, destructive purposes and to oppose its toleration.

In *The Insanity of Empire*, his 2004 book protesting the Iraq War, Bly writes, "I was surprised the other day as I read *The Light Around the Body*, a book of my own poems published in 1966, how little had changed since that time. We are still in a blindfold, still being led by the wise of this world." Finding poems from the 60s just as relevant as these published three decades later, Bly surmises: "We are still causing endless suffering with our well-known nonchalance" ("A Note About These Poems," n.p.). Yet Robert Bly has shaped thinking through language at different historical junctures with words that have roused citizens to take ethical action through the use of thoughtful language. I shall describe just a few instances to show that Bly has profoundly affected our perceptions and consequently swayed our very terms. These examples reveal how an individual's language awareness and facility can be responsible for social action.

When, in 1962, Wesleyan University Press published Bly's *Silence in the Snowy Fields*, both poets and critics were steeped in the precepts of New Criticism. Many discovered that inherited New Critical vocabularies, standards, and values were inadequate to respond to Bly's breakthrough volume. While they professed democratizing motives, American modernist New Critics—indeed, including Bly's teachers at Harvard—developed a poetics vocabulary that was university-taught and presumed to be universally available. Despite their avowed antipathy toward science, New Critics were immersed in current scientistic paradigms; thus, praise was based upon objectivist categories, the poem valorized as a self-enclosed object, machine-like, and existing apart from both poet and cultural context. Their putatively descriptive terms soon became prescriptive, and, as such, a leveling force. Bly's new vision and the poetic forms he created to contain that vision forced critics to grope for a way to describe that poetry, so different from such wonderful modernist poetry as Eliot's "Love Song of J. Alfred Prufrock." Neo-Romanticism or Deep Image poetry, for example, gained currency as descriptors apparently in tune with Bly's ideas about leaping poetry.

But just as Bly's quiet, predominantly rural poems differed from urban, self-ironizing poetry such as "Prufrock," they were also distinct from Romanticism. Although Bly's vocabulary lauded values apparently akin to those held by Wordsworth, for example, who states in his "Preface to Lyrical Ballads" that he took as much time avoiding "poetic diction ... as is ordinarily taken to produce it" (quoted in Perkins 323) and who describes the poet democratically (albeit irksomely) as "a man speaking to men" (325), Wordsworth's signature isolationism veers significantly from Bly's more responsive, communal perspective. The elevation of nature, typical of Romanticism, is coterminous with that movement's esteem of a poet's imaginative capacity as "different in degree" from other men's (327), largely equating, thereby, the status of the poem with that of the poet. Indeed, Wordsworth reveals poetry's rhetorical force, for example, in his sonnet "The World is Too Much With Us." Condemning cynical materialism, he states that "Getting and spending, we lay waste our powers;/ Little we see in Nature that is ours." Wordsworth finds himself "[f]or everything, out of tune." His recourse, however, is stamped by avoidance, as seen in his will to separate rather than act as an agent for repair. He avers that he would prefer being a "Pagan ... in a creed outworn," able to believe in Protean shape-shifting, or in the trumpeting Triton. This stated preference for retreat into the past reveals neither will nor initiative to involve himself in the work needed for change.

Even Bly's tiny poem "Watering the Horse," a poem that seems most Romantic in persuasion, and concludes in epiphany—a repeated Romantic strategy to reject religious and rationalist dogma pervasive in the 18th Century—shows how markedly his stance differs from Romantic reclusion. Although the poem's opening line, "How strange to think of giving up all ambition!" rejects a greed-based imperative—ambition—Bly proceeds—not to depart—but to immerse himself in nature by validating an alternate source of awareness at the present moment. He states, "Suddenly I see with such clear eyes/The white flake of snow/That has just fallen in the horse's mane" (*Silence* 46).

Rather than endorsing escape, this entire volume is in dialogue with its cultural context, including a relinquishment of more British vernacular and inscription of American idiom. Bly's mandate for awareness in his poem "Awakening" impels a need for historically contextual understanding "From the long past/ Into the present" (*Silence* 26). Never would he condone any excuse for the lack of awareness that ironically pervades our age of information. Being contained and content, proceeding chillingly with no understanding of history or concern for progeny, Bly avers, is the cause of our irresponsibility. In words that I think might be this generation's most potent metaphor, Bly labels the United States a "sibling society" (*The Sibling Society*). "Poem Against the Rich"(*Silence* 27) depicts a vertical dimension Bly states as lacking from a sibling society, showing that necessary awareness includes remembering the sad, historical past. Here Bly alludes to our sense of entitlement by having a so-called privileged domain in such evocative images as "weeping in the pueblos of the lily,/Or the dark tears in the shacks of corn." Bly, however, is not opting here for abandonment of any senses in this validation of intuition. He insists, rather, that we remain alert to sorrowful interiors, by exonerating the warriors—the army's interior. Bly apprehends, for example, that the expense of warfare is human lives and the land upon which they dwell, bemoaning the spectacle of "the sad rustle of the darkened armies,/Where each man weeps, and the plaintive/ Orisons of the stones." These sobering images have influenced both my conscience and awareness. There is no Thanksgiving available to me now untouched by those images, no desire to escape or ability to leave unacknowledged the fact that imperialism is inextricably tied to our pioneering of so-called virgin territory. These early poems have laid the ground, as well, for my despair regarding unprecedented military aggression taking place at this time.

Bly bristles against any form of retreat when he wrestles, for example, with what he describes in his poem "Silence" as "The sloth of the body lost among the wandering stones of/ kindness"(*Silence* 59). Opposing the superficial life, Bly concludes this book with a resounding invective against complacency. "Snowfall in the Afternoon" ends by devaluing a life lived without engagement: "All the sailors on deck have been blind for many years" (60). Certainly this is a quiet book in its presentation of a rural America with wintry snowfalls and orchards. But *Silence in the Snowy Fields*—packed with both feisty resistance and provisional reassertion—is no voiceless retreat. Instead, it endorses repair. Bly, always vigilant in redressing what our culture has occluded or debased, responds with inclusions, persuasively dismantling the exclusive authority of New Critical protocols. These different perspectives and vocabularies, therefore—gaining recognition by other poets as well as by the culture at large—have acted as a force to initiate different perspectives.

In many ways, Bly's second collection, *The Light Around the Body*, which won the National Book Award for Poetry in 1967, seemed terrifying, showing internal realms of sensitivity being conquered by external maneuvers devoid of humane motive. But again, to Bly there is always a deep connection between the country's ills and those of the soul, the interior and exterior realms being vitally dialogic. With its articulation of particular names, times, and places that historically signify culprits, locations, and material causes of American imperialism, *Light* differs radically from the spare, unpopulated poems in *Silence*. Assaults upon the administration are specific in such poems as "Listening to President Kennedy Lie about the Cuban Invasion," a poem that seems prescient now as it implores citizens to investigate the accuracy of official versions of actions that are taking place. Bly condemns "lying reporters," and concludes in dismay: "There is a bitter fatigue, adult and sad" (*Light* 16).

Bly shocked his audience when receiving the National Book Award in 1969 for *Light*, proclaiming, "I am uneasy at a ceremony emphasizing our current high state of culture. Cultural prizes, traditionally, put writers to sleep, and even the public. But we don't want to be asleep any more." Bly goes on to suggest: "In an age of gross and savage crimes by legal governments, the institutions will have to learn responsibility, learn to take their part in preserving the nation, and take their risk by committing acts of disobedience." He gave his award money to those resisting U.S. participation in the Vietnam War, denouncing the war as an act to destroy an old and rich culture, concluding that we have no right to congratulate ourselves for our "cultural magnificence" when we are "murdering" a culture in Vietnam ("Accepting," n.p.). How timely is this advice; how vital it is now to be culturally informed and ethically invested. To articulate our commitments, we must understand the context and force of current inscriptions and participate in their continual formation.

If my gesture will seem harshly polemic, I am sorry. My stance is fostered by a reverence for language, an understanding of its suasive power, and cultivated by a love of poetry that began seriously at seventeen when I read *Silence in the Snowy Fields*. As the root of polemic is *polemikos*, warlike, then my enemy is apathy in a battle waged against language deployed in the service of deplorable, unprecedented acts of military aggression. As my growing fear is that rhetorical devices are the means through which cultural lassitude is perpetrated with consequences that are globally decimating, I hope to describe and encourage language serving peaceful agendas. That an unquestioned empty signifier can take hold on public opinion may be seen in just one example of such linguistic engineering. The United States military has engaged in multinational assaults since 9/11. "9/11" locates a day, and its lack of factual content has allowed it to inspire the kind of inchoate "horror" well described in psychiatry and literature—think only of "the [undescribed] horror" in Joseph Conrad's *Heart of Darkness*. The lack of actual detail in this locution has resulted in outrageous racism and ethnic intolerance. The response to the tragic September 11, 2001 attack by terrorists on the Pentagon showed that Congress was focused upon might with hastily authorized expanded military force and emergency funding. As we proceeded to engage in unilateral preemptive strikes on so-called "rogue states," the character of the United States changed and is forever stained. Now in this so-named fight against terrorism, undermining constitutional and international law, the United States becomes a deeply discriminating force defying the rights of justice and civil liberties regarding such issues as immigration and internment. The loss of lives caused by U.S. military responses far exceeds the toll taken in this tragedy referred to by a date. An intentionally vacant carapace of the factual, "9/11," with its unlocatable "horrible other," has sabotaged a society and corraled it with collective fear. Meaningful rebuttal requires a habit of listening carefully to what is said and responding articulately and imaginatively to the matter. The character of this country never could have been sapped if we had voiced enough resistance. We could have and should have had enough population to listen carefully and speak out, and now we must.

As a force redressing this national agenda, Bly's castigation of pervasive racism as an ingredient underlying the Vietnam War should serve as a contemporary paradigm. Bly's words brought unalleviated shock and horror to awaken audiences through his expressive imagery. Bly's stance parallels a sentiment that Emmanuel Levinas—a wonderful philosopher of ethics—proposes we must endorse: the "other's" right to space, which must include an interrogation about assumptions we have concerning our own territorial rights. Bly's despair in the face of an ethical void involving racism is indicated in the very title of the poem "Counting Small-Boned Bodies" (*Light* 32). That taking responsibility for an Other has no boundaries shows throughout Bly's work, a moral imperative expressed also in Levinas's injunction that responsibility is such "that the alibi of my alterity cannot annul" (92). Bly exposes a loss of responsibility that allows us to devalue a people, a degrading disenfranchisement that may be based upon their distance from our lived environment. Bly's exposure of military language, here characterizing Vietnamese citizens as an almost different species, alerts us to the consequent savagery caused by such degradation. The rhetorical force of this poem has pounded audiences into both shock and tears, and is evoked emphatically by the incantatory force of the repeated line that begins three stanzas: "If we could only make the bodies smaller." I suggest incantation could be construed and chanted that would counter "9/11" and appall its use. Here, Bly writes:

> Let's count the bodies over again.
>
> If we could only make the bodies smaller,
> The size of skulls,
> We could make a whole plain white with skulls in the moonlight!
>
> If we could only make the bodies smaller,
> Maybe we could get
> A whole year's kill in front of us on a desk!
>
> If we could only make the bodies smaller
> We could fit
> A body into a finger-ring, for a keepsake forever.

This language does something. A poem that can infuriate can activate its audience.

What is annihilated by reading images of war's horror evinced as vividly as they are in Bly's epic and dramatic 1970 harangue *The Teeth Mother Naked at Last* is any capacity to remain aloof to atrocities committed against human beings partitioned off into some nebulous space of an abstract other. In an image that reverberates with the same power forged in Blake's "London" ("And the hapless Soldier's sigh/Runs in blood down Palace walls"), Bly describes the horrible consequences our military aggressions have wrought:

> But the room explodes,
> the children explode.
> Blood leaps on the vegetable walls. (7)

Bly exposes as deplorable both the language used to justify military action and implicitly the laxness tolerating and conditioned by evasiveness and abstraction. After Bly quotes President Johnson, for instance, as saying, "'Let us not be deterred from our task by the voices of dissent ....'"(9), he graphically depicts violent, blood-spurting scenes of murder. Later in the poem, with the resonance gained through the use of anaphoric litany, Bly condemns this military action as motivated by monstrous greed, and reveals how the deployment of abstraction works to obfuscate violence. "This is what it's like" begins the first four lines in section III. "This is what it's like for a rich country to make war, [...] to bomb huts (afterwards described as 'structures') [...] to kill marginal farmers (afterwards described as 'Communists')" (13). When the focus shifts to the vast differences between the two cultures, Bly demolishes any sense that stature is attained by affluence. Capitalism is imaged as a force destroying impoverished existence, as Bly envisions "what it's like to have a gross national product," to "send firebombs down ... from air-conditioned cockpits, [...] to fire into a reed hut with an automatic weapon" (14).

Stark and terrifying capacity for atrocious slaughter is brought home through Bly's foreboding cinematic imagery, again intertwining the public and private dimensions. Influenced by Arthur Koestler's rendering of Paul MacLean's theory of the three brains, Bly presents the brain as a terrifying structure housing devolution, posing a possibility of atavistic slippage into a subhuman species:

> If one of those children came toward me with both hands
> in the air, fire rising along both elbows,
> I would suddenly go back to my animal brain,
> I would drop on all fours, screaming,
> my vocal cords would turn blue, yours would too,
> it would be two days before I could play with my own
> children again. (20)

This poem, like many of Bly's poems, initiates resistances to all kinds of bifurcation, rejecting binary thinking that segregates populations by dividing a purported "us" from an abstracted "them" to separating national sentiment from private consciousness. What cannot be overstated here is the significance of reading such words as these. Bly's perpetual challenge to public discourse portraying the degraded victim in indelible language simply defies complacency. I know of no single person who has reached out to more diverse populations and who has informed us about different cultures so deeply and humanely. His gift has endowed us with loving regard for so many peoples. I know of no greater investment and I am in awe of that investment and the impact it has had. Anyone who has read these words will be unable to tolerate either the phrasing that lacks any moral equivalency and categorically excludes culpability or bear to watch the destruction brought on by systematic and governmentally sanctioned bombing.

New Critical strictures that a poet ought to be separated from his or her stance in the poem certainly are incommensurate to Bly's task here. At first, when Bly gave more than a half-dozen readings during the Vietnam War at rural, midwest Illinois State University, I felt uncertainty about Bly's performative presentation, including his donning of hideous masks. These readings forced me to acknowledge my own paradigmatic blinders. Audiences filled huge auditoriums, with unheard-of standing ovations after readings that often lasted more than two hours. Bly's work worked. Again, his signature personal immersion and involvement contributed to such success.

Besides this departure from both modernist stances and typical decorum at university revealing, I personally observed a wonderful consequence of Bly's trust in his intuition after a reading. I was driving Robert Bly to my house for a reception, navigating the winding single-lane parking lot of Illinois State University's Adlai Stevenson Hall. Without apparent cause, Bly suddenly directed me to "Stop!" Naturally, I did. He got out of the car and just stood there.

I am here with Robert Bly, while cars are skirting my car, and trailing to my house, for his reception. Minutes later, a man older than most students—in bib overalls, no less—emerges from the building in tears. When Bly approaches him, the man relates that he has never been to a poetry reading before and has never in his life been so moved. Of course, Bly proceeded to invite him to my home. So uncanny! So typical of Bly!

No rational explanation is sufficient to explain events clearly outside its logic. The question remains: How did Bly do both, what awareness was granted validity, when, after a poetry event during which he railed against current government aggressions, he knew that a man who needed him was *about* to become visible? Models I understood that accounted for perception in terms of signifier-signified couldn't yield any explanation for what I unquestionably, actually saw. Ambiguity lacks closure, precluding possibility when assumptions reify into reality paradigms bound by categorical thinking and sense data. A lesson learned once again from Robert Bly: one needs to retain a questioning mind; this is not some needless burden.

Bly's tutelage has influenced more than academics to appreciate varying sources of awareness and grant themselves permission to extend their vocabularies. Many of us attempting to keep up with his range of interests find and increasingly appreciate what could be construed as incompatible sources of authority. Bly hints at the implications and effects of exclusion brought on through specialization in *A Little Book on the Human Shadow* (1988), maintaining that we are born with "360-degree radiance" (17). Yet, as early as *Light*, in "Those Being Eaten by America," Bly finds "The light in children's faces fading at six or seven" (14). The cause of my worry shifted from performative style to academic restraint. I have come to fear the repercussions due to a lack of effective expression of outrage against such initiatives that since 2003, for example, have caused the death of 98,098-107,075 Iraqi civilians. (IBC, Iraqi Body Count reported as of 4 September 2010. "This data is based on 23,288 database entries from the beginning of the war to 4 September 2010.")

Always rejecting dichotomous imperatives about what should be embraced and what reviled, Bly continues to honor and recognize value inherent in presently inimical cultures, as seen, for example, in his collection *The Night Abraham Called to the Stars* (2004). Despite his nod in the poem "In Praise of Scholars" toward "hundreds of scholars [at] work in the basement," who are "good students of the ten thousand things" ("Without them we would be at war forever") (49), this volume's second poem, "The Wildebeest," more convincingly addresses Bly's perspective that "The essence of Reason's house is confusion"(3). The line "Arithmetic has failed to bring order to our sorrow" confirms Bly's awareness of reality that may be rationally inscrutable. The opening of "The Baal Shem and Francis Bacon" declares that "'The Five Ways of Knowing the World' worries me" (63). Rather astonishingly again, Bly confounds ordinary boundaries with a poem that embraces both Francis Bacon—reportedly the founder of inductive reasoning—and Baal Shem—a Jewish mystical, rather pantheistic rabbi, said to be the founder of Hasidic Judaism, whose capacity to enact miracles is legendary. Inscribing honorific recognition of vastly different times and cultures counters divisiveness, taking down both cultural and paradigmatic boundaries. Bly's continual struggle with cultural conditioning and intervention against received strategies and authorities seen in such a poem serves as a model for undertaking such a resistive task.

As a personal example of the influence Bly's language had on extending my parameters, I recognize that, although born and reared in a not too distant Midwest state, my urban, ethnic upbringing left me unfamiliar with the fabric of life presented in the rural poetic settings of his early work. The acquaintance and appreciation that I gained from Bly's distinct images of these silent landscapes and his portraits of its people prohibited my assigning or accepting abstract, generalized assumptions about an other. Similarly, both the men's movement and the volume *Loving a Woman in Two Worlds* (1985) caused me to revise my own precepts, principles I regarded as both conscientious and valid. While I don't question my motives, my contentions were situated in a previous historic moment. In my work at that time I already felt more inclined to depart from many past assumptions and adhere to more motile principles—openness, attentiveness, and becoming—more related to the theories developed by Gilles Deleuze and Felix Guattari. To suggest a nomadic pattern, they use the metaphor of the rhizome, whose paths of growth cannot be foreseen. Such a course counters paralyzing, foreclosing inscriptions. Deleuze and Guattari apply rhizomatic growth, which cannot be prepatterned, to subjectivity, which then would remain open to options that may be heretofore unscripted; that may, indeed, be imagined. My initial response to the men's movement, however, perpetuated a stance that I valued, that was grafted mainly from different voices in feminism. I thought, "That's all we need, another male initiation story." In his dissertation and a later essay published in *Centennial Review*, my son, Greg Harris, was a staunch and convincing supporter of the men's movement. And, obviously, history has shown that I was way out of step with my own culture. Bly was right on target to intuit that many of those who shared his antiwar sentiments, for example, had relinquished also some grounding for male energy. I don't need to rehearse the countless testimonials from men of all ages who regarded this movement as an almost saving grace.

Loving a Woman in Two Worlds triggered another reaction informed by various discourses against gender discrimination, such as the kind of voyeurism in cinema that typically poses the female as an object for the male gaze. For decades I fought that kind of objectification. But gradually I became aware that, if decontextualized and sedimented, even such a principled thought may foreclose imaginative openness and consequently be misappropriated. Despite my early misguided argument to the contrary (see earlier analysis of *Loving a Woman* in *The Incorporative Consciousness of Robert Bly*, 126-146), a woman being used as an object for a male subject, or as a body for speculation, is not what Bly describes in his love poems. More open and interactive engagement proved to be creative for me, generating new associations and responses. I saw in these poems a logic of embrace not reference, an embrace having affinity with a line from Rumi that Bly uses as the title of a section in his collection *The Soul Is Here for Its Own Joy* (1995), "Loving God Through Loving a Woman or a Man" (133). Bly's poems portray sexuality explicitly in bodies that are cared for and bonded in a real, physical, and, most poignantly perhaps, unidealized context.

Mine were difficult conversions, and I am thankful to Bly for words that demanded both renegotiation and revision. Here, too, I had an opportunity to realize that what remains valid and what should not be sustained cannot be codified in an objectified, atemporal space. The sensual symbolic elements in Bly's lovely poem "At the Time of Peony Blossoming" continue to move me—I have it on my wall, as do my children:

> When I come near the red peony flower
> I tremble as water does near thunder,
> As the well does when the plates of earth move,
> Or the tree when fifty birds leave at once.
>
> The peony says that we have been given a gift,
> And it is not the gift of this world.
> Behind the leaves of the peony
> There is a world still darker, that feeds many. (*Loving* 31)

One doesn't have to be well versed in the paintings of Georgia O'Keefe to understand the sexy yonic imagery of the peony blossom. It is a gorgeous poem, featuring sensual imagery that lasts and lasts.

"The Horse of Desire" concludes in imagery that is openly anatomical, here referring to the male.

> The bear between my legs
> Has one eye only,
> Which he offers
> To God to see with.
> The two beings below with no
> Eyes at all love you
> With the slow persistent
> Intensity of the blind. (*Loving* 65)

This imagery, again, is explicit, and the attraction is a physical force. That the sensuality within these poems is described as ordinary seems to invest the real with a sense of holiness—an oddity again not based in rational logic, but routinely accepted by Bly. In "The Good Silence," for example, Bly writes:

> I take your hand as we work, neither of us speaking.
> This is the old union of man and woman,
> nothing extraordinary; they both feel a deep
> calm in the bones. It is ordinary affection
> that our bodies experienced for ten thousand years.

Continuing later in the poem, Bly writes:

> And we did what we did, made love attentively, then
> dove into the river, and our bodies joined as calmly
> as the swimmer's shoulders glisten at dawn ...

In conclusion Bly states:

> And one day my faithfulness to you was born.
> We sit together silently at the break of day.
> We sit an hour, then tears run down my face.
> "What is the matter?" you say looking over.
> I answer, "'The ship saileth on the salte foam.'" (*Loving* 73)

The sexual imagery remains: ship, "salte foam," but once again Bly reveals the ordinary to be extraordinary—"[n]othing extraordinary" as this faithfulness, is signified here. This faithfulness, though, is born of such love that tears begin to flow. While I'm not convinced of the ordinariness attributed to such experience, I am responsive and totally engaged in the ecological momentum involved in taking physical care, and regarding the other with awe.

On a larger scale, the opportunity to recontextualize is clearly pertinent to the previously cited *The Soul Is Here for Its Own Joy*, Bly's anthology of sacred poems from a wide range of religious traditions, historical periods, and literary movements. Here, new perceptions arise from a book that for many crosses new thresholds. Through Bly's translations we encounter spiritual investments around the globe, from voices often previously unheard. As we become familiar with varying identities and cultural priorities, so do we access information that may encourage what is so urgently important right now: taking heed of widespread generalizations about national identities and reassessing their validity.

Understanding that language possesses such enabling valence ought also to impel us, as witnesses to this voice, to be in the service of articulate communication in any and every way possible. On October 17, 2004, Bly wrote an editorial column in the *Minneapolis Star Tribune*, stating: "We all know the invasion of Iraq was a hare-brained act, a colossal mistake." He then shifts to national grounds, describing the deterioration of the United States—"collapsing schools, ... failing factories ... huge increase of poverty"—and imploring citizens not to close their eyes, to take in the truth of "hundreds of soldiers in the coffin and millions of demoralized citizens." And he seeks action, surmising that "[w]e have all participated in the national and self-pleasing prevarication that a C-student can guide the country in a time of complicated issues ... that a man who doesn't read books can guide the fate of nations." He relates concomitantly the need to invest in the shaping of a literate, learned society whose spokespersons will speak deliberatively. In *The Sibling Society*, Bly refers to a study involving 1,200 subjects reporting that

> more skill and concentration was needed to eat a meal than to watch television, and the watching left people passive, yet tense, and unable to concentrate.

> Television provides a garbage dump ... that stuns the brain....
> (140)

Audiences remaining nonchalant about the misuse of language as well as their own use of language irresponsibly fail to discern geopolitical motives, and they absolve themselves of a citizen's duty to protest. We must analyze how such labels, such as "threats to security," shift focus and unconvincingly cause a sense of instability that frightens and subdues listeners. Attention to language generates perspicacious thought, as Bly avers in *The Lightning Should Have Fallen on Ghalib* (1999), stating in his introduction that "Ghalib's lines, so elegant and sparse, stretch the muscles that we use for truth, muscles we rarely use" (2). His sense that experience with language enhances discernment becomes clear in the following three-line stanza from "The Storyteller's Way":

> It's because the storytellers have been so faithful
> That all these tales of infidelity come to light.
> It's the job of the faithful to evoke the unfaithful. (*The Night* 85).

The teller has this job, and the audience, in turn, unlike "a man who doesn't read," has become better equipped for meaningful response. We allow countries to be endangered if we remain passive to public opinion being manipulated through such strategies as designating nations as threats. Indeed, as Bly states in "The Cry Going Out Over Pastures," "We cannot remain in love with what we cannot name ... " (*This Body*, 59), and I suggest that we could not bear the destruction of what we love. *The World Factbook*, published by the Central Intelligence Agency, estimates the population of Iran at 66,429,284 (July 2010, September 16, 2010 update). Yet the media uses the CIA's term and designates this country as a "rogue state," Iran being reductively insulted as simply a terrifying potential nuclear threat. Bly portrays a different Iran, relating a story of visiting the grave of Hafez in Iran and being amazed that a group of school children were there singing his poems by heart. The words of ancient poet Hafez, then, remain a significant vernacular within the

Iranian population. And the "news" of Hafez has come to Americans most prominently through Robert Bly. These words enter our consciousness of Iran differently than the widely heard military rhetoric, and enable us to withstand and oppose undermining representation imposed upon us. This one example shows subjectivity forming through attention to expressive language.

Significantly, this depiction portrays what value inheres in words that differ from abstract designations. Likewise, this should encourage careful enunciation and enable resistance to language that really severs the designated from such designation. Robert Bly brings cultural awareness using criteria of validity absent from our mass media representations, highlighting rich cultural voices and rituals. This poet's singular effort reveals the potential of such language to enlarge popular perceptions. I suggest that Bly's remarkable stance—his vigilance and moral obligation to take on the world with words—attests as well to an inherent capacity of literature to help shape national formulations.

Bly so encourages our participation in thoughtful reform, with the caveat, however, that resistance requires fluency. At the conclusion of his poem "Advice From the Geese," for instance, Bly warns:

> Give up the idea that the world will get better by itself.
> You will not be forgiven if you refuse to study. (*Insanity of Empire* 5)

Anyone reading his anthologies and translations would contest and disable representation of rich and varied cultures through the use of distortive, diminishing, and degrading abstractions. One cannot dismiss the ghazals of Ghalib as vague or foreign after reading *My Sentence Was a Thousand Years of Joy* (2005). Bly is enlarging an appreciation of poetic form as well, stating "[i]t slowly becomes clear that we are dealing with a way of adventuring one's way through a poem utterly distinct from our habit of textual consistency in theme" (*The Lightning* 5).

While wending his way along a path continually extending and rhizomatically winding, Bly sustains his unswerving signature motive: to redress inequity. He provides a model for refusing any assumption that there are overwhelming obstacles that keep citizens from including their voices. Is it possible to read Bly's words or to be in the habit of deliberative reading in general and not analyze underlying uses and motives in sweeping yet unspecific emotive language? We cannot tolerate cynical, emotive epithets to infringe upon constitutional protections, as "axis of evil" has been used to support administrative eavesdropping and attacks upon nations. Can we possibly allow the use of labels that sweep away particulars, such as 9/11, to justify assaults upon floating enemies? Can we tolerate an indulgence in programmed television that impairs reflection and deliberation, that reports and makes a visual spectacle of massive destruction while concomitantly running baseball scores along the bottom of the screen? That proffers such nonsense projects that have audiences passively sitting to watch a "reality" program? That allows the imperative of speed to arbitrate against mentation by using catchy sound bite slogans to supplant thoughtfulness? To allow news reporting to be replaced largely by rhetorical personalities?

And, how many "Ground Zeros" exist in Iraq, Iran, Pakistan, Afghanistan? What are the implications and complicities housed in phrases such as "pre-emptive strikes"? What "security reasons" or "states of exception" should trump constitutional provisions? Bly's refusal to separate literary composition from cultural-political invocation reveals the importance of attention to such language.

Clearly not restricted to "aesthetic" response or matters of "poetics," Bly's avowal that words can respond in "Call and Answer" is a rebuttal to the arena of nonchalance, inveighing us to have enough courage to resist an entire culture of passive reception. Acknowledging that refusing dormancy may involve protesting dominant discourse, Bly impels such active engagement, challenging us to participate in cultural dialogue with courage. This is a clarion call to use language as a catalyst for peace:

> Tell me why it is we don't lift our voices these days
> And cry over what is happening. Have you noticed
> The plans are made for Iraq and the ice cap is melting?

I say to myself: "Go on, cry. What's the sense
Of being an adult and having no voice? Cry out!
See who will answer! This is Call and Answer!"

We will have to call especially loud to reach
Our angels, who are hard of hearing; they are hiding
In the jugs of silence filled during our wars.

Have we agreed to so many wars that we can't
Escape from silence? If we don't lift our voices, we allow
Others (who are ourselves) to rob the house.

How come we've listened to the great criers—Neruda,
Akhmatova, Thoreau, Frederick Douglass—and now
We're silent as sparrows in the little bushes?

Some masters say our life lasts only seven days.
Where are we in the week? Is it Thursday yet?
Hurry, cry now! Soon Sunday night will come. (*My Sentence* 27)

Robert Bly may not be a committee's first choice to serve as National Poet Laureate if this honor mandates either reticence or blanket affirmation of United States policy. The humane ethos that pervades Bly's poetry is an ethos that remains borderless. His poetry, translations, and essays that engage international perspectives just might help inaugurate care for the other that is not constricted by national identities. It may enhance our own capacity to be neither beholden nor referential to predominant forms of representation. The great war now—of ecological proportions—ought to be waged against disengagement.

I suggest that we keep listening to Robert Bly who, now in his eighties, continues to be passionately driven to encounter and understand unfolding realities. Suggesting process, the poem "The Donkey's Ear" ends with a question. This poem, concluding the volume *Eating the Honey of Words* (1999), begins by stating, "I've been talking into the ear of a donkey. I have so much to say ...." The poem ends with a question indicating that Bly remains open to new venues: "Am I changing my road ... ?" (270).

Travelling along a changing road his entire life and driven by his felt cultural obligations to humanity without borders, Bly has tirelessly engaged our society with a capacity to affect social conscience. For this gift I am humbly grateful. For such a feat, in this turmoil of global warfare, Robert Bly, the first Poet Laureate of Minnesota, should be awarded the Nobel Peace Prize.

WORKS CITED

Bly, Robert. *Silence in the Snowy Fields*. Middletown: Wesleyan University Press, 1962.

—*The Light Around the Body*. New York: Harper, 1967.

—"Acceptance of the National Book Award for Poetry." <http://www.english.illinois.edu/maps/poets/a_f/bly/award.htm>.

—*The Teeth Mother Naked at Last*. San Francisco: City Lights, 1970.

—*Leaping Poetry: An Idea with Poems and Translations*. A Seventies Press Book. Boston: Beacon, 1975.

—*This Body is Made of Camphor and Gopherwood*. New York: Harper, 1977.

—*Loving a Woman in Two Worlds*. Garden City: Dial, 1985.

—*Selected Poems*. New York: Harper, 1986.

—ed. William Booth, *A Little Book on the Human Shadow*. New York: HarperCollins, 1988.

—*Iron John: A Book about Men*. Reading: Addison-Wesley, 1990.

—*What Have I Ever Lost by Dying?* New York: HarperCollins, 1992.

—ed. *The Soul Is Here for Its Own Joy: Sacred Poems from Many Cultures*. Hopewell: Ecco, 1995.

—*The Sibling Society*. Reading: Addison-Wesley, 1996.

—*Eating the Honey of Words: New and Selected Poems*. New York: HarperCollins, 1999.

—and Sunil Dutta, eds. *The Lightning Should Have Fallen on Ghalib: Selected Poems of Ghalib*. Trans. Bly and Dutta. Hopewell, Ecco, 1999.

—*The Night Abraham Called to the Stars*. New York: HarperCollins, 2001.

—*The Insanity of Empire: A Book of Poems Against the Iraq War*. St. Paul: Ally Press, 2004.

—"Editorial: The Emperor Has No Clothes." *Minneapolis Star Tribune*, 17 Oct 2004. <http://www.robertbly.com/news-editorial.html>.

—*My Sentence Was a Thousand Years of Joy*. New York: HarperCollins, 2005.

—and Leonard Lewisohn. *The Angels Knocking on the Tavern Door: Thirty Poems of Hafez*. New York: HarperCollins, 2009.

Deleuze, Gilles and Félix Guattari. *A Thousand Plateaus: Capitalism and Schizophrenia*. Trans. Brian Massumi. Minneapolis: University of Minnesota Press, 1987.

Harris, Greg. "Recontextualizing Iron John for the Il(mytho)literate." *The Centennial Review* 53.2 (Spring 1999): 353-376.

Harris, Victoria. *The Incorporative Consciousness of Robert Bly*. Carbondale: Southern Illinois University Press, 1992.

Hass, Robert. "The Consequences: An Interview with Robert Hass." *Guernica* (Jan 2008). http://www.guernicamag.com/interviews/429/the consequences_an_interview.

IBC. http://www.iraqbodycount.org (4 September 2010).

Levinas, Emmanuel. *Outside the Subject*. Meridian: Crossing Aesthetics. Stanford: Stanford University Press, 1994.

Perkins, David, ed. *English Romantic Writers*. New York: Harcourt, 1967.

The World Factbook. https://www.cia.gov/library/publications/the-world-factbook/geos/ir.html (20 September 2010).

ROBERT BLY'S POETRY: THE LATER YEARS

By Howard Nelson

I would like to dedicate this essay to the memory of John Unterecker, who asked me in 1980 to write a book on Robert Bly for the Columbia University Press series on 20th century poets. Jack was a small man of large energy, a Yeats scholar, biographer of Hart Crane, editor, professor, poet. He was also a generous man. I met him at an NEH Summer Seminar that he was leading. About half-way through, he asked me if I would be interested in writing a book for the Columbia series, of which he was founder and general editor. I was startled. Me, write a book for the Columbia series? But, I accepted. I didn't think of it in these terms at the time, but Jack's invitation was in a way a spiritual gesture. An older man showing interest and confidence in a younger man. The kind of act that Robert Bly has written about in detail, and told us much about. Maybe you could call it a kind of initiation. In any case, it was one of those acts of support that the younger man eventually comes to see for what it was, and never forgets.

At that time the Columbia series included books on Theodore Roethke, Hart Crane, Marianne Moore, Ezra Pound, Langston Hughes, Wallace Stevens, and E.E. Cummings. Looking at that roster, one might not expect that the next poet would be Robert Bly, but Jack was looking to the next generation. At the same time he was asking me about a book on Bly, he also had books on Robert Lowell, John Ashbery, and James Merrill in the works. Jack was not hemmed in by the partisanship of schools of poetry that was strong in those days. Unfortunately, the Columbia series died with Jack, but it was an important contribution. I think of him as a person who played his role well, one of the benevolent, liberal, ecumenical, large-minded priests of the church of poetry.

Once I started writing, the job was of course harder than I'd imagined. For one thing, besides writing about Bly's poetry itself, which I'd been reading intensely for ten years or so, I found myself responsible for fields of knowledge I did not know what you would call, *well*. For example, Jung. I had heard Bly say at a reading that Jung was "the greatest man of the last 500 years." It was one of those recommendations that catches your attention—a kind of statement that Bly has always been good at. So as I was writing along about the snow and the barns and dusks of *Silence in the Snowy Fields*, the book that had originally drawn me to Bly's work, with what felt like a mixture of deep pleasure and instinct; and as I was trying to be articulate about the poetry "in the white spaces between the stanzas," which was where Bly had said in a jacket note that the poetry in those poems would be found; and while I was trying to navigate the fierce visionary political and social poems of *The Light Around the Body*, and the subject of the Vietnam War, and the issue of whether it is possible to write poems that are both protest and poetry, which was a controversial question at the time—at the same time I was writing about these books which had arrived in my consciousness like oracles, I was giving myself a crash course in Jung. I knew I was also going to have to write about "Sleepers Joining Hands," a long poem that gave signs of being saturated in Jungian influence, and which sat in its book right next to a powerful essay about The Great Mother archetype. I also knew that Bly had said in the essay, "nor should anyone examine my own poems for evidence of [these ideas], for most of my poems were written without benefit of them," but I didn't quite believe him about that. As I read my commentary on "Sleepers" now, it seems conscientious but a little creaky. I can tell you that the chapter was in fact checked over by a certified Jungian, who said it was good—no problem. But my point is, it is a challenge in writing about Bly's work, more than with most poets, I think: the mind inside it is dynamic and far-ranging. It is like a horse—not one that settles into a particular pasture. It is a horse that likes to run, and which in its wanderings is always discovering new springs and groves. Well, the horse is a metaphor, and a little homage to Bly's critical essays, especially the early ones, which he would often conclude with an image rather than an abstract statement; for example, when he compared reading W.S. Merwin poems to finding a message in the kitchen left by a glacier, or when he said of James Dickey in his early books that he was "like a big moose adapted somehow to living beneath the water in some calm inland lake. The moose is constantly rising to the surface and breaking water so he can see his own huge horns in the sunlight, and giving a fixed and strange smile to the frightened bourgeoisie out fishing." My image isn't as good as those, but you get my drift: One of the challenges of reading Robert Bly's poetry is its expansive sense of boundaries, and how the horse is always getting out of the barn. You don't always find him where you expect him. This has remained true throughout his writing life.

When my book was published in 1983, Bly's most recent collection was *The Man in the Black Coat Turns*. Looking back at it, I see that in the final chapter I noticed the influence of fairy tales in some of the poems; also, an emerging theme of re-evaluation of the masculine. I wrote, "Bly entered the study of fairy tales through Jung, and it has been a major phase of his activities since. He has lectured widely on the subject, sometimes including the telling of a story in his readings, and in 1981 he began work on a book-length study of classic fairy tales as they apply to men...." I was on the right track there. We know what happened after that. *Iron John*. The men's movement, or the men's movements—whatever we may call it, some movement among men. Bill Moyers made his PBS program, "A Gathering of Men." There were many conferences, where men did in fact sit and listen to poems and folktales, and drum together into the night. They told their own stories, and sometimes shed tears. All of this was a phenomenon that was welcomed by satirists, *Newsweek* reporters, and other conventional thinkers, but something serious was going on. Many books were published, but it was *Iron John* that was the large, strange spark. If someone had said that a book based on the analysis of a fairy tale, a serious book, aimed at men, written by a poet, with many references to poems and poets, would become a national best-seller, a reasonable reaction would have been, "Not very likely," or "Impossible." But Bly managed to make exactly that happen, and if you want to point to a remarkable accomplishment in his literary career, they don't come more remarkable than that—nobody else could have done it.

Out of the conferences and the thinking about men's lives also came the anthology *The Rag and Bone Shop of the Heart*, edited by Bly with Michael Meade and James Hillman—a marvelous book, not only for its gathering of poems but also for its short, provocative essays, and for the conception of masculinity that the poems and the essays and the structure of the book itself set forth. Maybe it needs a few more sections, perhaps on Sports or Hunting or Cars and Trucks. But if the men of America read poetry more, and if they wanted a book as a resource on the male soul for themselves and for their sons, they already have it in *The Rag and Bone Shop of the Heart*.

But what about Bly's own poetry of this period? Three books appeared in the years around *Iron John*. There was *Loving a Woman in Two Worlds*, in 1985, a collection of love poems.

THE TWO RIVERS

Inside us there is a river born in the good cold
that longs to give itself to the Gulf of light.
And there is another river more like the Missouri
that carries earth, and earth joys, and the earthly.

The book tips toward the second river, about how "the loving man simmers his porcupine stew," and how the angel Gabriel loves honey but also enjoys "our own radishes and walnuts." What Bly seems to want in these poems is to create a mood of balanced passion and grounded love. There are several that describe the union between a man and a woman, the creation of "A Third Body," as one title puts it, but there are also constant reminders that the union is not perfect. In "Listening to the Koln Concert," he says that "animals/ abandon all their money each year"; for men and women in love, it is "their longing for the perfect" that needs to be abandoned, in order to "enter the nest/ made by the other imperfect bird."

There's a delicacy about these poems, and an indirectness when talking about sexuality. They prefer to speak through images of hummingbirds, or exchanging bread and salt, or ferns on the bank of a stream. Sometimes the images are a little precious, and sometimes they hit it just right. As an expression of desire, the simple lines that end the book's final poem, "In the Month of May," are both delicate and straightforward: "Along the roads, I see so many places/ I would like us to spend the night."

Also during this period Bly continued to work extensively in the prose poem. The original Kayak Press chapbook edition of *The Morning Glory* grew into a larger edition, and then became *What Have I Ever Lost By Dying?* in 1992. I'll say more about the prose poems later. And then there was, in 1994, *Meditations on the Insatiable Soul*. It was not a large book, but it was heavy. It had a lot of what Bly once referred to as "psychic weight." It is about as light or light-hearted as its title suggests: *Meditations on the Insatiable Soul*. The words sink into the page. The cover illustration was Blake's Behemoth, a primitive heavy-headed, deep-ribbed, thick-footed, hippopotamus-like creature, and it was a good choice for this book.

I take this book as a product of its time, in both personal and public terms. I also see it as a transitional book, holding some seeds that would flower later in very different ways. The poems are dense, and they don't feel entirely comfortable with one another. Even the poem that mentions "the gaiety of form" and "the glad body" do not feel especially gay or glad. "The gaiety of form lies in the labor of its playfulness," the poem says, but I feel more of the conscious labor than playfulness there. If you want true playfulness in form, wait, it will come—but playfulness is not a word that connects with *Meditations on the Insatiable Soul*. A beautiful and moving poem called "Gratitude to Old Teachers" begins in high spirits, but it quickly reveals an uneasiness, and the teachers are down below, in the deep waters of the lake. The poem that begins in buoyancy ends in depth and stillness.

The first poem in Bly's sequence about Wallace Stevens is here, but it is a criticism, not an homage. It calls Stevens to account for not paying enough attention to suffering: "As if we could walk always high above the world,/ No bears, no witches, no MacBeth,/ No one screaming, no one in pain, no one afraid." There is also a poem about a sculpture of St. George fighting the dragon, and the poem takes the side of the dragon, ending with a blessing upon "The swamp monster/ And the marsh hag/ Who bore him." Another spiny beast appears in a poem in which the poet and his father are swimming in the ocean together. Well, not together exactly—half a mile apart, and the beast is off in the distance, coming after both of them, and the ocean floor below is littered with old engine-blocks and broken farm machinery. There's foreboding and wreckage in these poems. And there is a prophetic, Whitmanesque-nightmare poem called "Anger against Children," which ends with the line, "The time of manifest destiny is over, the time of grief has come." The book's title poem, perhaps inspired by Whitman's great diatribe "Respondez," ("Let murderers, thieves, bigots, fools, unclean persons, offer new propositions!... Let freedom prove no man's inalienable right! every one who can tyrannize, let him tyrannize to his satisfaction!") gives this assessment of the state of the nation and the culture:

> Some ill-smelling, libidinous, worm-shouldered
> Deep-reaching desirousness rules the countryside.
> Let sympathy pass, a stranger, to other shores!
> Let the love between men and women be ground up
> And fed to the talk shows! Let every female breast
> Be photographed! Let the father be hated! Let the son be hated!
> Let twelve-year-olds kill the twelve-year-olds!
> The Great Lord of Desirousness ruling all.

Bly has always taken a Jeremiah-like view of American mass culture and political realities. *Meditations on the Insatiable Soul* is reminiscent of *The Light around the Body*, with bitterness to the tongue and heavy, ominous images for the spirit to absorb, even though the Vietnam War had ended.

I don't say that Bly wrote it for this reason, but if ever a book was likely to get a person off *People* magazine's list of "Most Intriguing People," where Bly had landed in the *Iron John* years, this would be it. The poet may be intriguing, but not in qualities that *People* magazine likes to emphasize. He's not charming; he's not trying to be likable or a "human interest" story; he doesn't say what people want to hear. Is the book public or private? There's not a simple answer to that, but perhaps we can feel in it the skin of a man who has faced criticism and ridicule for proposing that masculinity needs not only reexamination but also care. It may be that the burden of the public man is part of the weight of these poems. Some of the weight may come from having listened to many men tell their stories in an intensified atmosphere of ritual and grief.

Something else was happening as well: a man was coming to terms with his relationship with his own father. The public and mythological thought that went into *Iron John* was deeply tied to the private thought and emotion of contemplating one's own father—specifically, an aging father, a father approaching death. At men's conferences, much of the talk was about fathers, and in my experience at least, when poems were read, Bly's contributions usually included his gradually accumulating, slowly evolving series of poems about his father. It is these poems that are the center of gravity, and the most memorable, in *Meditations on the Insatiable Soul*.

They were written mostly in the skinny form of Neruda's *Odas Elementales*, but they have none of the sprightliness of Neruda's lines; Bly uses the narrow line for a different end. Instead of spontaneity, their movement down the page has a feeling of distillation, of trying to get down the essence of difficult feelings, with a determination not to allow any falseness or wishful thinking to slip in. In the midst of the sequence there are two poems that turn from the father to the mother, and there, a more tender tone enters. One of these, "Sitting with My Father and Mother," is the best poem I know about life—that is, the end of life—in those places we call nursing homes. But the tenderness toward the father is harsh. The poems do not come up with the answers we might want to hear; not recollections of good times together. Instead, there is something tough, bitter, and irresolvable in them. They are a powerful utterance. I think that's the right word—I don't want to suggest anything too lyrical. You can feel the effort to get this right, to say this truth. They do not tell the whole story. The father will continue to appear in years and poems to come. He will call home in dreams, from some other town where he stands alone on a cold street in the middle of the night. There will be a poem that notices "that lovely calm in my father's/ Hands, as he buttoned his coat" ("I Have Daughters and I Have Sons"). But this sequence of poems gives us something essential and difficult:

> If I do not wish
> To shame him, then
> Why not love him?
> His long hands,
> Large, veined,
> Capable, can still
> Retain hold of what
> He wanted. But
> Is that what he
> Desired? Some
> Powerful engine
> Of desire goes on
> Turning inside his body.
> He never phrased
> What he desired,
> And I am
> his son.
> ***
> Now you bring that
> Defiance to death.
> This four-year-old
> Old man in you does as
> He likes: he likes
> To stay alive.
> Through him you
> Get revenge,
> Persist, endure,
> Overlive, overwhelm,
> Get on top.
> You gave me
> This, and I do
> Not refuse it.
> It is
> In me.

They are about the intense knot of father and son, the recognition of how inextricable the father is, and they accept the father's rough gift.

The father in those poems is something other than a mentor. He is elemental, but not someone we choose, or who chooses us. The father is at the center of *Meditations on the Insatiable Soul*, but mentors are present too, in "Gratitude to Old Teachers" and in poems dedicated, in one way or another, to three of Bly's most important mentors: Joseph Campbell, Wallace Stevens, and William Stafford. In Bly's next collection, those last two step in and provide inspiration and guidance. They are not just acknowledged in individual poems; they are presiding spirits. I wonder what Wallace Stevens and William Stafford would say to one another if they were in a room together. I can imagine a cautious, reserved sort of conversation. But in Bly's next book, *Morning Poems*, they mingle in a different way, and the book is about as different from *Meditations on the Insatiable Soul* as it could be. From Stafford came the practice of writing a poem every day, in the morning—the discipline of just seeing what might come. It's not clear whether Bly did his writing as early as Stafford, who arose in the pre-dawn dark—but the book's title and opening poem announce the ritual: morning, coffee, the writing of poems, following whatever thread appears, under Stafford's belief (in the phrasing he took from William Blake) that any thread might lead to a kingdom. What kingdom? Blake said the thread might lead to Jerusalem. It's more like Stafford in these poems; a little more casual, less exalted than going to Jerusalem. In any case, what is found is some nourishment for the soul, found in the kingdom of the imagination. That's where Wallace Stevens comes in. Now there are several poems to Stevens, still with some complaints about him being too detached, and with some differences of opinion concerning statements Stevens made about the gods, but underneath, clearly, much admiration. There's a sequence of eight poems called "It's As If Someone Else Is with Me," about the act of writing poems (one of Stevens' favorite subjects), which says:

I've been thinking about these little adventures
In morning longing—these embarkations,
Excursions in round hide-boats on the sea [....]

Stevens would have taken some other craft, more elegant that a hide-boat, but otherwise the lines sound like something he might have said. He would have liked the words "embarkations" and "excursions"; they would have appealed to his exploratory mind. In another poem in the sequence, there are these lines:

It's morning and it's calm. And the man
Writes along, inviting this detail
And that—looking toward some playful life.
What life? Oh never mind—the life of language.
And thinking [....]

So it appears that Bly accepted the blessing of Stafford's disciplined casualness, and Stevens' reliance on imagination, and together they became the wellspring of a wonderful book. It is a book about mourning as well as morning, but there's more pleasure than sorrow now. The pleasure of writing, of reflecting, of being alone with language and one's thoughts—one's thoughts on this, and that, and the other. The pleasure is not just the poet's, but the reader's as well. I get many things from Bly's books, but for a sheer enjoyment, *Morning Poems* may be the best.

The satisfaction of articulation is one of the basic pleasures in poetry, even when the subject is far from any other kind of pleasure. For example, the poem called "The Russian," a magnificent story-poem about sufferings we can never fully fathom. Or a remarkable elegy for Jane Kenyon, "The Yellow Dot." It's very different from a standard elegy. It doesn't work through anecdotes or reminiscences. Its tone is not melancholy; it's firmer than that, a blend of realism and outrage, and some of that outrage is directed at God:

God does what she wants. She has very large
Tractors. She lives at night in the sewing room

Doing stitchery. Then chunks of land at mid-
Sea disappear. The husband knows that his wife
Is still breathing. God has arranged the open
Grave. That grave is not what we want,
But to God it's a tiny hole, and he has
The needle, draws the thread through it, and soon
A nice pattern appears. The husband cries,
"Don't let her die!" But God says, "I
Need a yellow dot here, near the mailbox."

The husband is angry. But the turbulent ocean
Is like a chicken scratching for seeds. It doesn't
Mean anything, and the chicken's claws will tear
A Rembrandt drawing if you put it down.

Where did "God's tractors" come from? And where the image of chicken claws? From living a long time in farming country, I suppose. But that doesn't explain them. Those images are both odd and brutal; they are accurate and striking descriptions of the indifference of the workings of loss in the world.

So there is no lack of seriousness in the book, but overall there is something easy-going, even light-hearted, about it. Not every poem is a major event. A few feel like exercises; more feel spontaneous and whimsical. For instance, a poem about clothespins, or a conversation with a mouse about the best position for sleeping. There is plenty of humor. I remember a sentence in the first piece I ever wrote about Bly, my Master's thesis: "There is no humor in Bly." At the time, Bly's only books were *Silence in the Snowy Fields* and *The Light Around the Body*. But it was a deficiency that he soon began to remedy—perhaps around the time he wrote a prose poem about watching a hockey game with his friend William Duffy. In *Morning Poems*, humor is simply a natural part of the tone and the mind. Most of all, the pleasure comes from a feeling of abundance—an abundant energy of thinking and imagination. Galway Kinnell wrote a comment for the book that catches it nicely: "There is a lot of human knowledge in this book, and at the same time it has the vigor of youth. How can that be?"

In a sense stronger and fuller and more mythological than our commonplace usage of the word, *Morning Poems* is a book of *musing*. There's a wealth of poems one could choose from to illustrate. It could be a wonderful, affectionate homage to the Norwegian poet Olav H. Hauge, whose poems Bly has translated. Or, one of the poems of supposing: "Suppose you see a face in a Toyota/ One day, and you fall in love with that face[...]" ("The Face in the Toyota"), or, "Well, let's say this morning is all of life there is—" ("Thinking about Old Jobs"). Or maybe one of the poems based in some psychological case study, such as "There Was a Man Who Didn't Know What Was His," or the one that begins, "I have been thinking about the man who gives in" ("It Is So Easy to Give In"), or "One Source of Bad Information": "There's a boy in you about three/ Years old who hasn't learned a thing for thirty/ Thousand years[....] Because of this boy/ You survived a lot. He's got six big ideas./ Five don't work. Right now he's repeating them to you" ("One Source of Bad Information"). Many possibilities to illustrate the musing, but I will go with this one, whose title in a way speaks for the whole book:

THINGS TO THINK

Think in ways you've never thought before.
If the phone rings, think of it as carrying a message
Larger than anything you've ever heard,
Vaster than a hundred lines of Yeats.

Think that someone may bring a bear to your door,
Maybe wounded and deranged; or think that a moose
Has risen out of the lake, and he's carrying on his antlers
A child of your own whom you've never seen.

When someone knocks on the door, think that he's about
To give you something large: tell you you're forgiven,
Or that it's not necessary to work all the time, or that it's
Been decided that if you lie down no one will die.

Sometimes you feel that you haven't accomplished anything in your life, and you should have. Sometimes our thoughts seem pitifully small, and life is dull, and having any big or original thoughts would only be a delusion anyway. We expect too much, and we expect too little, at the same time. Maybe you know the feeling. But between the poles of the sound of a hundred lines of Yeats, and the news that if we lie down it will be all right, no one will die, we can, for a while, be content. Relax; something interesting might happen. The world is rich, and we happen, for now, to be in it. The spirit of these poems is as generous as that.

Which brings me to two remarkable books, that I will talk about together—though they are not entirely similar, the first having a darker tone than the second. One might have expected them, but I didn't expect them. Bly had been talking about form for ten years or more. Even while he was writing much of his poetry in prose, he began putting in good words for poetic form. He had been talking about association in poetry for many years, at least since the influential essay "Looking for Dragon Smoke." He called it leaping. The only issue of his magazine to appear in the seventies (called, of course, *The Seventies*) was all about leaping. Always alert to possible models and inspirations from other traditions, and that he had also long been attracted to a kind of poetry that most of his contemporaries, Allen Ginsberg notwithstanding, would probably not feel comfortable with, and might be suspicious of: I mean poetry that is not just excitable but ecstatic, and explicitly caught up in a sense of the sacred. Who else brought Kabir into American English? When Bly did it, the results were quite amazing. I remember the crusty atheist Hayden Carruth saying in a review of Bly's Kabir versions that even though Bly wrote against his grain, he couldn't help but be won over by the energy of those poems.

All these strands were visible—form, leaping, the ecstatic, willingness to talk directly about God and the Guest and the road the soul is on. But still I was startled when they came together in an artistic opening, a creative burst. Freedom, structure, and spontaneity; praise, lament, homage, and zaniness; quickness, repetition, and unpredictability—all came together in a new kind of poem. Two books of many blank pages. Two books of poems of six stanzas, three lines per stanza; but within this regularity, radical disconnection, shooting from one thought to another in seemingly impulsive directions. They were like a sonnet sequence written by someone a little drunk—except that the speech of a drunken person is slack and slurred, and these poems are sharp and full of penetrating assertions. The form is Bly's adaptation of the ghazal, the form of Ghalib and Hafez. The books are the ones with the modest titles, *The Night Abraham Called to the Stars* and *My Sentence Was a Thousand Years of Joy.*

In spite of all the things that might have prepared me for them, they took some getting used to. I was somewhat familiar with the term and the form, but I was not really prepared for these ghazals, and not for whole books of them. Reading them one after another is enough to make one's head spin. Maybe that's the point. The main thing was the question of unity. What was the subject of the poem? Where were the transitions? Did the order of the stanzas even matter? I wondered if they had a coherent meaning, and often I wasn't sure what they delivered in terms of feeling.

After reading Bly's ghazals for a while, an image occurred to me: the poem is like a waterfall, and what we are used to calling meaning is like water flowing down over the ledges of the stanzas, arriving in some transparent, trembling pool. Where's the unity in that? There is one, but it's different from the anecdotal or the narrative poem—a poem with a clear dramatic situation. Others have compared ghazals to pearls strung on a string of a certain length, or the patterns in a carpet or tapestry, or a polyphonic or contrapuntal song. A translator of Hafez, Elizabeth T. Gray, advises the reader approaching ghazals "to question his or her own literary assumptions and to brandish lightly, at the outset, the templates of Western literary criticism."

I like that: "brandish lightly the templates." And that I guess is what I was learning to do reading Bly's ghazals, though I hadn't read the advice yet. But there are other problems besides a new sense of how meaning could be communicated, or even what meaning is. The poems had a wild assortment of titles, some lavish in their strangeness: "The Eel in the Cave," "Giordano Bruno and the Muddy Footprint," "The Cabbages of Chekhov." Others nearby would be called simply, "Brahms," or "The Shoehorn," or "The Pistachio Nut." And the titles often seemed arbitrary, taken from some detail halfway through the poem. Here again we might mention Stevens, Bly's eccentric poetic uncle, the aesthete, the master of the vivid, odd title, the creator of the phrase, "the essential gaudiness of poetry." There is a lot in these poems that is gaudy, high-spirited, kaleidoscopic. Even their self-deprecations have a certain gaudiness to them: "I am the grandchild of Norwegian forgetters./ I am the nephew of those who stole the onions."

And then there were the allusions. The nephew of the ones who stole the onions is in love with literature, music, art, and philosophy. In my book, in the chapter on *The Man in the Black Coat Turns*, I noted an increasing number of literary references, but I wrote, "Bly's allusiveness is not nearly as extreme as Eliot's or Pound's...." I think it's fair to say that in the ghazals, Bly caught up with and passed them in that department. The names of writers, artists, musicians, and historical and mythological figures are part of the basic vocabulary of these poems. I went through *My Sentence Was a Thousand Years of Joy* poem by poem and made a tally, and I came up with seventy-five separate references, with some of those names appearing more than once. By chance, or by some other guiding force, the list begins with Newton, the great dismantler of the world into predictable laws and components, and ends with Hafez, master of the ghazal, and perhaps the guiding spirit of these poems. Years later Bly would publish a collection of translations of Hafez, done in collaboration with the Sufi scholar Leonard Lewisohn. I had a conversation with Lewisohn once, and he said that the line between Bly's ghazals and their translations of Hafez is not an easy one to draw.

And then there was the gesture of turning and talking to himself at the end of some of the poems. Back when I was first reading Bly's Kabir versions, around 1970, I was struck by the way Kabir would step in at the end of the poem and mention his own name, and make a comment about what the poem had been leading up to: "How restless Kabir is all the time!/ How much he wants to see the Guest!" "Kabir says: Fantastic! Don't let a chance like this go by!" I thought, "Well, that's great, but an American poet couldn't get away with that. I should have known better. It takes some getting used to, but when Bly uses this gesture, the lines are by turns funny, interesting, and touching, and they are another expression of the essential gaudiness of poetry.

The ghazals resisted me in many ways, but I was won over by their boldness, and their colors, and their humanity. These poems are so striking and so out of step with the norms of contemporary American poetry, that I thought it would be interesting to see how people other than myself react to them. So I asked some poetry friends to read a selection of the ghazals that I put together. These people are poets and readers of poetry, devout parishioners, some of them perhaps deacons, probably mystics, possibly saints, out there in the church of poetry. Smart people, all of them, aware of Bly of course, more or less familiar with his work, but not immersed in it. I thought they would offer a little distance that I might not have.

My old creative writing teacher from college, who hammered home the lesson that every poem needs to have "a rational spine," turned out to have no hesitation about the reason or unreason of these poems. He wrote glosses on them that were succinct and convincing. And he said, "I come away from these poems with great admiration for their inventiveness, for the rightness of their startling pronouncements, the freshness of their language." Amen to that.

As to the allusions, a poet who works a day job as a hospital clerk said, "In these poems he keeps throwing around names like Mahler, Caedmon, and Kierkegaard. Most people have to look up who these people are. I think he wants us to learn something outside the poems. I had to go look up Caedmon and I found out how he was visited by a celestial visitor who appeared to him one night and taught him to sing. I couldn't help but think that this is Bly's way of educating me." Which I think is a good, non-defensive way of responding. I would add that all those allusions are a way of saying, "What would life be without the arts?" and that we can never say thanks enough to Rembrandt, or Herman Melville or Andrew Marvell, or Bach, or the skilled musicians who have played his music from his day to today.

I asked my friends specifically about meaning. What were they getting from these waterfall-like poems? One, a convert to Catholicism, a man who has spent some time in the psych ward, and who is one of the most profoundly and humbly religious people I know, said, "First of all, these are stories of redemption...These poems are about finding salvation, despite failure, despite fate, despite the purgatory of this life. They are all deeply religious." But another friend, who is in fact the Poet Laureate of the Episcopal Diocese of New Jersey, said, "Some of the lines make me feel sprightly joy—no kidding—and they convey a sense of ancient wisdom. But those lines just fill me for a moment with joy and then I am brought back down with an overwhelming sense of 'this is it.' His ending is all nihilism...." And another poet, whose day job is head administrator of a home for severely troubled children, a Quaker, said: "I wouldn't turn to these poems for solace....I think what I look for in poems is a change of the equation. Is there some way to pass through the polarities of success and ruin, happiness and despair—to some state of more evenness and stability? Maybe not. Bly doesn't suggest it."

Redemption, nihilism, solace: these are big words. And then there is that other word to put beside them: joy. Personally, I take the great theme of these poems to be the last word in the title, *My Sentence Was a Thousand Years of Joy*. Not joy alone, but also what we take to be its opposites: grief, sorrow, failure, ruin. When the book first appeared, I had trouble with the title. A thousand years of joy. That is a lot of joy. Maybe better not to mention it, if you have that much joy. I had a similar problem with the title of Bly's collection of sacred poetry, *The Soul Is Here for Its Own Joy*. I know the line is from Rumi, not someone I really want to get into a debate with—but maybe the soul is not here for its own joy, but for its own suffering, or maybe for the joy of others, or maybe the suffering of others. I don't take any of the comments that I've quoted lightly—not the words of Rumi, nor those of my friends. I wrestle with them, and consider them. But it is precisely in those questions of joy and sorrow that Bly's ghazals mean the most to me. I do not find them nihilistic, but it is true that they take us repeatedly up to a brink where our smallness looks out into the vistas of nothingness, or to use a word that appears in some of them, nonexistence. And it is precisely solace that I do find in them, as much as I find solace anywhere. For one thing, they include some of the sanest statements about mortality that I know: "I knew this friendship with myself couldn't last forever." "It's good if you become a soul and then disappear." "Robert, this poem will soon be over; and you/ Are like a twig trembling on the lip of the falls./ Like a note of music, you are about to become nothing." How sane these lines are; how free of dread and self-pity. I find such lines more consoling that anything I ever heard a minister say at a funeral.

The poems are fair to the messiness of our lives; they don't sell it short: "In our messy world, we all walk backward,/ Each holding a potato that points to the grave." A line like that is enough to give ballast to several appearances of the word "joy." As for "nonexistence," the poems meet it with good humor: "When each stanza closes with the same word,/ I am glad. A friend says, 'If you're proud of that,/ You must be one of the secretaries of nonexistence.'" They are eloquent in their acceptance of "ruin." Sometimes he goes too far: "The soul can never get enough of the taste of its own sorrow." I know some people who could rightly say, "Enough." "There is so much joy in losing the race." I know chronic losers who would disagree with that. Another friend, a woman who writes brilliant short poems, a veteran of relationship disasters, quotes the line "human beings take in the fragrance of a thousand nights of ruin" and comments, "I don't find ruin delicious. Is this something Bly learned in his men's groups or in his study of Jung??" She is a not an ironist. She is a passionate, burning, down-to-earth poet. She asks that question sincerely.

There are poets who try to get the opposites poised within a single poem, even in one or two lines—as Robert Frost did in "Birches," or as William Stafford did in "A Ritual to Read to Each Other": "...the signals we give—yes or no, or maybe—/ should be clear: the darkness around us is deep." But there's another kind of poem that uses a different method. The method that says things like, "Hurry!

The world is not going to get better!" and "Just keep shouting, 'My heart is never bitter!'" and "No one is as lucky as those who live on earth"—things as extreme as that.

The lines about joy are balanced, in a thoughts-pouring-down-among-the-ledges way, by line after line about sorrow and grief. Failure is relative, and quite likely. Grief and sorrow are part of the mix. But ruin is inevitable, and these poems accept that, and turn the acceptance into something that gives solace after all. Too much joy? No, about the right amount, just enough—as there are just enough stars in the sky on a starry night, as VanGogh saw; as Emerson saw, and said, "If the stars should appear one night in a thousand years, how would men believe and adore." A night like the one when Abraham first called to the stars.

Since I've mentioned Emerson, let me mention him again. I am outside my culture, my training, and no doubt my personality type, when I read Hafez. With Emerson I am closer to home. Bly is not the first American writer to admire and translate Hafez: Emerson loved Hafez, and saw him as the supreme exemplar of a quality he called "the superlative"—the state in which "the mind strings worlds like beads upon its thought." And while we are in Concord, I should mention Thoreau too. There is a book of Bly's that I think of as a perfect book: *The Winged Life: The Poetic Voice of Henry David Thoreau.* For some reason it gets left off the lists at the front of his books, but I think it is one of his very best. In it you get passages of Thoreau expertly chosen, and a commentary that is some of Bly's most astute criticism, both fresh and incisive. His assessment of Thoreau's life, personality, and thought seem to me as good as anything ever written about him. Even the physical book itself is a thing of beauty, with large pages and woodcuts by Michael McCurdy. We can use Thoreau also as a way of nodding to a part of Bly's work I've only alluded to so far: the prose poems. Since the Kayak Press edition of *The Morning Glory* in 1969, Bly has worked steadily in the prose poem, and among other things, it is the form in which he has most exercised the art of looking, of close physical observation—a discipline of which Thoreau was one of the masters. The prose poems, though they are not very long, have a spaciousness to them, with room not only for close description but also for family—the poet's own, and the one that includes ancient ancestors—"the last man killed by flu who knew how to weave a pot of river clay the way the wasps do....Now he is dead and only the wasps know in the long river-mud grief." That's a deft connection quickly made between the clay-pot-maker and the wasps. A recent collection gathers prose poems old and new, and puts them in new groupings that make them more impressive and enjoyable than ever. Those that tend toward high-flown swirling energy—especially the ones originally published in *This Body Is Made of Camphor and Gopherwood* – are more satisfying when they are set among the poems that focus on solid objects, such as a potato, a group of elephants, a rose, or a human skull. The prose poems combine description of the physical things and extravagant metaphorical thinking in a way that is rich in both perception and praise, and the new book's title, *Reaching Out to the World*, suits them very well.

Another category within Bly's work that needs to be mentioned is his short poems in the form Bly calls ramages, each dedicated to a particular sound or cluster of sounds. Twenty-four of them have been gathered in an exquisite little book called *Turkish Pears in August*. As I've mentioned, Bly in the 60's and 70's was often impatient with form, sometimes outright disdainful of it, but fairly soon he undertook to do justice to an aspect of poetic art he had undervalued. The ramage form was a space and a container in which to do that work. These are small resonating boxes of poems, modest, focused where the ghazals are impulsive. You could use them as little chants for meditation, or for the sheer pleasure of saying them. For example:

WANTING SUMPTUOUS HEAVENS

No one grumbles among the oyster clans,
And lobsters play their bone guitars all summer.
Only we, with our opposable thumbs, want
Heaven to be, and God to come, again.
There is no end to our grumbling; we want
Comfortable earth *and* sumptuous heaven.

But the heron standing on one leg in the bog
Drinks his rum all day, and is content.

I'll end with a personal story. A few years ago I experienced a house fire. When I arrived home, the firemen were in full force, smashing windows, pouring water into the house. It was a cold day in February, and as I stood in the snow watching, I could see that the fire had reached the middle section of the house, where my library was. And I thought, as the flames came up through the roof, "my books are gone"—and I thought, even as I stood there, that my books by Robert Bly were gone. I had, I think, a complete collection, going back to the first issue of *The Fifties* and his collaboration with James Wright and William Duffy, *The Lion's Tail and Eyes: Poems Written out of Laziness and Silence*. Ironic, that his earliest published collection was called that, since looking back at the body of his work now—poetry, poems, and translations; prose, criticism, social and mythological commentary—it would seem that laziness would be the one quality that he knows nothing about.

As it turned out, the destruction of the fire was not quite total. A few books survived. For example, I have in front of me a scorched, water-warped copy of Bly's *Ten Poems of Issa*, who also experienced a housefire, and worse losses than that. It is a strange and devastating feeling, seeing your house, so familiar, on fire. When I read the line, "the crop of ruin has been great," I think of standing in the snow watching that scene, and standing in the wreckage the next day, in the space where my books were, but the shelves now collapsed, all the books a blackened, frozen heap. It could have been worse. No one was hurt. Even the old, arthritic dog escaped, thanks to bold action by my neighbor. We were underinsured, but we managed to rebuild. Friends helped in many ways. Some boxes of books came in the mail, from Minnesota.

When I first started reading Robert Bly's poetry in 1968, I thought that someday I would awaken on a train, in Missoula, Montana, or some other place, utterly happy. Or that I would see a white flake of snow in a horse's mane, and that would be it, I would be satisfied, my mind a blaze of cool clarity. I was young; I had high hopes; and the book where I found the poems that gave me those thoughts and feelings, *Silence in the Snowy Fields*, had a powerful and mysterious vision. I still love that book, but I did not expect that I would ultimately find in Bly's poetry a guide for living in the ruins, all of the poems taken together a sort of wild and helpful handbook for living there. But that is what has happened, and I am both grateful and, you might say, joyful about that.

ROBERT BLY IN THE SHADOW OF HAFIZ

By Leonard Lewisohn

Introduction: 250 Years of English Literary Translation of Hafiz

Known as the "Tongue of Invisible Mysteries," Hafiz, who died in 1389, is generally considered to be the most eminent and famous of all the poets of Persia. During his own lifetime, his poems were internationally celebrated, his verses perused and collected by connoisseurs not only in Persia proper but in Ottoman Turkey and India. He still remains the most popular poet in Persian-speaking lands: Iran, Afghanistan, and Tajikistan.[1]

In the West, at least until the end of the 19th century in Germany and England, Hafiz was also very much a household name. E.B. Cowell, Professor of Sanskrit at Cambridge University and the Persian teacher of Edward Fitzgerald (famous translator of the *Rubaiyyat* of Omar Khayyam) felt no qualms in opening an article in the September 1854 issue of *Fraser's Magazine for Town and Country*, with the following rhetorical question:

> "Who has not heard of Hafez, the great Lyric poet of Persia?"

Prof. Cowell's audience were ordinary British men and women of one hundred and sixty years ago who flourished in the vicarages and country-houses of rural England and whose education was through autodidacticism rather than television.[2] Long before Cowell and Fitzgerald's day and age, for almost a century Hafiz had been a staple

1 See Leonard Lewisohn (ed.), *Hafiz and the Religion of Love in Classical Persian Poetry*, Prolegomenon 1, pp. 3-30 for an overview of Hafiz's life, times and literary stature.

2 See Peter Avery, "Fitzgerald's Persian Teacher and Hafez." Alas, even this simple level of common learning and popular culture—whether regarding European or Oriental poetry—has almost completely vanished in England today; a recent *Guardian* newspaper poll concluded that British students had the lowest score for reading poetry compared with students in other European countries, with only 8% saying they did so.

of British intellectual culture for when Sir William Jones published some of his first English translations of Hafiz in 1771, his *Grammar of Persian* had already been a "bestseller" throughout England for several decades.

Complementing Jones's 1771 translation, in 1787 J. Nott published his *Select Odes of Hafiz*. The various monthlies and quarterlies of rural England during the following – nineteenth – century were filled with well-informed opinions on the merits of Hafiz's poetry. There flourished an entire "Hafiz industry" in fact, his verse being relished by the ordinary reading public during the entire 19th and early 20th centuries although the names of most of Hafiz's translators of the period—H. Bicknell, H. Wilberforce-Clarke, Gertrude Bell and Walter Leaf—are barely known by us (nor are their renditions readable) today. Most of the English Romantics—Shelley, Keats, and Tennyson, to name just a few—were not only familiar with Hafiz's poetry, but regularly tried their hand at both the translation and imitation of his verse.[3]

In the mid-nineteenth century in the United States, the founder of the American Transcendentalist movement, Ralph Waldo Emerson, translated some four hundred lines of Persian poetry from Hafiz based on Hammer-Purgstall's German translation. Comparing Hafiz to Shakespeare, he wrote: "Hafiz is the prince of Persian poets, and in his extraordinary gift adds to some of the attributes of Pindar, Anacreon, Horace and Burns the insight of a mystic, that sometimes affords a deeper glance at Nature than belongs to either of these bards." The interest in Hafiz continued apace during the nineteenth century in the United States, and eventually "by 1900 a largely spurious, second-growth Hafiz stood beside the several approximations to the real figure."[4]

The working men and women behind this industry were all Victorian-period translators whose translations were usually of quite mediocre quality. One of the most popular of these works was an

3 See my "Correspondences between English Romantic and Persian Sufi Poets."

4 As G.M. Wickens pointed out, "Hafiz," p. 56.

anthology compiled by Louisa S. Costello (1799-1870) called *The Rose Garden of Persia* (1845), which was largely based on the translations of Sir William Jones done in the 18th century. Another well-known rendition of Hafiz by Clarence K. Streit (1896) was called *Hafiz: The Tongue of the Hidden*. Both works show the great care taken to translate his verse – but utterly tasteless results[5] came out of their convoluted attempts to turn Hafiz into a romantic Victorian poet. Save for Gertrude Bell (d. 1926) and Wilberforce-Clarke (d. 1905), all these translations have been out of print and circulation for over half a century.[6] Most of these translators' names are today largely unknown to us, although scholarly articles and specialist monographs about them can be found.[7] The industry of these Hafiz translators was certainly intense; there were, for instance, altogether 36 different poet-translators of the first poem in Hafiz's *Divan*, from the late 18th to the late 20th century listed by Parvin Loloi in her comprehensive critical bibliography of the subject entitled *Hafiz, Master of Persian Poetry*.[8]

Robert Bly's Engagement with Persian Sufi Poetry

One of Robert Bly's first excursions into Oriental poetry influenced by Sufism was his translation of the 15th century Indian antinomian poet Kabir (recast from Rabindranath Tagore's classic 1915 transla-

5 On Streit's Hafiz translation, see Loloi, *Hafiz, Master of Persian Poetry*, pp. 52-54.

6 See Gertrude Bell, *The Hafez Poems of Gertrude Bell* and H. Wilberforce Clarke (trans.), *The Divan-i-Hafiz*. John Yohannan in his Columbia University Ph.D. Dissertation of 1939 entitled "The Persian Poet Hafiz in England and America" traces the tradition of the translation of Hafiz into English from the late 18th century down to the early 19th century. See also Mahnaz Ahmad, *Persian Poetry and the English Reader from the Eighteenth to the Twentieth Century*; Julie Meisami, "Hafiz in English: Translation and Authority," as well as A.J. Arberry's introduction to his *Fifty Poems of Hafiz*, and its review and excellent critique by Eric Schroeder, "Verse Translation and Hafiz."

7 Their contributions are recorded, analysed and summed up brilliantly by Parvin Loloi, *Hafiz, Master of Persian Poetry: A Critical Bibliography*.

8 Parvin Loloi, *Hafiz, Master of Persian Poetry: A Critical Bibliography*.

tion *Songs of Kabir*)[9] first published in 1971 by the Seventies Press. Three decades later in the introduction to his translation of Ghalib's Urdu poetry (1999), after translating a number of other Oriental poets male and female influenced by Sufism, including the Persian Sufi poet Rumi and the Indian Bakhti poet Mirabai (1498-1565),[10] Bly reiterated his fondness for "Kabir's delight in God and the soul."[11]

I was aware of Robert Bly's skill as a translator of Kabir when I met him in person for the first time in the autumn of 1987 during a poetry reading held by the London Convivium for Archetypal Studies. He appeared on stage with the psychologist James Hillman, who I knew quite well, having read most of his works after spending a summer studying briefly with him in Zurich in 1970. During the intermission I approached Bly, who till then I had only admired from a distance, and introduced myself and presented him with a copy of a work on the esoteric symbolism of Persian Sufi poetry that I had just translated from Persian and published.[12] A few years earlier, I had been enthralled to find in Bly's *News of the Universe: Poems of Twofold Consciousness* correspondences and echoes of ideas from the Persian Sufi tradition in which I had been immersed for over a decade.

A few months before this encounter with Robert Bly at the reading, I had submitted my doctoral dissertation in the field of Persian Sufi literature at the University of London's School of Oriental and African Studies. Before falling in love with Persian poetry and going to Iran to study and live for five years during the 1970s (where I received my B.A. from Pahlavi University in Shiraz in Persian history in 1978), I had been absorbed in reading the modern European poets. At that time I had read Bly's criticism and essays in the literary journals he edited – especially *The Sixties* and *The Seventies* – and was particularly fond of his translations of my favorite German poets, Rainer Maria Rilke and Georg Trakl.

---

9 *The Kabir Book: Forty-Four of the Ecstatic Poems of Kabir*, Versions by Robert Bly.

10 *Mirabai: Ecstatic Poems* (with Jane Hirshfield).

11 *The Lightning Should Have Fallen on Ghalib: Selected Poems of Ghalib*, translated by Robert Bly and Sunil Dutta, p. 1.

12 *Sufi Symbolism I (The Nurbakhsh Encyclopedia of Sufi Terminology)* by Dr. Javad Nurbakhsh, trans. Leonard Lewisohn & Terry Graham.

During our chat in the intermission, we exchanged phone numbers. A few days later we met in private, and I suggested that, given his interest in Rumi and Sufi poetry, he might like to meet Dr. Javad Nurbakhsh (1926-2008), a Persian Sufi master of the Nimatullahi Order and psychiatrist who resided in London at that time.[13] Bly accepted my invitation. This meeting with Dr. Nurbakhsh soon developed into an intimate and long-lasting friendship between the master psychiatrist and master poet. Almost every year thereafter, when Robert and Ruth Bly returned to London to give readings and visit friends, they were regular visitors to the Nimatullahi dervishes in the Sufi center run by Nurbakhsh in Nottinghill Gate. We also remained in correspondence both by phone and letter, and saw each other regularly at least once a year, usually either in London or in New York.

In London, I introduced him to Pamela Travers, author of *Mary Poppins*, and also took him to see the great English mystical poet and Blake scholar Kathleen Raine, with whom he had previously been acquainted. He became very fond of Raine, visiting her every time he was in London, and until her death in 2004 maintained an occasional correspondence with her on matters of mysticism, religion and poetry.

In 1992, Prof. S.H. Nasr and I worked as conveners (with the Nimatullahi Research Centre in association with George Washington University) of a conference on "Persian Sufism from its Origin to Rumi" held at George Washington University in Washington, D.C. on May 11-13. I invited Robert Bly to grace our conference by contributing a poetry reading of his translations of Rumi. He kindly accepted and we spent much of the week before the conference together, working over his translations. Robert Bly told me that he was interested in working with me on translation of some of Hafiz's ghazals, thus beginning his long struggle to render the greatest medieval Persian lyricist into an acceptable American idiom. The reading held on May 12 was accompanied by two of the finest living classical Persian

13 See my obituary on "Javad Nurbakhsh: A leading Iranian Sufi, also a noted psychiatrist, author and medical clinic director" in *The Guardian* newspaper (London, Wednesday 7 January 2009).

musicians: Hasan Nahid (nay) and Muhammad Reza Lotfi (setar), and turned out to be an astounding success.

Although a number of the top Iranian scholars of Sufism in the audience looked askance at some of our idiomatic interpretations, Robert Bly's spirited declamation of our renditions of Hafiz during this reading generated much popular acclaim among the Americans present. We decided that it would be worthwhile to translate Hafiz on a more serious and regular basis. Translation of Hafiz's ghazals became our habitual work during his annual visits to London thereafter. Five of our translations of Hafiz first appeared in his anthology *The Soul Is Here for Its Own Joy* (1995).

In that same year (1992) when the first public reading of our Hafiz translations took place, Robert Bly's poetry anthology *The Rag and Bone Shop of the Heart*, edited with James Hillman and Michael Meade, was published. In his introduction to the 12th chapter on "The Cultivated Heart," he describes how the Troubadour poets and the radical love mysticism of medieval Provençal culture in France had been influenced by Arabic and Persian poetry:

> Much of the impulse for this movement came directly from Persian and Arabic piety and Muslim ideas of chivalry, which Spain and France absorbed. For many years, French scholars insisted that the first Provençal love poems came directly out of French folk life and owed nothing to the Arabs. Now we know that the early poems of Guillaume X were in fact virtual translations from the Arabic; the original Arabic poems, with the rhyme structure intact, have been found. Islamic civilization at its highest point encouraged and achieved marvellous cultivation of the lover's heart... American readers have adopted Rumi and Kabir and Mirabai poems with great joy recently, as if they were long-lost children. And they are.[14]

This statement clearly establishes the poetico-philosophical genealogy of ideas underlying Bly's renewed interest in Rumi and Hafiz during during the early 1990s. This genealogy does not belong simply to trends in the history of ideas nor to the fluctuating fashions

---

14 Robert Bly, James Hillman and Michael Meade (eds.), *The Rag and Bone Shop of the Heart*, p. 362.

of literary history, but rather figures as a kind of civilizational force whose origins are transcendental and divine as well as psychological and pertaining to the human soul. This force was best encapsulated, Bly posited, by the word *Amor* which "the people in the Provence region eventually adopted... to describe this new emotion in their minds with passionate delicacy and courteous affection."[15] This tradition of love had originally been elevated to the acme of its ethical and amorous perfection by Muslim poets' efforts to cultivate the "garden of the heart." Translation of Persian poetry was thus for Bly a communion with the Muslim muse originally sustaining his own tradition, an act of pilgrimage to the Islamic heartland and sources of erotic spirituality of the late Middle Ages and early Renaissance in the West. It was not just incidental that he concludes his introduction to this chapter on the Cultivated Heart with one of the verses by Hafiz that he had translated himself a few years earlier:

> How blessed is the man who like Hafez
> Has tasted in his heart the wine made before Adam.[16]

Metaphysically speaking, in Islamic thought the "wine made before Adam" refers to the pre-eternal covenant mentioned in the Qur'an VII: 172, where God asks the yet uncreated souls of Adam's offspring, "Am I not your Lord?" In their unconscious and uncreated state, they all ecstatically and drunkenly reply, "Yes *(bala)*!" Persian Sufi poets often liken this primordial event to a wine symposium that involves quaffing a cup of wine in intoxicated celebration of their acceptance of this covenant. In the case of Sufi ecstatics such as Hafiz, this pre-eternal intoxication—symbolic of the rapture of divine attraction that pulls man to God—has still not abated.[17] In reference to this same Qur'anic verse, the great Islamic scholar Henry Corbin (whose writings both Bly and Hillman admired exceedingly) observed that

15 *The Rag and Bone Shop*, p. 360.

16 *The Angels Knocking on the Tavern Door*, translated with Leonard Lewisohn, p. 25. In fact, Robert Bly was so fond of this line that he had originally entitled our book of translations of Hafiz as *Drinking the Wine Made before Adam*.

17 As Haravi, *Sharh-i ghazalha-yi Hafiz*, I, p. 629 notes.

we can see how "the religious conscience of Islam is centred upon a fact of meta-history."[18]

Obviously, it would have been impossible, without resorting to pedantic footnotes, to convey any of these subtle exegetical references and spiritual senses of this verse in our English translation. However, from our discussions and his own study of the Persian Sufi tradition, it is clear that Robert Bly was well aware of the metaphysical nature of such bacchanalian references in Persian poetry, the imagery of which he was to later introduce and interpret in his own poetry in his own unique way.[19]

Bly again quotes the same verse by Hafiz in his chapter on "What Is Vertical Thought" in *The Sibling Society* which appeared four years after his anthology *The Rag and Bone Shop of the Heart*). Alluding to its bacchanalian imagery, he ruminates:

> The sibling society is almost the pure antithesis of a Tibetan monastery. We have drunk beer so long that we have virtually forgotten the taste of real wine. Rumi and Hafez refer over and over to wine, which carries the flavor of the longing for God, the taste of the vertical, which is the afterflavor of ecstasy:
>
> How blessed is the man who like Hafez
> Has tasted in his heart the wine made before Adam.
>
> To become a genuine artist in our society is more and more difficult because fewer and fewer people "have tasted in their heart the wine made before Adam." Even if an artist creates a spiritual work, the readers are so flat, the art critics are so horizontal, that its "wine" is not recognized.[20]

To return to the early 1990s: It was during the first half of that decade that interest in Rumi in the United States really gathered mo-

18 See Paul Nwyia, *Exégèse Coranique et Langage Mystique*, p. 42.

19 Cf. this stanza *My Sentence Was a Thousand Years of Joy* (p. 37):

> Earth is the place where we've agreed to throw
> Away the gifts that Adam's grandfather gave us
> During the Dark Time before eternity was born.

20 *The Sibling Society*, pp. 210-11.

mentum.[21] *The Essential Rumi*, a compilation of translations by Coleman Barks and John Moyne, was published in 1995, and by 1998 it had sold more than 110,000 copies. Bob Summer, writing in *Publishers Weekly* in 1995,[22] informs us that another collection of Rumi translations by Coleman Barks and John Moyne (entitled *Open Secret*) had just sold 50,000 copies. Sales figures of this quantity *for poetry* were unprecedented in American publishing. Indeed, one would have to go back to the last two decades of the 19th century and the first three decades of the 20th century, when Fitzgerald's translation of the *Ruba'iyat* of Omar Khayyam became a publishing rage in the United States, to find a comparable craze over a Persian poet on the American literary scene.[23]

Coincidentally, it should be noted that Bly's infatuation with the poetry of Rumi and Hafiz and their influence on his verse (see below) stands directly in the tradition of the two founders of modernist English poetry, T.S. Eliot and Ezra Pound, both of whom were deeply absorbed in and influenced by Fitzgerald's translation of the *Ruba'iyat*. V.M. D'Ambrosio in her work *Eliot Possessed: T.S. Eliot and Fitzgerald's RUBAIYAT*[24] details extensively Khayyam's deep influence on Eliot. Pound claimed that "Fitzgerald's translation of Omar is the only good poem of the Victorian era,"[25] naming his own son "Omar Shakespeare Pound," comically underlining with typical hyperbole: "Just note the crescendo."[26]

Although Bly probably knew quite well of the translations of Rumi by Robert Duncan (1919-88, one of the founding members of the Black Mountain School), Coleman Barks's transcreations of R.A.

21 See Franklin Lewis, *Rumi: Past and Present*, pp. 587ff.

22 "Clear Some Shelf Space for Sufism," *Publishers' Weekly*, (January 9, 1995), pp. 33-35. Cited by Lewis, *Rumi: Past and Present*, p. 527.

23 On the Khayyam craze in the late 19th century U.S. see Mehdi Aminrazavi, *The Wine of Wisdom*, chap. 8.

24 New York: NYU Press 1989.

25 *Letters of Ezra Pound* (London 1951). Cited by Aminrazavi, *The Wine of Wisdom*, p. 262.

26 Aminrazavi, *The Wine of Wisdom*, p. 263.

Nicholson's prosaic scholarly translations of Rumi were, I believe, the most important influence on his interpretation of Persian poetry, at least before we began our work on Hafiz. In 1981, Coleman Barks and Robert Bly published 18 fragments from Rumi's poetry in a collection entitled *Night and Sleep: Rumi,*[27] some of which featured in his poetry reading in Washington on May 12, 1992. I remember Robert asking me at this time to find and translate for him the Persian originals of these poems in Rumi's *Mathnawi* for him. When I brought to his attention Nicholson's literal rendition of the original verses, and how different they were in letter and spirit from the *Night and Sleep* versions, I recall his astonishment. He collaborated with Coleman Barks on a number of other projects having to do with the translation of Rumi during the 1980s and 90s,[28] and used Barks' translations of Rumi in his two poetry anthologies: *The Rag and Bone Shop of the Heart* (1992: 13 selections from Rumi) and in his *The Soul is Here for its Own Joy: Sacred Poems from Many Cultures* (1995: 32 selections from Rumi) prolifically. The craze in the USA over the poetry of Rumi, whose translations have outsold all other poets, continues unabated today (2010).

Bly's deep appreciation of Rumi was evident in an article published in *The Times* (Oct. 26, 2002) newspaper in London, where he explained the relationship between Rumi's popular appeal among Americans at that time, before briefly commenting on his interest in translating Hafiz:

> People recognize that Rumi is not a New Ager babbling out happy quatrains, but his work depends on an immense knowledge of Muslim thought and theology and on a hardworking spiritual community in Konya, older and deeper than anything we have experienced in the West. During the past month, Rumi outsold every other poet in the US.
>
> The work on Hafiz is taking place now. One could say that his work is still more ecstatic and still more outspoken about crucial

27 *Night and Sleep: Rumi*, trans. C. Barks and R. Bly (Cambridge, MA: Yellow Moon 1981).

28 On which, see Lewis, *Rumi: Past and Present*, p. 588.

areas of disagreement in Muslim thought. Hafiz emphasizes his constant anger against the ascetics....[29]

This short article was published in conjunction with a conference on "Farid al-Din Attar (d. 1221) and the Persian Sufi Tradition" which I convened with Prof. Christopher Shackle at the School of Oriental and African Studies of the University of London (16-17 November 2002).[30] This conference was part of a larger program called "Intimations of Immortality: Mystical Yearnings in Iranian Poetry, Music and Art" organized by the Iran Heritage Foundation (IHF). The IHF also invited Bly to contribute another poetry reading of his translations of Rumi and Hafiz to this program. On Nov. 25, Bly gave a reading of his translations of Rumi and Hafiz to an audience of about 350 people at St. John's Church in Smith Square in London.

In the first part of the program, dedicated to Hafiz, he read from our translations, accompanied by the famous Iraqi Ud player Ahmad Mukhtar. In the second part, devoted to Rumi, he was accompanied by two young Iranian musicians Arash and Koorosh Muradi on the tambourak and setar.[31]

After Robert Bly's successful reading following the 2002 conference on 'Attar in London, we continued our work of translating Hafiz with even greater seriousness. Over the next four years, I was privileged to enjoy regular visits to Robert Bly's house in Minneapolis to work on Hafiz.[32]

---

29 *The Times* (Oct. 26, 2002); special supplement on "Mysticism: Intimations of Immortality: Mystical Yearnings in Iranian Poetry, Music and Art." I contributed a full double page spread with three articles to the same supplement (pp. 6-7): (1) on Hafiz entitled "Persia's rival to Shakespeare;" (2) on 'Attar: "Perfumed master of the religion of love;" and on Rumi: "Major-domo of Muslim mystical tradition."

30 Its proceedings I later edited (with Christopher Shackle) and published as *'Attar and the Persian Sufi Tradition: The Art of Spiritual Flight.*

31 The CD of this reading is currently (2010) being produced by Robert Simmons.

32 I spent a week in Minneapolis with him during January 2000; ten days during August 3-14, 2001, and again a week in September 2002. We also worked on Hafiz for 5 days in September 2003 in Mill Valley, CA., where he gave a poetry reading of our translations, accompanied by the renowned ethnomusicologist and specialist on Persian music Lloyd Miller, author of *Music and Song in Persia: the Art of Avaz.*

At the conclusion of our annual meetings, I always sent Robert Bly a fully updated status report on the readiness for publication of the individual ghazals that we had worked on. During the rest of the year we corresponded by post, phone and email about the meanings of select verses in the poems. By 2002, I had prepared twenty-two ghazals in a fully annotated form for him to use in our translation sessions. By mid-2005, our book of 30 Hafiz poems was practically finalized in the form that satisfied him, although it would take another year to perfect the translation of specific problematic verses, and another three years before it appeared in print. On Aug. 11, 2005, Robert Bly sent me an email in which he mentioned that he had just sent the preliminary manuscript of the poems off to HarperCollins:

> Shortly after I got back, I put together the old and new poems of Hafez that seemed to be going well, arranged them by the numbers in the edition that you use, got them all freshly typed and then sat down to read them. It was about nine o'clock at night, and when I got about halfway through I could feel myself getting dizzy. It was the sheer delight of the intensity of the poems and the wild variety of opinions and thoughts and the massive elegance of all infolding and outfolding from his personality. I jumped up and said, "This is one of the best books of poetry that's ever been!" I don't know that I'll have exactly the same experience when I read it again, but, as the wise people say, once is enough.

Our translation, which we eventually gave the title of *The Angels Knocking on the Tavern Door*, appeared in 2008 on the cusp of several important academic treatments of the Shirazi lyricist, for in the same year that we submitted our manuscript to the publisher, the most accurate and scholarly translation of the *Divan* of Hafiz in any European language – in French – by Prof. Charles-Henri de Fouchécour[33] appeared in print, and in the following year (2007), Peter Avery's full English translation of the *Divan*[34] came out. In early 2007 (March 30-April 1), I convened a conference on "Hafiz and the

33 C.-H. de Fouchécour, trans., *Hafiz de Chiraz: Le Divan: Œuvre lyrique d'un spirituel en Perse au XIVe siècle.*

34 Peter Avery, trans., *The Collected Lyrics of Háfiz of Shíráz.*

School of Love in Classical Persian Poetry at the University of Exeter, which later appeared as *Hafiz and the Religion of Love in Classical Persian Poetry* (2010).[35] Robert Bly's statement back in 2002 that "the work on Hafiz is taking place now" was indeed prescient.

The Three Steps of Translation of Hafiz

For me, the process of translating Hafiz with Robert Bly required painstaking background research. Even literal translation of one term, idea or image could consume hours of critical study. Perhaps having spent some two years in the early 1980s editing the *Divan* of the Persian Sufi poet Muhammad Shirin ("Shams") Maghribi (d. 810/1408), a contemporary of Hafiz,[36] which was later published by Tehran University Press, and having published a number of monographs, encyclopedia entries, and articles on other of Hafiz's great contemporaries and illustrious forebears among the Persian poets over the past twenty-five years, made the foolhardy – some would claim "impossible"[37] – task of translating Hafiz less daunting.

As translators, the basic symbolic topography of the Iranian poetic imagination as well as the technical symbolic vocabulary of Sufism[38] had been familiar territory to both of us for decades. We

---

35 Leonard Lewisohn, ed., *Hafiz and the Religion of Love in Classical Persian Poetry*.

36 *Divan-i Muhammad Shirin Maghribi*, Persian text edited by L. Lewisohn: see bibliography.

37 Hafiz, the argument runs, is untranslatable due to the formidable linguistic and cultural barriers that exist between classical Western Christian literature and Perso-Islamic *belles lettres* which remain insurmountable. See Dick Davis, "On Not Translating Hafez," and Shafi'i-Kadkani's similar views: "Dar tarjuma-napadhiri-yi shi'r," whose arguments for not translating Hafiz are restated by Islami-Nadushan, "Tarjuma-napadhiri-yi Hafiz."

38 See Leonard Lewisohn, "Ta'ammulati dar usul-i nazari u ravish-i tarjuma-yi ash'ar-i sufiyanih-i farsi," and also Javad Nurbakhsh, *Sufi Symbolism I: (Farhang-i Nurbakhsh)*, tr. L. Lewisohn and T. Graham. See also my remarks in "Hafez and His Genius," *The Angels Knocking on the Tavern Door*, pp. 81ff.

were both fully aware of the steepness of the mountain slopes to be scaled yet had our eye fixed on the sublime panoramas that could be seen from the peaks of Hafiz's angelic realm, where his language is transformed into the "Tongue of the Unseen" (*lisan al-ghayb*). Nevertheless, in homage and deference to all those learned Hafizologists, on whose shoulders all latter-day students of the Sage of Shiraz must stand, I prepared a literal, fully annotated translation of each ghazal for us to use as a crib. A score of Persian commentaries on the *Divan* of Hafiz were consulted for this, and countless glossaries and dictionaries of his terminology, historical studies, and literary monographs on key images, ideas, and terms in his lexicon perused.[39] Reference to the critical apparatus of twentieth and twenty-first century Iranian scholarship on the *Divan* was indispensable to me in illuminating the various contexts—literary, mystical, metaphysical, historical—of the poetry during the first stage of this translation, which involved writing a literal translation with annotated commentary on each poem.

It was clear to both of us that Hafiz's ghazals are multi-dimensional, replete with various layers of allusion—literary, symbolic, historical, ethical, political, scriptural-Qur'anic, etc.—often compounded within a single verse.[40] The historical, socio-political, theological, metaphysical and mystical, as well as the aesthetic and literary references in each of Hafiz's verses are often multifarious and usually recondite. When approaching Hafiz's Sufi lexicon, we well understood that it would be naïve and simplistic to interpret and de-

39 For publication details and a shortlist of the key works consulted during my preparation of the literal translations of each ghazal see the bibliography of my *Hafiz and the Religion of Love in Classical Persian Poetry.*

40 On this aspect of his poetic art, see Khurramshahi, "Uslub-i hunari-yi Hafiz va Qur'an," p. 7. G.M. Wickens in an intriguing article on "An Analysis of Primary and Secondary Significations in the Third *Ghazal* of Hafiz," made a preliminary study of this aspect of the multi-dimensionality and literary polysemy of his ghazals, although certain inconsistencies in his thesis were later strongly criticised by Mary Boyce, "A Novel Interpretation of Hafiz." Cf. Ashuri's analysis of the relationship between the sensual, spiritual, social, ethical, and political dimensions of meaning in Hafiz's ghazals in his *'Irfan u rindi dar shi'r-i Hafiz*, pp. 355-74.

code his language into literal one-to-one equivalences of symbols,[41] after the awful style of Wilberforce Clarke[42] for instance, but we did deem it necessary to familiarize ourselves with all the relevant connotative references in Hafiz's dictionary of terminology.

Neither of us found any previously published translations of Hafiz particularly useful. In particular, none of the classical Victorian translators of Hafiz who flourished during the last half of the 19th and first half of the 20th century mentioned earlier—a selection of whose versions were reproduced by A.J. Arberry in his *Fifty Poems of Hafiz* (first published in 1947)—had any effect, whether positive or negative, on kindling Robert Bly's interest in Hafiz. Although in selecting poems for us to work on and translate together, Robert Bly occasionally made use of Arberry's *Fifty Poems*, in general he viewed these Victorian verse renditions as tastelessly botched, abhorrent travesties of the art of literary translation, even if occasionally they did succeed in mimicking a verse's cadence or phrase's sense with some elegance.[43]

The two major poetic renditions of Hafiz ghazals into the type of modernist English verse favoured by Robert Bly were the translation by Peter Avery and John Heath-Stubbs entitled *Thirty Poems of Hafiz of Shiraz*, translated (London 1952), and *The Green Sea of Heaven: Fifty ghazals from the Díwán of Háfiz*, translated by Elizabeth Grey (Ashland, Oregon: White Cloud Press 1995). I gave Bly a copy of the Avery and

41 Purjavadi, "Rindi-yi Hafiz," *Bu-yi jan*, p. 238.

42 *Divan-i-Hafiz*, trans. H. Wilberforce Clarke. Finn Thiesen in his "Pseudo-Hafez: A Reading of Wilberforce Clarke's Rendering of *Divan-i Hafez*," has exposed how unreliable both as a literal translation and misleading as a commentary on the poetry is this translation.

43 To cite but one instance, when I gave Robert Bly a copy of Wilberforce Clarke's translation of the entire *Divan* of Hafiz, he wrote back to me: "I've never known anyone who has gone to the trouble of ruining Hafez's reputation so energetically as Wilberforce Clarke. However, I did hold my nose and go through the list [of his translations] that you sent..." (Letter of 24 July, 2001) However, it must be readily acknowledged that both of us stand on the shoulders of the three great British translators and scholars of Persian literature: E.G. Browne (1862-1926), R.A. Nicholson (1868-1945) and A.J. Arberry (1905-73); indeed all present-day translators of Persian poetry remain indebted to their pioneering studies.

Heath-Stubbs's translation back in the early 1990s. I believe he found this useful, although not always to his taste. He expressed considerable admiration for Elizabeth Grey's renditions, and occasionally he asked me to translate and do research on a certain ghazal after having read her translation of it.

Hafiz's symbolic lexicon details a well-known "visionary topography," as Daryush Shayegan so aptly dubs it,[44] that is reasonably well-mapped, being, as Alessandro Bausani has rightly proposed, the product of the paradoxical "social hermeticism" of classical Persian Sufi poetry, in contrast to the individualistic hermeticism of modern poetry, which is reckless and imprecise.[45] Just as Hafiz's terms have precise etymological derivations, equally they all possess a long history in Sufi symbolism.[46] Eric Schoeder underlines that "his [Hafiz's] *Divan* is permeated with Sufism; and the meaning of his life and work is primarily religious and metaphysical. Even an aesthetic critique of his verse which fails to show the intricacy of his metaphysical reference is aesthetically shallow, since much of his art is precisely the calculated weaving of multiple meaning."[47]

The first stage of this translation for me thus involved a kind of literary cartography: surveying the various layers of meaning (historical, aesthetic, mystical, metaphysical...) hidden within the ground of the poem. Very few Persian-speakers, let alone Westerners, understand the type of philosophico-theological thinking that underpins Hafiz's bacchanalian, romantic and erotic imagery, while those who do have the requisite 'learning of the Imagination' which inspired his poetry originally are as rare today as sightings of the phoenix.

The second stage of translation was now quite simple. Once the learned debates over a given ghazal in the critical literature had been surveyed, once the ghazal's bacchanalian and erotic images and symbols and key metaphysical, theological, political, mystical ideas had been researched and analyzed, each verse was then deconstructed into clear prose.

44 Shayegan, "The Visionary Topography of Hafiz."
45 Bausani, *Religion in Iran: from Zoroaster to Baha'ullah*, p. 256.
46 Purjavadi, "Rindi-yi Hafiz," in idem., *Bu-yi jan*, p. 238.
47 Schoeder, "Verse Translation and Hafiz," p. 216.

Finally, the third stage of the translation, which involved making a total linguistic reconstruction of the ghazal in the English language, the moods, sounds and rhythms of which are utterly alien to Persian, proved to be even more difficult than anything yet experienced. Fortunately, the labor involved in this final stage of translation rested on the shoulders of the poet, and my role here became merely one of being an interpreter of the subtle nuances of Persian words and the connotations of their various renditions in English. Whenever the idiomatic requirements of the English language or Bly's inventive genius occasionally demanded that new images be added to a verse or metaphors slightly altered in a poem, I took care to insure that the integrity of the higher "archetypal sense" (*ma'na*)[48] of Hafiz's verse remained intact in English. My sole concern was to be faithful to both the literal and anagogic senses of the poem, each verse of which we discussed word by word, phrase by phrase until we reached a text mutually agreeable to both of us.

The Art of Interpretation of Hafiz's Ambiguity: *Double Entendre*, Islamic Mystical Terms, Historical and Religious Allusions

Although Hafiz's poetry is notoriously difficult to interpret, most Westerners are unaware that it is easier for a native Persian to understand Hafiz's poetry than it is for an Anglophone reader to read Shakespeare. Whereas Shakespearean English to the modern speaker of English represents a quaint, archaic dialect at best and a dead language at worst, the contemporary language of Iran and Afghanistan is by and large exactly the same Persian spoken by Hafiz in 14th-century Shiraz. As Peter Avery points out, any cab driver in Tehran or Kabul can eloquently expound for you his favorite ghazal of Hafiz, which he normally has by heart down to its last syllable and symbol. But who has ever encountered a London or New York

48 See my *Beyond Faith and Infidelity*, pp. 181-83 for a discussion of this aspect of the aesthetics of Persian poetry.

cabbie capable of expounding even one verse from a Shakespearean sonnet?[49] Hafiz is everyone's best friend and hundreds of lines of his verse are on everyone's tongue in Persophone lands. Of course, each person intuitively appreciates him best, and everyone certainly knows him better than their neighbour does. Interpretation of Hafiz's poetry has always been socially hazardous. How many old friends have I found suddenly turn angry foe because my exegesis of the Shirazi master's verse was insufficiently reverential, or else saw my apprehension of covert sexual innuendos in his ribald metaphors a damnable profanation of their sacred national poet. How often an argument or applause have I won, how many vexing existential or metaphysical questions finally manage to settle by appropriate citation of a verse of his. To take umbrage at Hafiz's verse is sacrilege, for Hafiz always has the last word.

Nonetheless, modern university-educated rationalists in Iran and Afghanistan, since the early twentieth century at least, have ridiculed the metaphysical system behind Hafiz's poems and the religious and sacred aspect of his symbolism as a kind superstitious absurdity that is no longer within the range of intellectually respectable ideas. Today his spiritual and metaphysical teachings are quite often excluded from the curriculum of modern Persian literature departments in universities both East and West. The recondite nature of the sort of theological lore sustaining Hafiz's images and metaphors, which Robert Bly and I studied in detail while engaged in our work of translation, is best illustrated by specific examples. Since space does not allow more than discussion of a few lines, only four lines from one ghazal will be examined here.

Ghazal 64

I began by explaining to Robert Bly that this ghazal is celebrated both among both Christian admirers of Hafiz and scholars of com-

49 "Foreword: Hafiz of Shiraz," in Lewisohn (ed.), *Hafiz and the Religion of Love*, pp. x-xi.

parative religion as exemplifying the ecumenical spirit of the Persian Sufis.[50] My literal version of the first line was as follows:

Ru-yi tu kas nadid va hizarat raqib hast/
dar ghuncha-i hunuz u sadat 'andalib hast

No one has seen your face and yet there are a thousand chamberlains [already in waiting, on the lookout for you].

You are still [hidden] within the rosebud, and yet there are a hundred nightingales [ready to warble your praises].

The meaning of the couplet was far from clear to Robert Bly, who queried the significance of the term "chamberlain" (*raqib*). In considering the most appropriate rendition of this word, I had noted that in some of Hafiz's other ghazals the term *raqib* may also mean "rival," or even both "rival" and "butler" at once, since insofar as it is the butler/ doorkeeper who can refuse the lover access to the beloved, the butler may also be his rival. However, according to two contemporary commentators (Haravi and Khurramshahi) as well as the seventeenth-century traditional Sufi commentator Lahuri, the term in this context does not indicate a *rival* at all, but rather "doorkeeper," "butler," or "chamberlain."

Once we had come to understand the literal sense of the entire couplet, which now seemed fairly straightforward, we might have stopped there, but investigation of the ghazal's difficult mystical theology divulged the deeper spiritual structure of the verse, which now merited our careful consideration. The first three lines of this ghazal address the theological debate which raged in scholastic circles in mediæval Islam about whether it is possible to perceive God in *this world*.[51] Abu'l-Hasan 'Abd al-Rahman Khatmi Lahuri in his

50 See the Iranian Anglican Bishop G. H. B. Dihqani-Tafti's work on *Christ and Christianity Among the Persians: Masih va masihiyyat nazd-i Iraniyan*, III: *Dar nazm u nathr u hunar-i mu'asir*, who cites line 6 of this ghazal as demonstrating Hafiz's interest in Christianity.

51 On these debates, see Nasru'llah Purjavadi, *Ru'yat-i mah dar asiman*, who cites this verse as the epigraph for his whole study.

commentary on Hafiz's *Divan* written in India circa 1617, to which I frequently referred when preparing literal annotated versions for Robert Bly, places the verses in the context of these theological debates, stating:

> It should be understood that between the scholastic theologians *(mutakalliman)* and the gnostics whose knowledge is through direct experiental verification and realization *(muhaqqiqan)* a debate exists about whether the love of the devotee for God Almighty is valid. The theologians argue that it is invalid because love is established either by sight or hearing, and the devotee is not allowed access to God by either of these modes. ...According to the gnostics, a view which is contrary to the tenets of the theologians, the love of God for man and of man for God, both in respect to the Holy Canon-Law of Islam *(shari'at)*, the Sufi Path *(tariqat)* and the divine Reality *(Haqiqat)* is permitted and authorized, and this can be attested by many passages in the [Qur'anic] scripture and by numerous sayings of the Prophet. ...Now, in this verse, the discourse of the gnostic of Shiraz (Hafiz) is in agreement with the persuasion of the gnostics whose knowledge is through direct experiental verification and realization. ...The second hemistich of this verse is related to the first hemistich through the rhetorical device of repetitive 'folding and unfolding' *(laff u nashr)*, so that for example, [he states] "your true-divine face and visage has not been seen by anyone *in this world*, and yet there are a thousand lovers eagerly yearning for you." This situation is analogous to saying that your existence resembles an unopened rosebud that is being courted by a thousand nightingales. This is opposed to the customary practice of the nightingale that usually only falls in love with the rose once it opens up and blossoms and diffuses its fragrance abroad.[52]

Although Lahuri's commentary on this ghazal runs into many pages, it is clear that Hafiz intends to say that while God (the rose) in this world lies concealed beneath veils of majesty and glory (the thousand chamberlains), and so forever invisible to the optical sight and aural apprehension of man, nonetheless, despite His invisibility, He

52 *Sharh-i 'irfani-yi Divan-i Hafiz*, I, pp. 409-10.

still has a thousand lovers who love and yearn for Him with all their heart and soul.[53]

The mystical theology and key technical terms underlying the outwardly romantic "rose-and-nightingale" imagery of this verse having been deciphered, another dilemma presented itself: how best to convey Hafiz's image of a rosebud with a thousand doorkeepers in modern English poetry? After hours of discussion and several revisions, Robert Bly settled on the following translation:

> No one has ever seen your face, and yet a thousand
> Door-keepers have arrived. You are a rose still closed,
> And yet a hundred nightingales have arrived.

We both agreed that this summarized Hafiz's meaning quite succinctly. Although some of the theological implications of the verse outlined above may have been lost in translation, at least the poetic translation of this verse had forfeited nothing of its literal meaning.

However, the most problematic verse in this ghazal was the sixth, the literal translation of which, despite my detailed footnotes, remained unclear:

> *Anja kay kar-i suma'a ra jilwa midahand/*
> *naqus-i dayr-i rahib*[54] *u nam-i salib hast*

> There where they celebrate the affairs of the holy oratory, there is [also found] the monk's hermitage bell and the name of the cross.

The most difficult term to grasp in this verse is *suma'a*, translated above as "holy oratory," a word which can mean (according to context) either monastery, monk's cell, abbey, tabernacle, chapel, chantry, oratory, or house of prayer. The term's original connotation seems to have been a monk's chantry, more or less equivalent to the term "cloister" *(dayr)*, which is its Arabic meaning in the Qur'an

53 Cf. my "Hafez and His Genius," *The Angels*, p. 84.

54 Although Khanlari's *lectio* is *namus-i dayr-i rahib* (the honor of the monk's hermitage), in two of his MSS. *namus* is replaced by *naqus* (hermitage bell), which is the reading I have chosen, also following Qazvini's/ Ghani's edition of the *Divan*.

(XXII: 40), where the term first appears.[55] This verse in particular exposes Hafiz's interest in Christianity and Christian symbolism and is completely in the vein of the Persian Sufis' utilization of Christian symbols as ciphers to connote the higher realities of their esoteric Sufi doctrine.[56] But *suma'a* also has *extra*-Christian associations reflected in several other verses where Hafiz used the term to denote the Sufi meeting house (*khanaqah*).[57] In this verse in particular, it would have been illogical if not absurd to translate the term *suma'a* as *Christian* cloister or oratory: for the poet to have said that the Christian bell and cross are a necessary accoutrement of the *Christian suma'a* would have been redundant. The key to understanding this verse, many commentators state, lies in viewing it as an elaboration of the previous line (5) of the ghazal, which we had translated as:

Dar 'ishq khanaqah u kharabat farq nist/
har ja kay hast partaw-i ru-yi habib hast

In this matter of love, let's not put the Sufi gathering house
In this spot and the tavern in another; in every spot of the
    universe
Light shines out from the face of the Friend.

The eminent commentator Khurramshahi's prose paraphrase of verse six thus summarizes its gist quite well:

> However much there may be a distinction between the sacred rites and customs of Christianity and Islam, or for that matter, between any religion with other religions, there is a common unity and reality which all religions share. Even if the [Christian symbols of] 'cross' and 'bell' are not sacred to Muslims, ultimately they contribute to celebrate and amplify the lustre and eminence of the

---

55 Khurramshahi, *Hafiz-nama*, I, pp. 337-38.

56 See Leonard Lewisohn, "The Esoteric Christianity of Islam," pp. 127-56.

57 With this connotation (equivalent to *khanaqah*), its polar opposite had always appeared as "the Magian Temple" (*dayr-i Mughan*): see Khanlari, ed., *Divan*, ghazal 2:3 and Khurramshahi's analysis: *Hafiz-nama*, I, pp. 101-02.

> *suma'a*—so in this respect and context this term acts as a metaphor that conveys and unites one to [higher] Reality.[58]

Now how should one translate *suma'a*? As a Christian, or a Muslim Sufi temple?

Although in another ghazal where the term *suma'a* occurred (77:4) we had translated it as "hermit's hut," three eminent commentators had ruled that in this ghazal the term *must* here denote either "a house of Muslim worship,"[59] or "a Sufi house of worship (*khanaqah*)."[60] So here was an explicitly *Christian* term with definite *Muslim* and *Sufi* connotations. Because Hafiz in another verse had specifically used the term *suma'a* to denote an Islamic place of worship—the Sufi *khanaqah*—and associated Sufis with the *suma'a*,[61] we decided that it was entirely appropriate to translate the term *suma'a* as "the *Muslim* cloister."[62] No doubt, the deliberate religious ambiguity of the term in Persian has certain other poetic associations and symbolic dimensions that will forever remain lost in translation, but if we had attempted to preserve that ambiguity in English, our translation would have appeared either exotic and fatuous—arcane at best, meaningless at worst. Thus, in deference to the opinion of the majority of commentators on the line, we decided to specify its meaning in our English translation. The discussion on the meaning of the term *suma'a* in this line, having taken well over an hour, Robert Bly and I at last settled on:

---

58 Khurramshahi, *Hafiz-nama*, I, p. 338.

59 Husayn 'Ali Haravi, *Sharh-i ghazalha-yi Hafiz*, I, p. 279. Lahuri, commenting on another ghazal (77:4; *Sharh-i 'irfani*, I, p, 574) translated in this collection, states clearly that although "etymologically speaking, *suma'a* does indeed signify a Christian space of devotion or a Zoroastrian temple, in this context it refers to a *Muslim* place of worship because it is juxtaposed to *kanisht* ...which is a Jewish or Zoroastrian temple."

60 Isti'lami, *Dars-i Hafiz*, I, p. 228.

61 His reference, e.g., to *sufiyan-i suma'a-dar* (Khanlari, ed., *Divan*, ghazal 215: 7) in particular; also ghazal 368:2 which refers to the Sufi customs of the *suma'a*. See also Khurramshahi, *Hafiz-nama*, I, p. 102 for several other references in which *suma'a=khanaqah*.

62 This is also the second definition of the term given in the *Farhang-i farsi-yi Mu'in* (Tehran: Amir Kabir 1375 A.Hsh./1996), II, p. 2174.

> There where the good work of the Muslim cloister
> Is celebrated, we celebrate as well the bell
> Of the monk's cell and the name of the Cross.

Each line of every ghazal in *The Angels* was subjected to the same exhaustive treatment. Once I had translated and presented to Robert Bly all the important exegetical scholarship available on a given ghazal, he then proceeded to compose several versions of a given line which he read aloud to me. Several hours of debate and argument later, one, or a combination of several, of these lines would be chosen as the final translation; in some cases, if necessary, an entirely new version would be prepared. Since our schedules rarely allowed us to allocate more than two weeks per year to discuss Hafiz, several drafts of ghazals were inevitably made, each of which we then reworked over the course of several years on the basis of new research.

Robert Bly in the Shadow of Hafiz

Sufism has been a key formative influence on Bly's own thought and verse over the last two decades. The central Sufi concept most frequently found in his prose and poetry written in the last two decades (1990-2010) is the notion of the *nafs*, which in Sufi doctrine, literally means 'soul', but in the technical sense, refers to the drives which predominate in an unregenerate psyche – what eighteenth-century faculty psychology dubbed "carnal passion." Bly usually translates the term as "the greedy soul" or the "insatiable soul" in his works. In the first chapter of *The Sibling Society*, he devotes seven pages to the *nafs*,[63] and in *The Night Abraham Called to the Stars* mentions the concept in six different places.[64] The *nafs* is one of the most dominant psychological motifs in his later poetry.

63 Bly, *The Sibling Society* (Reading, MA: Addison-Wesley Publishing Co. 1996), pp. 21-28.

64 *The Night Abraham*: p. 31, stanza 3 ("Lord of Greed"); p. 37, stanza 2 ("greedy souls"); p. 51, stanza 3 ("greedy soul"); p. 55, stanza 2 ("growing soul"); p. 57, stanza 4 ("greedy soul"); p. 61 stanza 4 ("greedy soul"). *My Sentence*: p. 25, stanza 5 ("greedy soul").

Bly's immersion in the writings of the classical Sufis shows in his direct mention of the sayings by or stories about a number of classical Sufi figures in his two books of ghazals, including the likes of Rabi'a (d. 801),[65] Abu Sa'id (d. 1048),[66] and Shabistari (d. after 1340).[67] It should be recalled that *The Night Abraham Called to the Stars* was itself dedicated to Dr. Nurbakhsh, to whom Bly remained much attached until his death in 2008. He also dedicated an entire poem to the classical Persian Sufi singer Shahram Nazeri whose music he greatly admires.[68]

During our fourteen years of work on translating Hafiz, a number of rhetorical and doctrinal elements were clearly appropriated by Robert Bly from Hafiz's ghazals for use in his poems. Hafiz in particular was one of the key influences on both the form and the content of his two later collections of poetry: *The Night Abraham Called to the Stars* (2001), and *My Sentence Was a Thousand Years of Joy* (2005).

In *The Night Abraham Called to the Stars*, there are several direct references to verses, ideas, or images directly taken from Hafiz. One of these occurs in the following two stanzas from "The Way the Parrot Learns," where he writes:

> Trainers once placed a parrot before a mirror,
> And a man behind. The parrot, assuming
> A parrot was speaking, would learn to talk.
>
> Perhaps if God would put up a mirror
> And sit behind it, and talk, I could believe
> That those words of mercy were coming from me.[69]

These stanzas present Bly's own exegesis on Hafiz's verse:

> *Tuti-sifat par pish-i ayina dashta-am*
> *An-chi ustad azal guft hamam miguyam*

---

65 *My Sentence*: p. 57.

66 *My Sentence*: p. 87.

67 *My Sentence*: p. 83.

68 *My Sentence*: p. 61 "Listening to Shahram Nazeri."

69 *The Night Abraham Called to the Stars*, p. 37. N.B. There is a misprint in the last line. *Read*: "Around those days when *we* danced in the road."

> Like a parrot I have been kept before the mirror.
> I but repeat what the Eternal Teacher dictates.

He also directly refers to this same verse by Hafiz (which, strange to say, is not found in any of the ghazals that I worked on with him) in the following stanza:

> I don't know if you've heard the buff-chested grouse
> When he drums on an old log. He is like Hafez
> Repeating something he has heard from his teacher.[70]

Another key doctrine of the Sufis expressed in the poetry of Hafiz is the denigration of rationalism, intellectualism and reason in favour of the *furor* of love and the glorification of ecstasy. Thus Hafiz advises:

> Ask not of us more than obeisance
> To lunatics: the master of our sect always
> Said rationalism was all wickedness.[71]

The same theme appears as well in this verse:

> The holy court of love is a thousand times higher
> Than the house of reason. Only a man who holds his soul
> Lightly on his sleeve can kiss the threshold of that court.[72]

(Incidentally, under the rubric of "Learning to Love Excess"[73] in Bly's essay on "Six Disciplines that Intensify Poetry," we find the parallel Western literary tradition underlying this doctrine described in detail). In the first line of the second poem in *The Night Abraham Called to the Stars*, Bly thus expresses this quintessential Hafizian notion:

> Once more the murky world is becoming confused. Oh
> The essence of Reason's House is confusion,
> So this development is like the owl becoming more owlish.[74]

---

70 *My Sentence*, p. 95.
71 *Diwan-i Hafiz*, ed. Khanlari, ghazal 48: 4 (my translation)
72 Bly and Lewisohn, (trans.), *The Angels*, p. 55.
73 *The Thousands*, ed. Robert Bly, no. 1 (2001), pp. 33-40.
74 *The Night Abraham Called to the Stars*, p. 3.

And in the next stanza of the same poem, he reiterates the same Sufi privileging of love at the expense of reason:

> Arithmetic has failed to bring order to our sorrow.
> Newton is not guilty, because the man who
> Invents the knife is not responsible for the murder.[75]

The same theme recurs in other poems in this collection, as, for example:

> We value addition and subtraction too much
> Ten thousand Newtons wrapping their equations
> Around the serpent's tail can't replace a single lover.[76]

Or:

> The ink we write with seeps in through our fingers.
> What we call reason is the way the parasite
> Learns to live in the saint's tract.[77]

The last two stanzas are heavily indebted to several verses of Hafiz in our translation where the same concept is clearly enunciated:

> The hot brand which we have pressed onto
> Our lunatic hearts is so intense it would set fire
> To the straw piles of a hundred reasonable ascetics.

Further evidence of this appears later on in the same ghazal by Hafiz where the originals of the terms "parasite" and "reason" mentioned above by Bly can be found:

> ...The man next door, whom I have called a parasite
> Of reason and an intellectual is—thanks to God—
> Like us, actually faithless and without heart.[78]

---

75 *Ibid.*
76 *The Night Abraham Called to the Stars*, p. 11.
77 *The Night Abraham Called to the Stars*, p. 47.
78 Robert Bly and Leonard Lewisohn, *The Angels*, pp. 15-16.

Similarly, in the first poem in *My Sentence Was a Thousand Years of Joy*, Bly appropriates the Sufi notion of the superior rank of the lover in human civilization, "Westernizing" it in the process by applying it to the low position of the lover in the European Middle Ages:

> Those lovers, skinny and badly dressed, hated
> By parents, did the work; all through the Middle Ages,
> It was the lovers who kept the door open to heaven.[79]

Another key theme in Hafiz's poetry is his emphasis on the centrality of "erotic melancholy" or "love's grief" (*ghamm-i 'ishq*). The Persian poet's view that the woes and sorrows of love comprise paradoxically its delights and blessings, since these ultimately deepen one's comprehension of *Eros* and the erotic, are clearly expressed in a number of verses by Hafiz in our translation, for example:

> The Sultan of Pre-Eternity gave us the casket of love's grief
> As a gift; therefore we have turned our face
> Toward this wrecked caravanseri that we call "the world."[80]

And:

> The jealousy of love has severed the tongues
> Of all the Gnostics. How could it be that the mystery of His grief
> Ever settled down to the people walking along the street?[81]

Robert Bly echoed Hafiz's sentiments and expressions precisely in his own poetry. Thus, in "A Poem for Andrew Marvell," he writes:

> Twice this morning I've kissed Marvell's book.
> He's glad for the mourners—whose eyes are blessed
> By grief, who "weep the more and see the less."[82]

In "Tightening the Cinch," he says:

---

79 Bly, *My Sentence Was a Thousand Years of Joy*, p. 3.
80 Bly and Lewisohn, trans. *The Angels*, p. 15.
81 Bly and Lewisohn, trans. *The Angels*, p. 57.
82 Bly, *My Sentence*, p. 5.

> While they saddle the horses, just keep shouting,
> "My grief is a horse; I am the missing rider!"
> The grief of absence is the only bread I eat.[83]

It should be stressed that there is no verb in English for "eating grief," whereas in Persian a verb with exactly this connotation and conjugation (*gham khwurdan* = to "eat grief," i.e. to grieve) does exist. Bly has obviously rendered this Persian verb—one constantly used by Hafiz, and which he knew of from our discussions—into English in his own idiosyncratic manner in this stanza.

Another key Sufi theme found in Hafiz is the doctrine of accepting blame and reproach in love, in line with the *malamati* tradition which opposes the conventions and institutions of orthodox religious piety and abstinence.[84] While translating Hafiz, we frequently discussed the Shirazi poet's *malamati* doctrines, in which the lover typically praises selflessness as constituting the essence of the spiritual path and glories in the pursuit of notoriety and the incurrence of public blame. In the following verse from the end of his poem "The Greek Ships" in *My Sentence Was a Thousand Years of Joy*,[85] we can find Bly's own personal *malamati* ethic enunciated:

> Go ahead; throw your good name into the water.
> All those who ruined their lives for love
> Are calling to us from a hundred sunken ships.[86]

The key images and ideas in this stanza seemed to have been borrowed directly from the two opening stanzas of this ghazal from our translation of Hafiz:

> I'm notorious throughout the whole city
> As a renegade lover; and I'm that man who has
> Never darkened his vision by seeing evil.

83 Bly, *My Sentence*, p. 25.

84 For a discussion of *malamati* doctrine in Hafiz, see my *Hafiz and the Religion of Love*, Prolegomenon 2, pp. 36ff.

85 Bly, *My Sentence*, p. 19.

86 Bly, *My Sentence*, p. 19.

> Through my enthusiasm for wine, I have thrown the book
> Of my good name into the water; but doing that insures that
> The handwriting in my book of grandiosity will be blurred.[87]

Aside from these Persian Sufi images and ideas, Bly also adopted a number of formal elements of Persian lyric poetry and poetic devices from Hafiz's ghazals for use in his own verse.

The first of these elements is the poetic device of 'indirect symbolic allusion' (*isharat*), in which various abstract figures, such as the Lover, the Lunatic, the Puritan, Preacher, Ascetic, etc., are used by poets like Hafiz to symbolize various spiritual or psychological types of human beings. An example of Bly's use of this device from the Persian ghazal can be found in this stanza:

> The Pharoah's wives touch the mud with their toes.
> You and I float in Moses' cradle. Dear friends, you and I
> Are parted by a thin skin from the ignorance of the Nile.[88]

Here, we need to recognize that in Sufi poetry Moses functions as a symbol of the dry pedant or hyper-rationalist, typifying one who exalts reason at the expense of imagination and intuition, resembling Blake's Urizen ("your reason"). In this stanza, Bly is saying that the egocentric self or the "insatiable soul"—described at length in the opening chapter of *The Sibling Society*—is constricted and bound in Moses's cradle, being swaddled and stunted by the immaturity of his own worldly reason. The repetition of the phrase "you and I" twice in the second line above is a thoroughly Sufi gesture; in fact it is a direct translation from Persian of the phrase *man u ma* (I and thou, mine and thine), referring to the selfish and self-absorbed ego, a phrase which fills many of Hafiz's ghazals.

The second device adopted by Bly from Hafiz's ghazals is what the Arabic rhetoricians and theorists of poetry call the "return to the opening verse" (*radd al-matla'*), in which all the key technical terms, images, and sometimes, the entire phrase and distich are repeated

87 Bly and Lewisohn, trans. *The Angels*, p. 21.
88 Bly, *The Night...*", p. 9.

at the end of the ghazal exactly, or in a similar fashion, as they were voiced in the opening line. This device is also found in English poetry although it is extremely rare.[89] We see Bly's use of this device in the first stanza of his poem "When We Became Lovers":

> Do you laugh or cry when you hear the poet sing?
> "Out of the warmth of the spring, and out
> Of the shine of the hemlocks..." It's the hemlocks then.[90]

In the final stanza of the poem, he repeats all the key words and themes ("warmth of the spring," crying, laughing, hemlocks) over once again.

Likewise, his poem "In Praise of Scholars,"[91] begins with the line: "Furry shadows are bringing gifts to the door" and the concluding stanza again repeats the same line: "The furry shadows are bringing gifts to the door."

However, the two best-known poetic devices which Robert Bly adopted from the Persian ghazal form are the signature verse (*takhallus*) at the end of the ghazal and repetition of the rhyme word at the end of each couplet.

The *takhallus* is the signature verse of the ghazal in which the poet finishes off his poem by "signing off" with his *nom de plume*. In *My Sentence Was a Thousand Years of Joy* Bly frequently employed this device, with "Robert" being repeated in the concluding stanza in fifteen of the forty-eight poems of the collection.[92]

The most important formal element of every ghazal is the repetition of the rhyming word at the end of every couplet. In *The Night Abraham Called to the Stars* Bly appropriated and utilized this device in

89 Carl Sandburg's (d. 1967) poem "Evening Waterfall" in which the two opening lines: "What was the name you called me?—/ And why did you go so soon?" are reiterated as its concluding verses, exemplifies this device in English poetry.

90 Bly, *The Night...*", p. 13.

91 Bly, *The Night...*", p. 49.

92 Bly, *My Sentence*, pp. 5, 13, 23, 29, 47, 51, 53, 65, 67, 75, 79, 83, 85, 87, 95, where "Robert" is repeated in each concluding stanza.

five different poems.[93] Interestingly enough, in one of these poems, he employed exactly the same word ("separation") that Hafiz had used as the key rhyming word in one his ghazals (*firagh*). In *My Sentence Was a Thousand Years of Joy* this device is featured in seven poems as well,[94] in one poem even proudly acknowledging his use of this poetic device taken from the Persian ghazal:

> When each stanza closes with the same word,
> I am glad. A friend says, "If you're proud of that,
> You must be one of the secretaries of non-existence."[95]

Lastly, in both collections of poems published in the first decade of the 21st century, Robert Bly took over the three-line stanzaic form that he had discovered and perfected during our translation of Hafiz during the 1990s to replicate the Persian hemistich or couplet form (*bayt*) found in Hafiz's ghazals, and successfully applied this stanza form to all the poems in *The Night Abraham Called to the Stars* and *My Sentence Was a Thousand Years of Joy*.

Robert Bly's appropriation of these rhetorical aspects of the Persian Sufi ghazal tradition and integration of them into his own English verse has been extremely successful. Since Fitzgerald's creative remodeling of the *Rubaiyyat* of 'Umar Khayyam into English quatrains in the 19th century, and Lorca's *Casidas* written in imitation of Arabic *qasidas* and Gunnar Ekelöf's poems in imitation of Ibn 'Arabi's and Ibn Farid's Arabic Sufi verse, and Louis Aragon's infatuation with Jami's *Leili va Majnun* (all works well known to Bly) in the 20th century, Bly's original re-adaptation of Hafiz's Persian verse for the uses of his own poetry is unprecedented, representing the most important impact that classical Persian poetry has had so far

93 Bly, *The Night...*", where various words or phrases recur at the end of every stanza. On pp. 61 ("it's already too late"); on pp. 81 ("separation"); on p. 85 ("faithful"); p. 91 ("listening"); p. 93 ("Amen"); p. 95 ("dawn") are repeated.

94 Bly, *My Sentence...*", p. 17 ("so many times"); p. 23 ("It's all right"), p. 61 ("it's already too late"); p. 87 ("existence"); p. 89 ("faithfulness"); p. 93 ("non-existence"); p. 97 ("joy").

95 Bly, *My Sentence...*", p. 93.

on modern European and American poetry of the 21st century. In my opinion none of the previous great literary translators of Hafiz and Rumi into English, whether Basil Bunting, John Heath-Stubbs, or Robert Duncan, have even faintly managed to match Bly's achievement and innovations in English poetry based on the classical Persian ghazal tradition.[96]

96 Regarding the creative adaptations of classical Persian poetry into English, only Peter Russell in English has achieved a similar success, although his achievement has not enjoyed Bly's public recognition.

Bibliography

Mahnaz Ahmad, *Persian Poetry and the English Reader from the Eighteenth to the Twentieth Century* (M. Litt. Dissertation, University of Newcastle upon Tyne, U.K. 1971).

Mehdi Aminrazavi, *The Wine of Wisdom: The Life, Poetry and Philosophy of Omar Khayyam* (Oxford: Oneworld 2005).

A.J. Arberry, *Fifty Poems of Hafiz*, (Cambridge: Cambridge University Press 1977).

Daryush Ashuri, *'Irfan u rindi dar shi'r-i Hafiz* (Tehran: Nashr-i Markaz 1381 A.Hsh./2003).

Peter Avery, "Fitzgerald's Persian Teacher and Hafez," *Sufi: A Journal of Sufism*, Issue 6 (1990), pp. 10-15.

__________, trans. with John Heath-Stubbs. *Thirty Poems of Hafiz of Shiraz* (London: Archetype Press reprint 2006).

__________, trans. *The Collected Lyrics of Háfiz of Shíráz* (London: Archetype 2007).

Alessandro Bausani, *Religion in Iran: from Zoroaster to Baha'ullah*, tr. J.M. Marchesi, (New York 2000).

Gertrude Bell, *The Hafez Poems of Gertrude Bell* (reprinted Bethesda, Maryland: Iranbooks 1995).

Robert Bly. *The Kabir Book: Forty-Four of the Ecstatic Poems of Kabir, Versions by Robert Bly* (The Seventies Press 1971).

________. With James Hillman and Michael Meade. Eds. *The Rag and Bone Shop of the Heart* (New York: HarperCollins 1992).

________. *Mirabai: Ecstatic Poems* (translated with Jane Hirshfield), (Boston: Beacon Press 2004); *Mirabai Versions* (Red Ozier Press 1980). Expanded version: Penland, NC: Squid Ink 1993).

________. *The Soul Is Here for Its Own Joy: Sacred Poems from Many Cultures* (Hopewell, NJ: Ecco Press1995).

________. *The Lightning Should Have Fallen on Ghalib: Selected Poems of Ghalib*, translated by Robert Bly and Sunil Dutta (Hopewell, NJ.: Ecco Press 1999).

________. *The Angels Knocking on the Tavern Door: Thirty Poems of Hafez*, translated by Robert Bly and Leonard Lewisohn (New York:

HarperCollins 2008).

________. *The Sibling Society* (Reading, Mass.: Addison-Wesley Publishing Co. 1996).

________. *The Thousands: A Magazine of Poetry and General Opinion*, ed. Robert Bly, no. 1 (2001).

________. *The Night Abraham Called to the Stars* (New York: HarperCollins 2001).

________. *My Sentence Was a Thousand Years of Joy* (New York: HarperCollins 2005).

________. (trans.) with Leonard Lewisohn. *The Angels Knocking on the Tavern Door: Thirty Poems of Hafez* (New York: HarperCollins 2008).

Mary Boyce, "A Novel Interpretation of Hafiz," *Bulletin of the School of Oriental and African Studies*, XV (1953), pp. 279-288.

H. Wilberforce Clarke (trans.), *The Divan-i-Hafiz* (reprinted Bethesda, Maryland: Iranbooks 1998).

Dick Davis, "On Not Translating Hafez," *New England Review*, vol. 25/1&2 (2004), pp. 310-18.

G. H. B. Dihqani-Tafti, *Masih va masihiyyat nazd-i Iraniyan*, I: *Sayr-i ijmali dar tarikh;* II: *Dar shi'r-i farsi dawran-i sabk-i kuhan;* III: *Dar nazm u nathr u hunar-i mu'asir*, (London: Suhrab 1992-94), 3 vols.

Charles-Henri de Fouchécour (trans.), *Hafiz de Chiraz: Le Divan: Œuvre lyrique d'un spirituel en Perse au XIVe siècle*, introduction, commentary and translation (Paris: Verdier 2006).

Elizabeth Grey (trans.), *The Green Sea of Heaven: Fifty ghazals from the Díván of Hafiz* (Ashland, Oregon: White Cloud Press 1995).

Shams al-Din Hafiz. *Diwan-i Khwaja Shams al-Din Muhammad Hafiz*, ed. Parviz Natil Khanlari, (Tehran: Intisharat-i Khawarazmi 1359 A.Hsh./1980), 2 vols.

Husayn 'Ali Haravi, *Sharh-i ghazalha-yi Hafiz*, (Tehran: Nashr-i Naw 1367 A.Hsh./1988), 4 vols.

Muhammad 'Ali Islami-Nadushan, "Tarjuma-napadhiri-yi Hafiz," *Hafiz-pazuhishi*, IX (1384 A.Hsh./2006), pp. 19-26.

Muhammad Isti'lami, *Dars-i Hafiz: Naqd u sharh-i ghazalha-yi Khwaja*

Shams al-Din Muhammad Hafiz, (Tehran: Intisharat-i Sukhan 1382 A.Hsh./2003), 2 vols.

Baha' al-Din Khurramshahi, "Uslub-i hunari-yi Hafiz va Qur'an," *Darbara-i Hafiz: bar-guzida-i maqalaha-yi Nashr-i Danish (2)*, ed. Nasru'llah Purjavadi, (Tehran: Nashr-i Markaz-i Danishgahi 1365 A.Hsh./1986), pp. 3-20.

__________. *Hafiz-nama: sharh-i alfaz, i'lam, mafahim-i kilidi va abyat-i dushvar-i Hafiz*, (Tehran: Intisharat-i Surush 1372 A.Hsh./1993).

Franklin Lewis, *Rumi: Past and Present, East and West: The Life, Teachings and Poetry of Jalal al-Din Rumi* (Oxford: Oneworld 2000).

Leonard Lewisohn (trans.) with Terry Graham. *Sufi Symbolism I (The Nurbakhsh Encyclopedia of Sufi Terminology)* by Dr. Javad Nurbakhsh (London, Khaniqahi Nimatullahi Publications 1986).

__________. *Beyond Faith and Infidelity: the Sufi Poetry and Teachings of Mahmud Shabistari*. (London: Curzon 1995).

__________, editor with Christopher Shackle, *'Attar and the Persian Sufi Tradition: The Art of Spiritual Flight*, ed. (London: I.B. Tauris & the Institute of Ismaili Studies 2006).

__________, editor, *Hafiz and the Religion of Love in Classical Persian Poetry* (London: I.B. Tauris 2010).

__________, Correspondences between English Romantic and Persian Sufi Poets: an Essay in Anagogic Criticism," in *Temenos Academy Review*, 12 (2009), pp. 185-226.

__________, "Homam-i Tabrizi," in *Encyclopædia Iranica*, XII/4 (2004), pp. 434-5.

__________, "Sufism and Isma'ili Doctrine in the Persian Poetry of Nizari Quhistani (645–721/1247-1321)," in *Iran: Journal of the British Institute of Persian Studies*, XLI, (2003), pp. 1-23.

__________ . (ed.) *Divan-i Muhammad Shirin Maghribi*, Persian text edited with notes, introduction, and index; Wisdom of Persia Series XLIII, (Tehran: McGill Institute of Islamic Studies, Tehran Branch; London: SOAS 1994).

__________, "The Life and Poetry of Mashriqi Tabrizi (d. 1454)."

Iranian Studies. XXII/ 2-3. (1989): 99-127.

________. "The Life and Times of Kamal Khujandi." in Maria Subtelny (ed.) *Annemarie Schimmel Festschrift (Journal of Turkish Studies*, vol. 18, Harvard University 1994), pp. 163-76.

________, "Ta'ammulati dar usul-i nazari u ravish-i tarjuma-yi ash'ar-i sufiyanih-i farsi," translated by Majd al-Din Kayvani, in *Kimiya: Daftari dar adabiyat u hunar u 'irfan*, ed. Husayn Ilahi Qumshihi and Sayyid Ahmad Bihishti, (Tehran: Intisharat-i Rawzana 1382 A.Hsh./2003), pp. 354-86.

Parvin Loloi, *Hafiz, Master of Persian Poetry: A Critical Bibliography*, (London: I.B. Tauris 2004).

Bruce Lawrence. "Can Sufi Texts be Translated? Can They be Translated from Indo-Persian to American English?" *Islamic Culture*, VXIV/3-4 (1990), pp. 25-46.

Abu'l-Hasan 'Abd al-Rahman Khatmi Lahuri, *Sharh-i 'irfani-yi ghazalha-yi-i Hafiz*, edited by Baha' al-Din Khurramshahi, Kurush Mansuri, and Husayn Muti'i-Amin, (Tehran: Nashr-i Qatra 1374 A.Hsh./1995), 4 vols.

Julie Meisami, "Hafiz in English: Translation and Authority," *Edebiyat*, VI (N.S. 1995), pp. 55-79.

Paul Nwyia, *Exégèse Coranique et Langage Mystique*, (Beirut: Dar El-Machreq 1970).

Nasru'llah Purjavadi, *Bu-yi jan: maqalaha-yi darbara-yi sh'ir-i 'irfani-yi farsi*, (Tehran: Intisharat-i Markaz-i Danishgahi 1372 A.Hsh./1993).

__________. *Ru'yat-i mah dar asiman: barrasi-yi tarikhi-yi mas'alih-i liqa' Allah dar kalam va tasawwuf*, (Tehran: Nashr-i Danishgahi 1375 A.Hsh./1996).

Eric Schroeder, "Verse Translation and Hafiz," *Journal of Near Eastern Studies*, VII/4 (1948): 209-221.

Muhammad Rida Shafi'i-Kadkani, "Dar tarjuma-napadhiri-yi shi'r," in Vali'ullah Darudiyan (ed.), *In Kimiya-yi hasti: Majmu'a-i maqalaha va yad-dashtha-yi Ustad Duktar Muhammad Rida Shafi'i-Kadkani*, (Intisharat-i Ayidin 1385 A.Hsh./2006), pp. 125-33.

Daryoush Shayegan, "The Visionary Topography of Hafiz,"

translated by Peter Russell, *Temenos: A Review Devoted to the Arts of the Imagination*, VI (1985), pp. 207-32.

Clarence K. Streit. Trans. *Hafiz: The Tongue of the Hidden* (New York: The Viking Press 1928).

Finn Thiesen, "Pseudo-Hafez: A Reading of Wilberforce Clarke's Rendering of *Divan-i Hafez*," *Orientalia Suecana*, LI-LII (2002-2003), pp. 437-59.

G.M Wickens, "An Analysis of Primary and Secondary Significations in the Third *Ghazal* of Hafiz," *Bulletin of the School of Oriental and African Studies*, XIV/3, (1952), pp. 627-38.

______________. "Hafiz," *Encyclopedia of Islam*, 2nd Ed., (Leiden: Brill 1986), vol. 3, pp. 55-57.

______________. , "The Frozen Periphery of Allusion in Classical Persian Literature," *Literature East and West*, XVIII/2-4, (1974), pp. 171-90.

RELEASING BIRDS TO THE AIR

By Coleman Barks

I had never even heard Rumi's name before attending Robert Bly's Great Mother Conference in 1976. Robert often brings to those gatherings some new enthusiasm he has found. In June of 1976 it was a book of Rumi translations published by the University of Chicago, done by the Cambridge Islamicist, A. J. Arberry. Robert thought it would make a good afternoon writing exercise to try and rephrase Arberry's scholarly language into an American free verse poem in the tradition of Whitman. As he handed me my copy, he said, "These poems need to be released from their cages." I forget which poem I worked on that afternoon, but throughout the rest of that summer and into the fall I would spend part of each day in the region of Rumi's poetry. It was a most delicious form of play, and sublime relaxation. It felt familiar and excitingly new and fresh and mysterious. I claim now that it was the presence of Shams Tabriz that I was feeling, coming through the poetry. After a year of this deep daily delight, a lucid, precognitive dream came. May 2, 1977. In the dream I am sleeping on the bluff above the Tennessee River, five miles north of Chattanooga, where I grew up. I wake up inside the deam, still asleep but in a lucid state. A ball of light rises off Williams Island and comes over me. It clarifies from the inside out to reveal a man sitting crosslegged with a white shawl over his head, which is bowed. He raises his head and opens his eyes. *I love you*, he says. *I love you too*, I answer. Then the landscape, the curve of the river there and Williams Island, feels soaked with dew, and the dew is love. I felt the *process* of the dew, which was just completely natural and ordinary for that time of night, but, it is difficult to explain, I felt the whole forming process as *love*. The exchange and the knowing of that moment is really the only credential I have for working on Rumi's poetry, along with the fact that I met that teacher, the Sufi Bawa Muhaiyaddeen, a year and a half later, in September of 1978. He told me to continue the Rumi work. *It has to be done*, he said.

It is a strange thing to have done with thirty-four years of one's life, to have spent it rephrasing scholarly translations, John Moyne's most importantly, but also those of Arberry, Nicholson, and Nevit Ergin. But I would have been a fool not to, given such a radiant encouragement. Certainly, I have been a fool in other ways, truly, but I have been faithful with the poetry. Life goes so fast. It is a grace to have something you love to do while the trees on the bank go hurtling by. I'll look at a few more Rumi lines before the waterfall. Being seventy-three frees one up some from old ways of wasting time: finishing a book, Rousseau's *Confessions*; going to a funeral, a colleague I wasn't that close to; getting an honorary degree, no thank you. No more for me. There is a synchronicity involved with my connection with Rumi that Robert likes to hear me tell. At the age of six I was a geography freak. All I wanted for Christmas was a globe and an atlas. I had memorized all the capitols of all the countries in the 1943 *Rand McNally Atlas*. I grew up on the campus of a boys' preparatory school, and the teachers were always testing out this odd expertise. "Bulgaria," someone would call out as I went across the quadrangle to the dining hall. "Sophia." "Uruguay!" "Montevideo," I never missed. Finally the Latin teacher, James Pennington, decided this perfection had gone on long enough. He found a country that didn't seem to have a capitol, on his classrom map anyway, and called it out, "Cappadocia!" The look on my face, he said, *named* me. From then on, he and others, people to this day in Chattanooga, call me *Cappadocia*, or *Capp*. I am named for what I do not know, for my ignorance. It has come to me, finally, that the central city in south-central Anatolia, in Cappadocia, was Iconium, now Konya, where Rumi lived and is buried. Rumi's name itself refers to "Rum, the Roman-influenced area." Sometimes the universe plays a joke on us, to see if we will get it.

A PERFECT NEW MOON
—for Robert

Over the house next door, as I walk out,
just where the sun set earlier,
is a new moon supremely level
like a thinnest jewel gondola
with fitted over itself, prow to stern,
the circular sail that first made us want
to make something new, to say or sing
a reminder that we have this inside us,
this sailing membrane-embrace,
so now we can be and love
its beauty and never fail to.
We may be sure of something.

AS THE DEW

I have tried to write
in praise of the dew
and what it does,
and what it do,
condensing nightair
into invisible eyedroppers
of cold water that wash
the hands of the grassblades.

It is that
sudden wet breakage
that we love.

APPENDIX I

A FEW TRIBUTES FROM FRIENDS OF ROBERT'S NOT PRESENT AT THE "ROBERT BLY IN THIS WORLD" SYMPOSIUM

ROBERT BLY: AN APPRECIATION BY JANE HIRSHFIELD

A few years ago I received a small book in the mail. It held in its pages some long-unpublished poems by Robert Bly, going back to the start of his writing life. Poems coming from, as the preface describes it, "that quiet time before the Vietnam War captured our attention." He was writing then on his farm in Minnesota—a farm which has since become one of the mythic places in American literature—and in the introduction he describes these early poems as modelled after the Chinese classical poets, particularly Tao Yuan Ming.

Here is one:

FALL NIGHT

Fall night. Assyrian cities
Of blackbirds asleep in the trees.
Rabbits stretch up, eating the late leaves.
Water goes farther down into the earth.
Clouds cover half the Milky Way.

This unassuming, set-aside piece, more sketch than poem, shows just how much Robert's contribution to American poetry was ripening within him from the start. Its lines carry the watermark of what was perhaps his first gift to American literature: faith in the unfettered image as a wellspring of malleability, openness, and infinite depth. For me, to read "Assyrian cities of blackbirds" is to feel the heart leap at the marriage-joy of accuracy and expansion. To then travel with those blackbirds into sleep is to feel the self let down its guard and enter, in safe accompaniment, the peace in which still deeper heart-work can be done.

Another of Robert Bly's root-stock contributions is here as well: a birthright connection to the full range of the world's cultures. No small part of the personal debt that successive generations of poets continue to feel for Robert Bly stems from this sense of world-community he brought us. The landscape into which I came of age as a young writer included Neruda and Lorca, Mirabai, Kabir, and Rumi,

Rilke, Tranströmer, and Holderlin within its natural vernacular and range of possibility in no small part because Robert, and the circle of poets he was part of, had made that possible. They did this through their alive and breathing translations and through their insistence that American poetry liberate itself from the provinciality of an English-limited world.

Next, let us notice this early poem's psychological and spiritual dimensions. The creatures of earth, the hungry rabbits, stretch upward for nourishment. The clarity of water meanwhile travels inward and down. At the poem's end, we look up to find a sky half stars, half clouds: both an actual view, seen with the eyes, and a portrait of our human condition. What other weather would we want for our lives? If there were only stars, there could be no rain to sustain earth's creatures in their appetites and needs, no life-bestowing gift of leaves. If there were only clouds, we could not perceive the vast and glimmering realm that is also our true existence.

So there it is: a lifetime foretold in the first unfurling leaves of the seedling poet. Decades later, Robert Bly's poems still honor both sides of a life—the homely and the ecstatic—as essential:

> Like a bird, we fly out of vastness into the hall,
> Which is lit with singing, then fly out again.
> Being shut out of the warm hall is also a joy.
>
> ("Stealing Sugar from the Castle")

It is quite impossible to summarize the joyous plenitudes that Robert has given—news of the leaping image and the seven holy vowels; the example of political awareness and of a continual responsibility taken for our larger cultural choices; the love of the teachings of Jung, of Trickster, of the Sufis; the early ecological awareness and the awareness of the heart's own ecologies, of the need for wholeness in the feelings of men as well as of women; the necessary reminding of a culture's need for elders; the forging of communities of mutual conversation, instruction, and singing; the inclusion of sitar, of tabla, of dancing, of story; the indefatigable and generous decades given to magazine publishing and teaching.

Robert Bly – as only a very few others have done – has changed the world for all who now share it, has altered the lives even of many who never read his work directly. But I turn again to read his poems and I think: Here is the really important news. Rabbits reach upward. Rain travels into the earth. We need both stars and clouds.

We do what we must to keep the earth alive and our own species awake to its own full nature, for our own rescue and joy, and for the rescue and joy of those who will follow. This is the vow Robert Bly has always embodied, living as he has in sentinel alertness. In his ninth decade now, he remains for me both exemplary and beloved: a man, as he wrote in one of the wild-woven three-line ghazals of his recent years, still in love with the setting stars.

⋆ ⋆ ⋆

FORMER US POET LAUREATE DONALD HALL ON ROBERT BLY

... It was Robert Bly I met first [at the editorial board of *The Harvard Advocate*], and he has remained my dearest friend, from an evening when we collided and talked about Robert Lowell and Richard Wilbur. He was rather bright, you might say, and otherwise he was a Robert Bly who would be unrecognizable now. A veteran of the Navy (whom I took to be twenty-five; he had just turned twenty-two), he was always serious and spoke barely opening his mouth. He wore a three-piece suit and a narrow striped tie, and advised me to wear more conservative neckwear. At first I knew him as a critic, and his demeanor was critical. Within a year he was Bob Bly the poet. He dropped the Harvard manner and wardrobe, wore checkered shirts, and laughed out loud. He and I spent hundreds of hours together, talking poetry, reading each other's things, tirelessly critical, rewriting each other's work. In those first years we talked constantly of Yeats and quoted him at each other. We wrote poems that suggested an Irish ancestry. We also took lessons from the new young poets, Bly from the pentameters of Robert Lowell in *Lord Weary's Castle*, and I from the elegant stanzas of Richard Wilbur. We saw each other every day. After college we continued to visit each other—in Minnesota, in Michigan, in New York, in New Hampshire, at various poetry occasions—as well as writing each other something like twenty thousand letters. Fifty-odd years later, this friendship endures at the center of our lives. By this time we have shown each other our poems—celebrating and damning, writing lines for each other—from the '40s into the '00s."

—from *Unpacking the Boxes*, Houghton Mifflin, ©2008, used for *Robert Bly in This World* by special permission of the author.

* * *

HUGH VAN DUSEN, ROBERT'S EDITOR AT HARPER-COLLINS

I have now been an editor in book publishing for over fifty years and edited hundreds of books in that time, some of them very distinguished if I say so myself. But [the poetry anthology] *The Rag and Bone Shop of the Heart* is the one I am proudest of, and I've said that many times—not just for the convenient purpose of this conference. It's the one that I am sure has made the greatest contribution to the lives of the thousands of men who have read it. I salute Robert and Jim Hillman and Michael Meade for their work (as Robert calls it) and am grateful for the chemistry between them which made this book possible.

—for the occasion of the conference *Robert Bly in This World*

⋆⋆⋆

FROM POET MYRA SHAPIRO, FOR ROBERT

When I asked my husband to join me for a trip to Greece and Sicily with the poet Robert Bly, he said no. In his experience poets always mumbled, head down in the text of their books, and they were humorless. Not this poet, I assured him. Into our marriage came Robert's generous spirit; he hath made us to laugh, and cry, and love.

—author of *I'll See You Thursday*, Blue Sofa Press, and *Four Sublets: Becoming a Poet in New York*, Chicory Blue Press.

⋆⋆⋆

KIM STAFFORD: A POEM FOR ROBERT BLY

A PRAYER BY THE TIGRIS

—for Robert Bly

Let me be light from the morning star,
the glimmer between worlds.
I am what you cannot see—at midnight
or noon. I am the child in war
putting my candle in a paper boat
at the call to prayer. My mother says
when I die I will be a secret.
Little boat, you are my sister.
I put light in. Go find me
a place to be. Allah is great;
you are small. Go tell them
your brother is here. My mother
my father, we—we are a secret,
we are a boat, we are a light.
We are the star that sees you.
What we lost will be you,
my mother says.

—First published as a broadside by Lone Goose Press. Sent by the author, the son of Robert's great friend the poet William Stafford, on the occasion of *Robert Bly in This World*.

⋆ ⋆ ⋆

FROM NILS PETERSON, POET LAUREATE OF SILICON VALLEY, CALIFORNIA

Congratulations ... on getting it together [*Robert Bly in This World*]. No living American poet deserves it more than Robert. No living American poet has done more to increase the language and the gesture of poetry. In the introduction to *Driving a Herd of Moose to Durango* I wrote, "Falstaff says, 'I am not Only witty in myself, but the cause of wit in other men.' Surely something of the same could be said of Robert, – he is not only a poet but he is a cause that poetry is in others." Certainly that is true of me. So ... good work for a good man.

—Professor emeritus of Creative Writing at San Jose State University, author of two poetry collections, named official poet laureate of Silicon Valley in 2008, sent on the occasion of *Robert Bly in This World*.

APPENDIX 2

THE POET COMES HOME

THE POET COMES HOME: RECKLESS YOUTH. WAR PROTESTER. TRANSLATOR. MEN'S-MOVEMENT GURU. THROUGH IT ALL, ROBERT BLY'S ENDURING PASSION HAS BEEN FOR HIS POETRY.

By Laurie Hertzel, StarTribune Staff Writer

Outside the bus, bare fields. A barn, a silo. A cloudy sky, the early-morning sun trying to push through.

Inside the bus, poets. They take turns at the microphone, standing up and facing the other passengers, reciting poems, telling stories, passing out snacks. When the bus rounds a curve, they lurch and grab a seatback for balance, and laugh. They have come from all over the country to take this trip to the western Minnesota farm town of Madison.

The reason is Robert Bly. There he is, in the front of the bus, staring out the windshield at the flat land and farms of his childhood, one arm draped around the shoulders of his sweet-faced wife, Ruth.

The journey on this Sunday in April is the culmination of a four-day symposium on Bly's life and work, hosted by the University of Minnesota. The night before, Bly and Georgia poet Coleman Barks gave a reading in Willey Hall, Bly in a blue shirt and colorful vest, accompanied by drum and sitar.

Now, Barks takes the microphone as the bus crosses the Minnesota River and white pelicans fly up, startled. Bly stares straight ahead as the poets rumble west.

Robert Bly, Minnesota's poet laureate, is wealthy and world-famous, unusual things for an American poet to be. Some know him for his poetry, or his translations of poetry, or his work against the Vietnam War, or the audacious literary magazine he and schoolteacher Bill Duffy started in the late 1950s. He won the National Book Award in 1968 for his second collection of poetry, *The Light Around the Body*, and donated the prize money to the antiwar movement.

But most people, it would be safe to say, know him for *Iron John*, the book that catapulted him to mainstream fame. Published in 1990, it was an international bestseller, captivating thousands of men, drawing them to conferences to talk about their fathers and their emotions. It also launched a thousand jokes about men drumming and weeping in the forest. ("Ah, I don't care," Bly says, shrugging.) This month marked the 25th men's conference in Sturgeon Lake, Minn., and Bly was there, leaning on a cane (he broke his hip this summer), retelling the legend of Iron John. He is proud of that work—and proud of the Great Mother-New Father Conference on goddesses and mythology, which, at 35, is even older.

But it is poetry that has his heart.

He has published more than 20 collections of his own poetry, and more than a dozen collections of poetry in translation. When he talks about other things, it is with great politeness, but with distance. There are long silences. Could he be bored? Sooner or later (and it's usually sooner), the conversation clicks around to poetry, and his rich, slightly nasal voice warms and his sentences sharpen and he talks with enthusiasm, he talks without stopping. Thoughts about his own poetry merge with thoughts about translating other people's work and then double back; it's all connected, in Bly's lively mind.

He has been translating poetry since the 1950s, when he was in Norway on a Fulbright scholarship. Encountering a world of unknown foreign poets was eye-opening, with their wild imagery and freewheeling style that ignored the staid rules of meter and structure that governed traditional English and American poetry.

"There wasn't much translation being done at the time I started," Bly says. "And so I was able to do some new versions of Pablo Neruda and César Vallejo and all of these unbelievable people from the Spanish language, though I did some in German with Rilke, as well.

"When you do translation, it changes your mind, and you can see how a person from another culture would respond with ideas and references and images which you would probably never learn in your own culture.

"So that was wonderful, and I saw that it had a good effect on my own poems, especially the use of images as a form of discourse. Instead of saying, 'I went to school, and I did this, and so on,' with the use of images, all other things can come in. I met a kangaroo and he told me his name and I asked if he had any children, and I married one. You know. You can say all kinds of things with images that are partially true.

"But everything else we say is partially true, too. They may as well be partially true in a kind of flamboyant way."

Bly likes wild. He has never been terribly interested in stodgy, or obedient, or tame. "Our major literary influence is England. And they are not very famous for being wild, you know," he says. "So one or two metaphors in a poem would be enough, whereas in South America, 16 metaphors in one line is a good idea. And so you sort of have to be careful you don't get run over by a South American poet when he comes toward you. But I love that kind of wildness there."

Wildness in a poem, he says, doesn't interfere with meaning. Quite the contrary. "In England, most of the meaning is killed by everybody being too tame." He chuckles. "That's not true of all the English poets, but in general, I think wildness is a positive characteristic, and it allows you to say things about life that would not ordinarily come in. And, of course, I think of some parts of T.S. Eliot's as being wild, too. 'I've been born, and once is enough. You don't remember, but I remember. Once is enough.'

"I love that."

Bly and Duffy were pretty wild themselves, back when they started their magazine in Duffy's farmhouse in the autumn of 1957. They were in their 30s then, Bly tall, dark-haired, with dark-rimmed glasses, Duffy short and talky, with a mustache. Neither can say precisely when the idea came to put out a magazine of poetry written "in the new way," but Bly had written letters about it when he was still in Norway.

The plan was to publish a magazine of Scandinavian, European and South American poets in translation, and of certain American poets. They had a particular aversion to university poets, whom they saw as safe and stodgy and protected by the institutions.

The arrival of the first issue of *The Fifties* in the summer of 1958—small in size, a print run of only 1,000, published in the middle of nowhere by a couple of nobodies—was electrifying. The first issue stated firmly, "The editors of this magazine think that most of the poetry published in America today is too old-fashioned."

People paid attention right away. "When I read Robert Bly's magazine, I wrote him a letter," James Wright told the *Paris Review* in a 1975 interview. Wright, who won a Pulitzer Prize in 1972 and died in 1980, was teaching at the University of Minnesota at the time, and though he had received the Yale Younger Poets Award, he had grown uncomfortable following in the traditional footsteps of earlier American poets.

His letter to Bly "was 16 pages long and single-spaced, and all he said in reply was 'Come out to the farm,'" Wright said.

Two of Wright's poems appeared in the second issue of *The Fifties*. The back of the magazine carried this note: "James Wright decided this spring to abandon what he calls 'nineteenth century poetry,' and the poems printed here are the first he has written in the new manner."

All kinds of people wanted to be published in *The Fifties* (later named *The Sixties*, and then *The Seventies*), but few were accepted. Established poets, tenured professors, the dreaded "poets with three names," whom Bly and Duffy mocked mercilessly: All were rejected. Bly and Duffy have a million stories about the two audacious young men who deliberately, sometimes cruelly, rejected the work of some of the most famous literary lions in the country. And it is true that they rejected many great poets—James Dickey, Denise Levertov, Ted Kooser. But it's also true that those poets were young then, not yet well known.

Duffy was living in Pine Island, down by Rochester, at the time, and Bly would drive over from western Minnesota, where he lived with his first wife, Carol Bly, and they'd stay up all night going through submissions. "We'd get drunk and sit up and send them all back in one night," Bly says. "Bill was a genius in writing rejection slips. 'Dear Mr. Johnson, These poems remind me of old socks, Yours sincerely, William Duffy.'

"And then they'd write us insulting letters and we'd print the letters instead of the poems. We were not responsible. We were simply reckless."

Those flippant rejections were reserved for poets the magazine had no interest in. Talented poets were handled more respectfully. "If there ever was any glimmer of promise, the rejection note would become more detailed," says Mark Gustafson, a Twin Cities scholar who is writing a book about the magazine. " Robert would say, 'I liked this line, I liked that line; please try us again.'"

Duffy, who now lives in White Bear Lake, seems a bit galled by their cockiness of 50 years ago. "Who would have thought that two farm boys who cultivated corn and milked cows would become part of something so great?"

As the Bly Express (as the bus has been nicknamed) rumbles up the road, Bly narrates his life, and heads swivel. "I was born up in that little house," he says, as they pass a small house with peeling white paint set back in the trees. Swivel.

"This is not the way it used to look," he says a few minutes later. "It looks like South Dakota now." Swivel. This landscape is in Bly's bones, in his poetry, steeped, especially, in his early work, *Silence in the Snowy Fields*, published in 1962.

Madison is 150 miles west of the Twin Cities. It is not just where Bly grew up, it is also where he settled down with Carol after the Navy, after Harvard, after a couple of years in New York, after Norway. By then, Bly's father, Jacob, had sold the family farm and had bought three smaller farms. "One he kept for himself, one he gave to my brother, Jim, because he knew he was going to be a farmer, and one he gave to me because he knew I wasn't going to be," Bly says.

He points out his old farm, with its red farmhouse, and the spot where his writing studio once stood in a grove of trees. The studio was hauled over to the Lac Qui Parle County Museum 10 years ago, with Bly's books and furniture intact. It is where Bly wrote *Silence in the Snowy Fields*, and where his four children played on the wooden floor, separated from their father by a curtain so that Bly could think. The studio served as a guest house, too, and Wright and his wife, Anne, spent their honeymoon there. Anne later recalled how Robert invited them on a walk: "'Come on, Annie and Jim, we're going to lie down in the grass and listen to the animals.' Robert said we might hear mice or rabbits. But we never heard anything but the wind."

Four deer run straight up the road in the midmorning sun. "Jim Wright and I were standing by a corncrib over there"—Bly points, heads swivel—"Jim opened the door and a squirrel jumped out with one leap. And Jim put that into an amazing poem. Wherever you are, you try to make a heaven of it."

As the bus pulls up to the museum, the writing studio comes into view, a sweet clapboard building painted blue. It now bears a giant photograph of Bly's face and the words "Robert Bly Studio" in serious black and white. Bly looks at it and then speaks lightly, ironically. "And there's the log cabin in which he was born."

As a boy, during planting season, Bly and his older brother, Jim, helped plow the fields, sometimes staying out on the tractor until long after dark. When they stumbled into the house at 10 or 11 p.m., exhausted and dirty, their father was waiting—maybe he'd just come in from planting, too—and he'd fix them something to eat. An act of kindness for the tired boys, as their mother slept peacefully in the other room.

And some mornings, when Robert was struggling to crawl out of bed and head back out, his father would say, "No, no, you need to read a little bit. You stay in bed this morning and read."

That's how Bly tells it, anyway. These days, his stories about his father are steeped in benevolence. That memory of his father fixing a late-night meal for Bob and Jim, "that was a kind of male hospitality," Bly says, "and that's one of the reasons I've done the men's work, because you're invited into a place where men are not competitive, but hospitable."

There was a time, 20 or 30 years ago, when his stories about his father weren't so benign—there was anger and the memory of alcoholism and pain. But Bly is 82 now, and he has done a lot, and written a lot, and thought a lot and, yes, worked through a lot. The man who wrote *Iron John* now talks about his father in a much less complicated way. He talks about his father with love.

Inside the museum, chairs are packed tightly in rows. Half the town has turned out to see the man whom many still call Bobby. The air is fragrant with coffee, and sunlight streams through old lace curtains. There are too many people, and there's a delay while someone drags in more chairs. Everyone is squished together, but it's a pleasant squished-togetherness. Everyone wants to pay homage to Bobby Bly.

Bly listens while poets—Jim Lenfestey, Patricia Kirkpatrick, Anne Wright—take turns at the microphone, telling stories. Bill Duffy talks about how James Wright lounged in a hammock one afternoon while Bly repaired Duffy's basement door. Wright didn't help, but by the end of the day, he had produced a magnificent poem: "Lying in a Hammock at William Duffy's Farm in Pine Island, Minnesota."

"I never thought that I would be associated with something so phenomenal," Duffy says.

And then it is the townspeople's turn. Wilt Gustafson, who once swapped 15 bales of hay for a subscription to *The Fifties*, presents Bly with a bouquet of flowers. They hug, and Bly says, "You know we've made a little progress when men are presenting flowers to one another."

Bly's niece, Julie Ludvigson, recalls seeing Bly on the farm back in the day, steering the tractor with one hand, holding an open book in the other. "And then when he'd get over the hill, sometimes it'd be a long time before he'd come back."

Finally, Bly himself gets up and reads Wright's hammock poem, his right hand beating out the rhythm like a symphony conductor, and then another Wright poem ("Unbelievable. How can he do this? It all makes sense. How does he get there?"), and he thanks the town for turning out. "I'm so happy to be in the room with some of my relatives. Most of them thought I'd never amount to much."

It is ghazals that have captivated Bly in recent years—a Mideastern form of poetry that allows 36 syllables to make a point, and then the writer must move on to the next point. "In Iranian, in Farsi, they do that in two lines of 18 syllables each," he says. "So we tried that, but you cannot extend an American line beyond 12 or 13 syllables or the line begins to fall apart. So we did three 12-syllable lines. And the next stanza needs to be about something else. Well, then you've got six or seven stanzas. This requires a lot of athletic ability."

He plans to include ghazals in his next book, *Talking Into the Ear of a Donkey*, which he has been working on for several years and which, he says, is almost done. It will be his 23rd collection of poetry. He has also written nine books of nonfiction, edited seven anthologies and published many chapbooks and more than a dozen books in translation. His poem "Courting Forgetfulness" was published last summer in the *New Yorker*; "I Have Daughters and I Have Sons" will appear there later this year. He has published steadily throughout his life. One critic said in the New York Times, "I know of no contemporary poet ... who is so unafraid to write about joy."

At 82, he does not admit to worrying about his legacy ("Ah, I don't care," he says again) or about getting old ("Did I say I was old?"). These are not things he is interested in talking about. He wants to talk about the poems, and he lets the poems say what he will not. He picks up "Keeping Our Small Boat Afloat" and reads it aloud. His warm, sweet voice grows stronger as he reads. His right hand dips and sways.

> Each of us deserves to be forgiven, if only for
> Our persistence in keeping our small boat afloat
> When so many have gone down in the storm.

He sets it aside, picks up another poem, this one unfinished. " Robert, stop complaining. You've already been luckier than you deserve.... " His voice trails off as he studies the words.

"Even though our lives are more and more scruffy, the angels are still sending messages to Joseph. Maybe I ought to mention which angels, I don't know....

"There's no telling how many hours are left to us. Well, I think it's a poem about getting older, you know." He says this as though this is a surprising discovery, although it is his own poem.

"It's all right if we are scruffy and badly dressed. There's no telling how many hours are left to us.... Hmmm. That's probably the main thought. We're all growing more old and goofy each day."

He looks up. “It’s nice to be able to write a line like that. It’s saved by the word ‘goofy.’”

Bly picks up the first poem and reads it again. Jim Wright has gone down in the storm. Carol Bly has gone down in the storm. Rilke and Neruda and Vallejo have all gone down in the storm. But Bly’s small boat still rides proudly across the swells.

Look to his poetry. That’s where his answers lie. But—why? Why poetry? Why not prose? The question stops him, but only for a moment.

“What’s the point in dancing? Why not just walk around?”

(Original publication Date: September 27, 2009 Page: 01E Section: VARIETY Edition: METRO, StarTribune)

APPENDIX 3

ROBERT BLY CHRONOLOGY

CHRONOLOGY

1926 Robert Elwood Bly born December 23 to Jacob Thomas Bly and Alice Aws Bly in Madison, Minnesota.

1944 Graduates from high school and enlists in Navy, where he is strongly influenced by men interested in poetry.

1946-47 Attends St. Olaf College in Northfield, Minnesota.

1947-50 Attends Harvard, graduating with a BA, magna cum laude. Works on *Harvard Advocate* staff, delivers class poem.

1951-53 Lives alone in New York City, writing, reading, and supporting himself with part-time jobs.

1954 Moves to Iowa City and enrolls in MA program at University of Iowa.

1955 Marries Carolyn McLean. They move to a farm in Minnesota.

1956 Returns to Iowa City, where he submits book of poems, *Steps Toward Poverty and Death*, as Master's thesis. Receives master's degree.

1956-57 Fulbright Fellowship in Norway. In Oslo library he discovers work of Spanish surrealist poets that will transform his own style.

1958 Publishes first issue of *The Fifties*; meets James Wright.

1959 Works on *Poems for the Ascension of J. P. Morgan*, some of which will turn up later in *The Light Around the Body*.

1961 Publishes first Sixties Press book, *Twenty Poems of Georg Trakl*, translated with James Wright.

1962 Birth of first daughter, Mary. First major book of poems, *Silence in the Snowy Fields*, published. *The Lion's Tail and Eyes: Poems Written Out of Laziness and Silence* and *Twenty Poems of César Vallejo* published.

1963 Birth of second daughter Bridget. Amy Lowell Traveling Fellowship in England, France, and Spain. Guggenheim Fellowship.

1966 Organizes with David Ray national organization, American Writers Against the Vietnam War. Edits *A Poetry Reading Against the Vietnam War* and *Forty Poems Touching on Recent American History*.

1967 Birth of first son, Noah. *The Light Around the Body* published.

1968 Receives the National Book Award for *The Light Around the Body* and turns prize money over to the War Resisters League. *Twenty Poems of Pablo Neruda* published.

1969 *Forty Poems of Juan Ramón Jiménez* published. *Tennessee Poetry Journal* publishes special Bly issue.

1970 *The Teeth Mother Naked at Last* published. *Twenty Poems of Tomas Tranströmer* published. Lives with family in California, writes *Point Reyes Poems.*

1971 Birth of second son, Micah. *Neruda and Vallejo: Selected Poems* (with James Wright and John Knoepfle) published. Publishes first Kabir versions, *The Fish in the Sea Is Not Thirsty*.

1972 Guggenheim Fellowship.

1973 *Sleepers Joining Hands* published. *Lorca and Jiménez: Selected Poems* published.

1974 Teaches course in hometown titled "The Discoveries of Freud and Jung and How They Apply to Life in Madison, Minnesota."

1975 Publishes first large collection of prose poems, *The Morning Glory*. Also publishes *Leaping Poetry* and *Friends, You Drank Some Darkness: Three Swedish Poets*. Organizes first annual Conference on the Great Mother.

1977 *This Body Is Made of Camphor and Gopherwood* published. *The Kabir Book* published.

1978 Bly is subject of two documentaries, *A Man Writes to a Part of Himself* by Mike Hazard and a PBS Bill Moyers production.

1979 Robert and Carolyn Bly divorce; *This Tree Will Be Here for a Thousand Years* published.

1980 Marries Ruth Ray and moves to Moose Lake, Minnesota; *News of the Universe* and a book of interview, *Talking All Morning*, published. James Wright dies.

1981 *The Man in the Black Coat Turns* and *Selected Poems of Rainer Maria Rilke* published. Special double issue of *Poetry East* published in honor of Bly.

1982 Teaches at first annual men's conference in Mendocino,

California.

1983 Publishes *Times Alone: Selected Poems of Antonio Machado. Eight Stages of Translation* published.

1985 *Loving a Woman in Two Worlds* published.

1986 *Selected Poems* and *A Little Book on the Human Shadow* (with William Booth) published.

1987-88 Leads with Michael Meade, James Hillman, and Robert Moore workshops and conferences for men, developing material that will become *Iron John*.

1989 A Bill Moyers documentary on Bly, *A Gathering of Men*, brings men's work to public eye. Companion documentary with Bly and Michael Meade, *On Being a Man*, produced by KTCA-TV, St. Paul, Minnesota.

1990 *Iron John: A Book About Men* published. Essay collection, *American Poetry: Wildness and Domesticity*, published.

1991 *Iron John* rises to top of New York Times bestseller list. Bly is vocal critic of the Gulf War.

1992 *What Have I Ever Lost by Dying? Collected Prose Poems* and revised version of *This Tree Will Be Here for a Thousand Years* published. Edits *The Rag and Bone Shop of the Heart* with Hillman and Meade. Festschrift *Walking Swiftly* published in honor of 65th birthday.

1994 *Meditations on the Insatiable Soul* published.

1995 Anthology of spiritual poems, *The Soul Is Here for Its Own Joy*, published.

1997 *Morning Poems* published.

1999 *Eating the Honey of Words: New and Selected Poems* published. Translations, *The Lightning Should Have Fallen on Ghalib* (with Sunil Dutta), published.

2000 Wins McKnight Foundation Distinguished Artist award. Edits *Best American Poetry 1999* (Scribners).

2001 First book of "American" ghazals, *The Night Abraham Called to the Stars*, published. Translations *The Half-Finished Heaven* (Tomas Transtömer) and (with Robert Hedin) *The Roads Have Come to an End Now* (Rolf Jacobsen) published. *Air Mail*, collection of Bly/Tranströmer correspondence, bestseller in Sweden. *The Thousands #1* published by McKnight Foundation in honor of Bly's

75th birthday.

2004 *The Insanity of Empire* published. Selected translations, *The Winged Energy of Delight*, published.

2005 Second book of ghazals, *My Sentence Was a Thousand Years of Joy*, published.

2007 *Turkish Pears in August: 24 Ramages* published.

2008 *The Dreams We Carry: Selected and Last Poems of Olav H. Hauge* (with Robert Hedin and Roger Greenwald) published. *Angels Knocking on the Tavern Door: 30 Poems of Hafez* (with Leonard Lewisohn) published. Bly's translation of Ibsen's *Peer Gynt* staged by Guthrie Theater.

2009 *Reaching Out to the World: Collected Prose Poems* published. "Robert Bly in This World" symposium at University of Minnesota.

2011 *Talking into the Ear of a Donkey* published.

(This chronology compiled by Thomas R. Smith, drawing on Howard Nelson's chronology in *Robert Bly: An Introduction to the Poetry*, Columbia University Press, New York, 1984, with contributions by James P. Lenfestey.)

CONTRIBUTOR NOTES

COLEMAN BARKS was born in 1937 in Chattanooga, Tennessee. He has since 1977 collaborated with various scholars of the Persian language (most notably, John Moyne) to bring over into American free verse the poetry of the 13th Century mystic, Jelaluddin Rumi. This work has resulted in 21 volumes, including the bestselling *Essential Rumi* in 1995, two appearances on Bill Moyers's PBS specials, and inclusion in the prestigious *Norton Anthology of World Masterpieces*. The Rumi translations have sold over a million copies. It is claimed that over the last fifteen years Rumi has been the most-read poet in the United States. In the fall of 2010 HarperOne published *Rumi: The Big Red Book*, which collects all of the work on Rumi's ghazals and rubai that Barks has done over the past 34 years. Dr. Barks has taught American Literature and Creative Writing at various universities and published seven volumes of his own poetry. The University of Georgia Press published *Winter Sky: Poems 1968-2008* in 2008. In 2009 he was inducted into the Georgia Writers Hall of Fame. He is now retired Professor Emeritus at the University of Georgia in Athens. He has two grown sons and four grandchildren, all of whom live near him in Athens, Georgia.

WILLIAM BOOTH lives on Kabekona Lake in northern Minnesota where he worked with Robert Bly on *A Little Book on the Human Shadow* and where he and his wife, Nancy, enjoy visits from children and grandchildren. He has acted as Robert Bly's unofficial audio archivist for many years and contributed to *Walking Swiftly: Writings and Images on the Occasion of Robert Bly's 65th Birthday*.

DANIEL DEARDORFF is a "Singer" in the old sense of the word, which involves being a musician, a storyteller, and a maker of ritual. He has been a composer and a performing artist for more than four decades. As an independent scholar of myth, Deardorff's emphasis is on the performative aspects of mythic expression. He is the author of *The Other Within: The Genius of Deformity in Myth, Culture, and Psyche*.

He also the founder of The Mythsinger Foundation www.mythsinger.org and the Mythsinger Consortium www.mythsinger.net, an online community devoted to myth, ritual, and the mythopoeic arts.

WILLIAM DUFFY was born in 1930, graduated from Carleton College, founded *The Fifties* with Robert Bly, taught high school for 38 years (last 27 in Grand Marais). Retired to White Bear Lake, Minnesota, with wife Marilyn of 47 years to be near sons Michael and Patrick and their families. Published in *The Lion's Tail and Eyes, The Fifties, The Sixties, Poetry of Chicago, San Francisco Review, Great River Review*, etc.

RAY GONZALEZ is a professor in the English Department at the University of Minnesota. He is the author of 10 books of poetry including, most recently, *Faith Run* (University of Arizona Press, 2009) and *Cool Auditor: Prose Poems* (BOA Editions, 2009). He is the author of three books of nonfiction, including *Renaming the Earth: Personal Essays* (University of Arizona Press, 2008) and *The Underground Heart* (2002), which received the 2003 Carr P. Collins/Texas Institute of Letters Award for Best Book of Nonfiction. He is also the author of two books of short stories: *The Ghost of John Wayne* (2001) and *Circling the Tortilla Dragon* (2002). He is the editor of 12 anthologies including *Sudden Fiction Latino: Short Short Fiction from the U.S. and Latin America* (W.W. Norton, 2010) and *No Boundaries: Prose Poems by 24 Poets* (2002). He has served as Poetry Editor of *The Bloomsbury Review* since 1980. He received a Lifetime Achievement Award in Literature from the Border Regional Library Association in 2003.

MARK GUSTAFSON is a writer and teacher. He has a Ph.D. in Classics and has taught in Michigan, Indiana, Iowa, and Minnesota. He has published widely in the areas of Classical Studies and contemporary poetry. A bibliography of Bly's magazine and press, *The Odin House Harvest*, is forthcoming from Red Dragonfly Press. *The New Imagination*, a narrative account of the same, will follow.

VICTORIA FRENKEL HARRIS is Professor Emerita of English at Illinois State University where she taught American poetry, gender studies, and social theory for 33 years, focusing often on the vital relationship between poetry and culture. She has written chapters and presented papers at international conferences on the work of Robert Bly as well as Adrienne Rich, Denise Levertov, Jorie Graham, and James Wright. With Eva Goldschmidt Wyman, Harris translated *Los poetas y el general: voces de oposici"n en Chile bajo Augusto Pinochet*, and edited a critical study of Carole Maso. Harris is the author of the critical study *The Incorporative Consciousness of Robert Bly* (1991).

MIKE HAZARD The documentary *A Man Writes to a Part of Himself* was made by Greg Pratt and Mike Hazard in 1978. Pratt is currently professor of Business Communication and Business English in the Graduate School of China and the Graduate School of Business at Sungkyunkwan University in Seoul, Korea. Hazard has continued to make videos with writers and poets, including Frederick Manfred, Thomas McGrath and Eugene McCarthy, as artist in residence at The Center for International Education (www.thecie.org).

LAURIE HERTZEL is senior editor for books and special projects at the *Star Tribune* in Minneapolis, and the author of *News to Me: Adventures of an Accidental Journalist*. Her short fiction has appeared in *North Dakota Quarterly* and *South Carolina Review*, among other places, and her short story, "Snapshots," won the Thomas Wolfe Fiction prize. She is co-author, with Mayme Sevander, of *They Took My Father: Finnish Americans in Stalin's Russia*. She first met Robert Bly back in the 1960s when her father brought him to the University of Wisconsin-Superior for a seminar on North Country Writers. She met him for the second time in 2009, when she profiled him for the *Star Tribune*. There are not many opportunities for a journalist to sit in someone's living room and listen to him talk about the use of images as a form of discourse, but this was one of them, and she cherishes it.

JANE HIRSHFIELD is the author of six books of poetry, including *After* (HarperCollins, 2006), named a "best book of 2006" by *The Washington Post*, *The San Francisco Chronicle*, and England's *Financial Times*, and *Given Sugar, Given Salt* (HarperCollins, 2001), a finalist for the National Book Critics Circle Award. She is also the author of *Nine Gates: Entering the Mind of Poetry* and three books collecting the work of women's spiritual poetry from the past, including *Mirabai: Ecstatic Poems* (Beacon, 2004), co-translated and edited with Robert Bly. She has received fellowships from the Guggenheim and Rockefeller Foundations, the National Endowment for the Arts, and the Academy of American Poets, as well as the Poetry Center Book Award, the Commonwealth Club of California's Poetry Medal, and other honors. Her seventh poetry book, *Come, Thief*, will appear from Knopf in 2011. She lives in the San Francisco Bay Area.

LEWIS HYDE is a poet, essayist, translator, and cultural critic with a particular interest in the public life of the imagination. His 1983 book, *The Gift*, illuminates and defends the non-commercial portion of artistic practice. *Trickster Makes This World* (1998) uses a group of ancient myths to argue for the kind of disruptive intelligence all cultures need if they are to remain lively, flexible, and open to change. Hyde's most recent book, *Common as Air*, is a spirited defense of our "cultural commons," that vast store of ideas, inventions, and works of art that we have inherited from the past and continue to enrich in the present. A MacArthur Fellow and former director of undergraduate creative writing at Harvard University, Hyde teaches during the fall semesters at Kenyon College, where he is the Richard L. Thomas Professor of Creative Writing. During the rest of the year he lives in Cambridge, Massachusetts, where he is a Faculty Associate at Harvard's Berkman Center for Internet and Society.

PATRICIA KIRKPATRICK has published *Century's Road* (Holy Cow! Press), two poetry chapbooks, and books for young readers, including *Plowie: A Story from the Prairie* (Harcourt) illustrated by her sister, artist Joey Kirkpatrick. Her poems appear in many anthologies, most recently *The Poet's Guide to the Birds* and *She Walks in Beauty* (forthcoming), as well as literary magazines. Her awards include fellowships from the National Endowment for the Arts, Bush Foundation, Minnesota State Arts Board (1988 and 2010), and McKnight Loft Award in Poetry (1989 and 2006). Currently she teaches at Hamline University and is Poetry Editor for *Water~Stone Review*.

JAMES P. LENFESTEY is a writer based in Minneapolis. After a career in academia, advertising and journalism on the editorial board of the *Star Tribune*, where he won several Page One awards for excellence, he has continued to publish poems, commentaries, reviews and articles. Since 2000, he has published a book of personal essays, four poetry collections and edited a poetry anthology. He has served on many non-profit boards, and co-chaired the campaign to purchase the Robert Bly Archives for the University of Minnesota Libraries, and coordinated the 2008 conference "Robert Bly in The World" at the Elmer L. Andersen Library. He is founder of the Ojai Poetry Festival in Ojai, California, chairs the Literary Witnesses poetry series in Minneapolis, and teaches a summer poetry course on Mackinac Island, Michigan.

DR. LEONARD LEWISOHN is Senior Lecturer in Persian and Iran Heritage Foundation Fellow in Classical Persian and Sufi Literature at the Institute of Arab and Islamic Studies of the University of Exeter in England where he currently teaches Persian language, Sufism, the history of Iran, as well as courses on Persian texts and Persian poetry in translation. He specializes in translation of Persian Sufi poetic and prose texts. He is the author of *Beyond Faith and Infidelity: The Sufi Poetry and Teachings of Mahmud Shabistari* (London: Curzon Press 1995), and the editor of three volumes on *The Heritage of Sufism*, vol. 1: *The Legacy of Medieval Persian Sufism*, vol. 2: *Classical Persian Sufism from its Origins to Rumi*, vol. 3 (with David Morgan): *Late Classical Persianate Sufism: the Safavid and Mughal Period* (Oxford: 1999), covering a millennium of Islamic history. He is editor of the *Mawlana Rumi Review*, an annual journal devoted to Jalal al-Din Rumi. He is also editor (with

Christopher Shackle) of *The Art of Spiritual Flight: Farid al-Din 'Attar and the Persian Sufi Tradition* (London: I.B. Tauris 2006), co-translator with Robert Bly of *The Angels Knocking on the Tavern Door: Thirty Poems of Hafez* (New York: HarperCollins 2008), and editor of *Hafiz and the Religion of Love in Classical Persian Poetry* (London: I.B. Tauris 2010). Dr. Lewisohn has contributed articles to the *Encyclopedia of Love in World Religions*, *Encyclopedia of Islam*, *Encyclopedia Iranica*, *Encyclopedia of Philosophy*, 2nd Edition, *Encyclopedia of Religion*, 2nd Edition, *Iran Nameh*, *Iranian Studies*, *African Affairs*, *Islamic Culture*, *Journal of the Royal Asiatic Society* and the *Temenos Academy Review*.

HOWARD NELSON is Professor of English at Cayuga Community College in Auburn, NY. He is the author of *Robert Bly: An Introduction to the Poetry* (Columbia University Press), and editor of *On the Poetry of Galway Kinnell: The Wages of Dying* (University of Michigan Press) and *Earth, My Likeness: Nature Poetry of Walt Whitman* (North Atlantic Books). His poems appear in numerous anthologies and several collections, most recently *The Nap by the Waterfall* (Timberline Press). www.howardnelsonpoet.com.

JOHN ROSENWALD lives in Farmington, Maine, where he serves as co-editor of the *Beloit Poetry Journal*. Before his retirement in 2010 he served as Professor of English for 35 years at Beloit College in Wisconsin. As Fulbright Professor of American Culture and Literature, he has taught in China at Fudan, Nankai, and Zhejiang Universities. Recent work involves collaborative translation of contemporary Chinese poets and organization of exhibitions of Chinese peasant artists. His poems and translations from German and Chinese have appeared in numerous journals. With his wife, Ann Arbor, he has been a frequent participant at Robert Bly's Annual Conference on the Great Mother and the New Father since the first conference in 1975.

THOMAS R. SMITH is a poet, teacher, essayist, and editor living in River Falls, Wisconsin. He is a poetry advisor in the Foreword Program at the Loft Literary Center in Minneapolis, where he teaches. He is the author of six poetry collections, most recently *Waking Before Dawn* and *The Foot of the Rainbow*, both from Red Dragonfly Press. In 1992, he edited his first book on Robert Bly, *Walking Swiftly: Writings and Images on the Occasion of Robert Bly's 65th Birthday*. He is also the editor of *What Happened When He Went to the Store for Bread*, a US selection of the Canadian poet, Alden Nowlan. As a college student in 1969, he heard Robert Bly for the first time at a Poets Against the War reading at the University of Minnesota. This outing was led by his English teacher, James P. Lenfestey. He posts poems, essays and news at www.thomasrsmithpoet.com.

GIOIA TIMPANELLI is a writer, poet/storyteller, sometimes lecturer in literature, and one of the founders of the current world-wide revival of the art of storytelling. She was given the Women's National Book Award for her lifelong work in the oral tradition and the Maharishi Award for "promoting world harmony wherever she goes by enlivening within the listener that field of pure consciousness that is the source of all stories." She created, wrote and broadcast eight literature series on Educational Television for which she won two Emmy awards. She has published many articles and essays in the USA, Canada, and in Italy. *Sometimes the Soul, Two Novellas of Sicily*, published by W.W. Norton, won an American Book Award, and her new novel, *What Makes a Child Lucky*, published by W. W. Norton, is again about Sicilian place and soul. Among many awards she received the Brooklyn President's Award for "lifelong dedication promoting Italian Language, literature, poetry and culture." She writes, "Praise and Joy to Robert Bly for his Poetry and his amazing work in this world and with deep Thanks and Praise for his blessed friendship in and out of our 17-year collaboration. Robert told me once that he 'finds scattering stones in the moonlight with friends a comforting thing.' Salve!"

ANNE WRIGHT was born in New York City and has lived there since 1957. A graduate of Wheelock College with a major in early childhood education, she taught young children in Connecticut, Rome, Paris, and New York, as well as adults at New York University for 42 years. She met poet James Wright on April 28, 1966. They were married a year and a day later. She edited (with Robert Bly) James Wright's *Selected Poems* and (with Saundra Rose Maley and Jonathan Blunk) *A Wild Perfection: The Selected Letters of James Wright*, both from Wesleyan University Press. She was also a contributor to *Walking Swiftly: Writings and Images on the Occasion of Robert Bly's 65th Birthday*.